Recovery of Your Self-Esteem

A GUIDE FOR WOMEN

CAROLYNN HILLMAN, C.S.W.

A FIRESIDE BOOK

Published by Simon & Schuster

New York London Toronto Sydney

FIRESIDE
Rockefeller Center
1230 Avenue of the Americas
New York, New York, 10020

Designed by Black Angus Design Group
Manufactured in the United States of America
19
Library of Congress Cataloging in Publication Data
Hillman, Carolynn.
    Recovery of your self-esteem : a guide for women / Carolynn
Hillman.
        p.   cm.
    "A Fireside book."
    Includes bibliographical references
    1. Women—Psychology.   2. Self-respect in women.   3. Nurturing
behavior.   I. Title.
    HQ1206.B425   1992
    158'.1'082—dc20   92-885
                                                             CIP
ISBN-13: 978-0-671-73813-6
ISBN-10:   0-671-73813-5

Poems and journal entries on pp. 131–36 copyright by Rose —1992
Poem on pp. 60–62 copyright by Ayanna —1992

Dedicated to
my mother, Lillian Hillman,
who taught me how to nurture myself

Acknowledgments

I wish first and foremost to thank the women in my practice who have trusted me enough to allow me to enter their lives while they courageously faced their most painful feelings and experiences. They have taught me much not only about the pain of feeling defective and inferior, but also about the strength we all have to recover from the unhappiness and morass of self-deprecation and self-hate, and to move on to be able to love, cherish, and value ourselves. I want to thank each and every one of them for enriching my life by sharing their lives with me.

I especially want to thank "Rose" for allowing me to include her poignant poems and journal entries, "Ayanna" for her moving poem, "Diane" for being willing to let me share so much of her personal voyage with the readers, and "Lois" for her careful reading of the manuscript. The women presented in this book are all real, though some are in composite form. In all cases all identifying information has been changed to maintain confidentiality.

I am also grateful to my colleagues and friends who read my manuscript in whole or in part, and who generously offered their reactions, suggestions, and encouragement: Isabel DeMaster, Renana Kadden, Zenith Gross, Rita Sherr, and Adele Holman. I especially want to thank Dr. Shelley Ast, for her inestimable help with the manuscript as well as for her unfailing belief in the importance of this book and the value of what I had to offer.

In addition, I am appreciative of the people in my life who have believed in this book from the inception, and were ever ready to encourage and nurture me: especially my husband Steve Harrigan and daughters Nurelle and Robyn, also my mother Lillian Hillman, sisters Sara Schutz and Shelly Warwick, brother Henry Hillman, my friends, and the members of the Feminist Therapy Collective in New York City, and of the Bergen County Women Therapists in New Jersey who provided a great deal of support and encouragement.

I also want to express my gratitude to Zenith Gross for her invaluable help in the writing of the book proposal, to Eileen Fallon for enthusiastically believing in this book and placing it with a publisher, and to my editor Kara Leverte for her support and vision.

Contents

Introduction

$\mathcal{I}$am a middle-aged, middle-class, professional woman. I graduated from an Ivy League college, and subsequently completed a two-year masters program, a four-year psychoanalytic program, and two years of training as a sex therapist. I live in New Jersey in a house that I like with my supportive husband, two delightful children, and our much loved cat; and have a private practice of psychotherapy in New York City that continues to offer me challenge and fulfillment. If that weren't enough, I am reasonably attractive and in excellent health. In short, I would seem to have it all—everything a woman needs to feel good about her life and herself.

Why then, I wondered over the years, *don't* I feel better about myself? Why does it take so little to make me feel unattractive, pushy, selfish, and rejectable? As I established my practice, I imagined that my clients thought that I had it all together and generally felt serene, confident, unflappable; bubbling over with high self-esteem—and sometimes this was true. But other times I felt like a mass of insecurities for which no reassurance was enough. I noticed, too, in my practice how women across the board, whether or not they were outwardly successful, similarly struggled with feelings of inferiority and inadequacy.

My rising feminist consciousness, which started in the late sixties when I was in graduate school, certainly provided much insight into why women so often have low self-esteem: We find it hard to value ourselves because we are raised in a society that disempowers us and views us as inferior. However, this feminist analysis, while supplying some crucial understanding, still left unanswered for me the question of what an individual woman could do to help herself. Yes, it would help immeasurably if society in general and men in particular valued women equally, but despite the best political efforts of many women, such enlightenment is clearly still a long way off. What are we to do in the meantime?

As I was struggling with the issue of self-esteem in myself and in my practice, I became increasingly aware of how many of the women I was treating had a hard time nurturing themselves. They would be compassionate, accepting, respectful, and supportive towards many people in their lives, praising and encouraging them, while themselves they berated and belittled.

With experience it became increasingly clear to me that these two issues—nurturing yourself and self-esteem—were intricately linked. Over the nearly twenty-five years I have been practicing psychotherapy I have developed a number of techniques and approaches to assist women in building self-esteem. This book is the result of that process. I hope you find it helpful.

I would be interested in learning your response to the steps to self-esteem, and in your personal experiences in raising your self-esteem. You can write to me c/o Fireside Press, Simon and Schuster, 1230 Avenue of the Americas, New York, New York 10020.

PART I

The Importance of Self-Nurturing

In my work as a therapist as well as in my personal life, I find that understanding something intellectually is often the first step toward change. First I have to understand why my vacuum cleaner is making that funny noise, or why I feel angry or upset, and then I can take action to fix the vacuum or to deal with what is bothering me so that I can feel better. Similarly, understanding why we feel deficient, inferior, or worthless helps us realize what the problem is and makes it easier to take the steps we need to raise our self-esteem.

I have begun, therefore, with an examination of why we as individuals, and women as a group, are prone to low self-esteem, and with an explanation of the general principles underlying the ability to feel valuable and worthwhile. From this foundation, you the reader can move on to the second part of the book, which offers specific, hands-on steps designed to increase your self-esteem. The third part focuses on how to maintain your self-esteem in stressful circumstances: when anxious, depressed, raising children, making love, and in the workplace.

First let's look at why self-esteem can be so problematic.

⇥ CHAPTER 1

Being There for Yourself

Marcy was laid off from work. After a month of fruitless job-hunting, she feels like a nothing and a nobody.

Nancy's three children are late getting off to school, despite her waking them on time, continually urging them to hurry, and finally yelling at them. After they leave she sits with her head in her hands, feeling like a nag, a screaming meanie, and an inadequate mother.

Linda gets up her courage and phones the man she met at last week's singles party. He says he is too busy preparing a case for trial to make any plans at this time. She hangs up and feels embarrassed, ashamed, unattractive, undesirable, and unlovable.

Karen, a vice president for marketing, writes a report that includes her recommendations for increasing sales. Her boss decides to go with Charlie's recommendations instead. Karen spends the next week in a funk, questioning whether she's fit for her job.

Sally has struggled with her weight all her life. She diets down almost to her goal, then gradually puts the weight back on, plus a few more pounds. When her weight reaches what she considers panic proportion, she frantically starts dieting again. Whenever she is more than five pounds above her optimal weight, she feels fat, ugly, unattractive, and undeserving.

Elaine is driving to work when her car sputters, stalls out, and won't start up again. She turns to her husband beside her and berates him for not taking better care of the car, though he knows no more about cars than she does.

Marcy, Nancy, Linda, Karen, Sally, and Elaine are all competent, likable women; yet they all have fragile self-esteem. However others may view them, inside they feel deficient and inadequate. Whenever something goes wrong, they are sure they're to blame. Even Elaine, who seems to react by blaming her husband and not herself, does so to ward off feelings of inadequacy. Her sense of self-worth is so shaky that she can't bear thinking herself responsible for one more difficulty, so whenever anything goes wrong, she looks for someone else to blame. These women are like many of us.

When we react to disappointment with self-blame or by blaming others, it is because we do not have an ample inner reservoir of self-liking and self-appreciation to weather whatever storm we're in. We are not grounded enough in our sense of self-worth to be able to take responsibility for what we contributed to our troubles without condemning ourselves totally. Nor are we secure enough in ourselves to recognize the role that people and events beyond our control have played in our difficulties, rather than blaming ourselves for not having been able to control the uncontrollable. Instead, when things don't go the way we want them to, rather than being there for ourselves, most of us blame ourselves, dredging up all the things we think are wrong with us.

We may blame ourselves for a few "glaring" faults, or we might have a long mental list of our failings, such as: socially awkward, timid, unassertive, fat, clumsy, ugly, dull, boring, dumb, lazy, overemotional, aimless, fearful, selfish, unambitious, disorganized, unworthy, and unlovable. Some of us have gone through our entire lives feeling not good enough, or no good at all, often without a clear idea of what's really wrong. There's just this feeling that, deep down, there is something terribly wrong with us, some nameless thing that is defective or missing.

We long to feel better about ourselves. We know that the more we like ourselvés, the better we will feel, and the more others will like us. It is common knowledge that people with high self-esteem have an aura about them that makes them attractive and desirable. Yet, to many of us, realizing our worth seems a goal beyond our reach. Despite our discouragement, however, most of us don't give up. We keep thinking that, if only we could correct what's wrong with us or our lives, *then* we would approve of ourselves.

As a teenager I was overweight, young-looking, and awkward. I longed to be sophisticated and sought-after, and thought that, if only I were older and thin and had the right clothes, then I would be glamorous and popular. By the time I hit thirty, I realized that no matter how old, thin, or smartly dressed I might become, I would never be sophisticated. My personality is more warm and forthright than it is charming and coolly contained. I decided I needed to learn to feel good about myself as I was, rather than continuing to long for the elusive sophistication that I had believed would make me desirable.

Many women erroneously believe, like I did, that they don't appreciate themselves at present because they haven't accomplished enough to merit feeling good about who they are. They think that, in order to value themselves, they first have to *do* more: lose weight, get married, earn more money, get a promotion, obtain a degree, have children, be a better mother, acquire poise, or produce something wonderful. However, in many cases even reaching these goals doesn't provide the desired results.

Many high achievers remain on a treadmill where, no matter how much they achieve, they feel it's not enough. They just keep needing to do more and more to fill their inner sense of inadequacy. Often, despite receiving the respect and admiration of others, inside they feel like imposters, and live in terror of failing the next time, thereby exposing their deficiency. They look at each achievement as something that only increases others' expectations of them, setting them up for a harder fall when their unworthiness is revealed. They long to feel content and pleased with themselves, but self-contentment is the one thing they cannot achieve.

Self-esteem can come only from the inside, from inner acceptance and approval. If this self-approval is not there, then the effects of outside commendation and rewards last only as long as the kudos keep rolling in. When they cease, the achievement junkie suffers a dramatic drop in self-esteem, and often becomes depressed. **To be truly anchored in feelings of self-worth, we need to approve of ourselves for who we are.**

Women are especially vulnerable to feeling inadequate and depending on the approval of others for our sense of self-worth. Society, rather than valuing us as full human beings and empowering us, socializes us to focus on attracting, giving to, and pleasing others. We are "good girls" if we do as we're told, keep our voices down, willingly help out, and mind our manners. Advertisements and the media constantly barrage us with the message that we are to be beautiful and desirable, that our purpose in life is to snare and keep a man, and that failure to do so or the choice of other options means we are deficient and inadequate. Co-dependency, a problem that has received a lot of attention in recent years, involves getting your sense of self-worth from the approval of others, rather than generating it from within yourself—but this is precisely what women are taught to do. It is therefore not surprising that so many of us have limited or fragile self-esteem. We need to challenge our upbringing and culture in order to learn to value ourselves for who we truly are.

If you've ever rehashed your day in your mind, thinking about all the things you should have done better and telling yourself how inadequate you are, then you know how this self-recrimination drains time and energy from your life. If you've ever procrastinated before doing a task, and then spent the day (or week or month) feeling guilty, then you know how guilt can sap your strength, and sour your free time. It is quite common for women from all walks of life and with varying degrees of accomplishment to waste their time and energy making themselves feel deficient and therefore miserable.

Usually, though, a woman is not aware that she is actively undermining herself and eroding her self-esteem. Instead, she may think she has a "poor self-image," or a "guilt complex" that is beyond her control. The good news is that nothing could be further from the truth. You are not the helpless victim of unmanageable internal forces. If you don't value yourself, it is because you are actively treating yourself in a critical and belittling manner. Let me explain:

A helpful way to understand what happens when you feel bad about yourself is to consider yourself as having an inner-caretaker and an inner-child. Your inner-child contains your feelings, wishes, desires, and needs. Your inner-caretaker's job is to care for you as a parent would: to see that you eat right, get enough sleep, show up on time, act ethically and morally, and fulfill your responsibilities. When your inner-caretaker sees you stumbling, she tries to get you to straighten up and fly right. However, she can do this in very different ways.

Some of us, the lucky ones, have an inner-caretaker who gives constructive criticism and advice while being understanding, accepting, compassionate, encouraging, supportive, and approving. Others of us, the less fortunate, carry within ourselves an inner-caretaker who is really an inner-critic, who tries to help us by being disparaging and demeaning.

Our inner-critic is the part of us that is always telling us what we might have done, and could have done, and should have done . . . telling us how other people are better and luckier than we are, and how we are inferior . . . telling us that no matter how hard we try, we'll never succeed because we just don't have what it takes, and success is for other people, not for us.

Can you recall hearing the voice of *your* inner-caretaker? Think of a time when you were under pressure . . . feeling stressed . . . had things to do, decisions to make . . . were unsure of what to do and how to handle things. Perhaps your caretaker soothed you . . . told you to calm down and take a break . . . told you that your decisions are usually sound, but also that it's all right to make mistakes . . . told you that you are a valuable, likable person and will remain so, no matter how things turn out. If your inner guardian talked to you this way, you won't have any trouble remembering how helped and supported you felt.

However, maybe your inner voice addressed you differently . . . told you that you always get overexcited, that you can't handle pressure like others can . . . that you can't make good decisions because you really don't know what you should know . . . told you that you'd better not make a mistake because then everyone will know how incompetent you really are . . . told you that you really are no good or unlikable and don't have what it takes, and now everyone will know it. If your inner-critic talked to you this way, you will remember how this added to the pressure you were under, and how much harder it was to operate effectively.

We all have our vulnerable spots, areas in which we feel particularly unsure of or bad about ourselves. These are the areas where our inner-critics continually criticize us. In my case, I'm vulnerable to feeling "fat" (I've struggled and see-sawed with my weight all my life), pushy (it's sometimes hard for me to find the dividing line between being assertive and overinsistent), selfish (it's not easy to balance my needs with those of others), impatient (I don't like waiting), and rejectable (based on some childhood experiences). My inner-critic, when left unchecked, is ever ready to push my buttons in these areas by interpreting events as proof that I'm too fat, pushy, selfish, impatient, and rejectable—in short, that I'm just not worthy.

If you dislike yourself, it is because you, like so many of us, have an inner-critic constantly telling you that you're inadequate and unworthy, that you should have done it better, acted better, felt better, or looked better; telling you that other people are much more capable than you and that whatever you accomplish isn't enough, that doom is just around the corner and that, if you make one wrong move, you'll slip into the abyss of rejection and abandonment.

Self-esteem can develop only if you turn this inner-censor into a loving, nurturing guardian. The ten steps described in part 2 will show you how to do just that. You will discover how to recognize and appreciate your good points, and how to be supportive and understanding towards yourself when you are having difficulty. You will learn how to give yourself credit and praise for the things you *do,* rather than criticize yourself for what you don't do; how to encourage yourself as you take steps to attain your goals, and not berate yourself if you stumble on the way. Most importantly, you will learn to give yourself the appreciation and respect that you are longing for. When you nurture yourself, you give yourself what you need to feel confident and capable, and create for yourself the conditions under which you will thrive. Then you will value yourself for who you are, not for what you accomplish.

Paradoxically, you will also be able to accomplish more and to feel better about the things that you do. This is the magic of self-esteem—the better you feel about yourself, the less you need to prove your worth to others and to yourself, so the more energy you have available for accomplishing things, having fun, and—as you come full circle—feeling good about yourself.

This is not a quick and easy process—a few exercises and your sense of self will be radically and permanently changed. We all know that life doesn't work this way. Change always takes time and repeated effort. You didn't learn to dislike yourself in a week, and you won't unlearn it in a week either. But you *can* do it! The steps in this book, synthesized from nearly twenty-five years' experience in helping women come to terms with and feel positive about themselves, are designed to give you the tools you need to treat yourself with the compassion and understanding that foster self-approval, growth, and success, which I define as:

> Success is being happy first with yourself, and
> secondly with your life.

I firmly believe that what we really want and need, once our basic requirements of food and shelter are adequately satisfied, is a life where we feel good about ourselves, about what we are doing, and about the people around us. However, we cannot feel good if we are not happy within. Without inner assurance, no accomplishment ever seems enough—and it is hard to be close to others if we feel unworthy and are in inner conflict.

I know this is different from the common way success is defined and measured. After all, I am putting wealth, fame, status, achievements, or accomplishments in, at best, a secondary role. This is because there is no point in "having it all" if it doesn't make you happy, and if you are not happy with yourself, then all the accomplishments in the world are not going to make you so. There are many people who are rich and famous, the envy of others, but who never feel successful within. (A tragic example would be Christina Onassis, heir to the vast fortune amassed by her Greek shipping tycoon father Aristotle; she had four failed marriages and died at age thirty-seven. Her huge fortune and jet-set life-style could not enable her to find a fulfilling relationship or give her the inner contentment that she so needed).

Money, fame, and achievements are only of value when integrated into a positive sense of self. Otherwise the outwardly "successful" person remains discontent and unfulfilled. No amount of money, no degree of fame, no long list of achievements ever fills the hollow inner space.

When you learn to nurture yourself, you learn how to feel good about yourself as you are, freeing your energy to go after what you want. You will live not primarily in the future ("I'll be happy once I . . . make a lot of money, or advance in my career, or find the right person to share my life with"), but in the present, enjoying yourself and feeling good about yourself even as you strive for more.

This will put you in what I call the *Success Cycle,* where nurturing yourself leads to increased self-esteem and hope, which leads to positive efforts for which you take credit and feel good and successful, which leads to more self-nurturing.

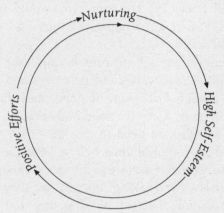

This may seem simple and self-evident; however, it is often difficult to put into practice. Many intelligent, wise, sensitive, knowledgeable women don't give themselves the nurturing they need to feel good about themselves and to take positive steps, but attack themselves instead. They criticize and berate themselves, believing harshness to be the best way to motivate themselves to change. They try to prod themselves into achievements by constantly focusing on their deficiencies, and fear that if they stop harping on their shortcomings, they will give up on improving themselves and do nothing.

Perhaps you feel this way, too. Do you use your energy to put yourself down, rather than using it to cope and grow? Do you seek the support and approval of others, without recognizing that it is you yourself from whom you most need encouragement and acceptance? Do you resent others or the world for not rewarding you, but ultimately blame yourself for not doing more and being so unworthy? Do you command yourself, "Do something impressive, then I'll approve of you?" Then you know that such behavior works about as effectively as telling a plant, "First grow, and then I'll water you."

Of course, you wouldn't treat a friend the way you treat yourself. If a friend were upset, you would respond with warmth, comfort, and support, rather than by putting her down. You know that what a person who's disturbed or frustrated needs is encouragement and hope. The last thing you would say to a depressed friend is, "You're just a hopeless failure." So why do you treat yourself that way?!

Many women cannot self-nurture because we have been brought up to think that we should be givers and not takers. Society teaches women that giving is good, and that taking is selfish. At dinner we dish out the food and serve ourselves last. In life, too, we feel that we need to first take care of everyone else and fulfill all our responsibilities before we're allowed to give to ourselves. And we never seem to have done enough to merit approving of ourselves and taking. Instead, we strive to live up to society's expectation that we be all-giving and all-capable (women are supposed to be able to do everything as long as we stay out of men's domain and don't step on their toes in ours), and we inevitably come up short. This starts the self-critical cycle where we try to help ourselves by picking on ourselves and reciting our litany of faults.

When this self-punishment doesn't work, and in fact backfires—lowers our self-esteem and makes us feel hopeless and helpless—the only solution we often see is to criticize ourselves more, thinking that the fault lies not with the technique, but with the too-gentle application of it. Thus, even as we desperately want to break out of our misery, we dig ourselves into a deeper hole. This is the *Failure Cycle,* a self-perpetuating circle where self-perceived failure leads to self-belittlement, which decreases self-esteem. Low self-esteem produces feelings of hopelessness and despondency, which sap the energy and faith needed to strive and achieve, thus producing more failure.

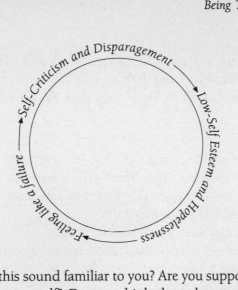

Does this sound familiar to you? Are you supportive to others, but berate yourself? Do you think that whatever you do is just not good enough, or no good at all? When you make a mistake, do you tell yourself, "What a jerk I am," rather than supporting yourself? Do your good points seem ordinary and your failings all-important? Do you measure yourself and your accomplishments with an ever-expanding ruler that always manages to be at least a foot taller than you are?

Since birth all of us have been surrounded by people evaluating us and pronouncing judgments about every aspect of our beings and our performances. Parents, siblings, relatives, teachers, clergy, bosses, peers—there is no end to the number of people ready, and over-willing, to let us know how we do, and especially how we don't, measure up. Society puts out additional messages via its institutions and media. What are we to do with all this input? How can we tell how we measure up? Which opinions of us should we accept and which reject? How are we to tell which criticisms are sincere, well-meant, and accurate, from those which are sincere and well-meant but misguided? Which evoked by jealousy and competition? Which sparked by the desire to keep us submissive? The possibilities are endless. How are we to develop an accurate self-appraisal out of all this input?

. . .

Women in the failure cycle, women who habitually feel disappointed in themselves and their accomplishments, have made order out of this confusion by developing a simple set of *failure guidelines:*

1. If other people criticize me, they're absolutely correct in their assessment. They have delved into my heart and soul (even if they've just met me) and have accurately seen through to my inferiority.
2. If people praise me, it's because they've been taken in by my "surface" virtues (hard work, talent, pleasant manner, looks, etc.). When they get to know me better, they will change their opinion.
3. Whatever I accomplish doesn't matter. What matters is what I have not accomplished.
4. My accomplishments are due to luck, my failures to incompetence and inadequacy.
5. If I am not a total success, then I am a failure. There is no middle ground, no so-so, no becoming, no points for effort.

Accompanying these guidelines is an important assumption: If I do not live up to my expectations, then I am worthless and deserve nothing, and certainly don't deserve to be nurtured.

These guidelines can be reduced down to their lowest common denominator, which is: "If I did it, it can't be worth much." Thus many women trap themselves in a vicious cycle—they desperately long to prove to themselves and others that they can be and are successful, then use rules for evaluating the results of their efforts that are totally stacked against them, and leave them no option other than to see themselves as failures when they fall short of attaining superhuman accomplishments.

"But," I can hear you object (as I've heard so many women

in my practice object), "I'm not asking for superhuman accomplishments. I just want the things that seem to come so easily to other people: a fulfilling career, or a good relationship, or the ability to deal effectively with my children, or to be at ease with people, or not to be anxious or depressed. Everybody else can do this. Why not me? It must be because there is something wrong with me."

These objections, however, miss the point. The aims in themselves are not superhuman. What's unrealistic is the expectation that you will be able to realize your goals without support from yourself. When you measure each step you take with harsh, perfectionist criteria, you are holding yourself back from success. The way to grow and change so that you can get what you want out of life is not by criticizing yourself, but by helping yourself to feel good about the person you are.

Let's see the failure cycle in action by examining some typical self-critical attitudes:

"Everybody else can always handle things, but I'm always messing them up."
"Everybody else is moving forward, and I'm the only one standing still."
"I should have done better."
"I'm not good enough."
"I'm worthless."
"I shouldn't have made this mistake."
"I'll never be able to learn this."
"I'm a terrible mother/child/lover/wife/worker."
"I hate the way I look."
"I don't deserve to get this good thing."
"I don't deserve to live."
"The problem with me is that I'm always feeling sorry for myself."
"I should have accomplished more with my life by now."
"What a failure I am!"

Obviously these thoughts are far from being good motivators. In fact, they lead to a dead end. If you think that you're always messing up, you're bound to feel that trying anything is pointless, since you're sure you'll mess that up too. If you believe that everyone else has been surging ahead and you alone have been standing still, then how can you feel there is any hope of trying to catch up at this "late" date? If you feel you're not good enough, or undeserving, then how are you going to summon up the courage to try to forge ahead? If you believe that you cannot learn, then you will want to avoid further anticipated failure by not attempting to master anything new. Most immobilizing of all is believing you're a failure. In this society where such stress is placed on competition and achievements, personal as well as professional, what shame you heap on yourself when you label yourself a failure! Holding yourself in such low regard, all you can feel is dejected, depressed, and hopeless—dead-end emotions that make positive action impossible.

If you doubt the validity of this, verify it yourself: **Read the above quotes again, slowly, as though you were talking about yourself—pretend that this is truly how you regard yourself—and see how you feel.**

How does attacking yourself this way make you feel? Are you depressed? Discouraged? Despondent? Let yourself experience that this is the inevitable result of attacking yourself. No one reacts to being put down and berated by feeling buoyed up, confident, and ready to go out there and meet the world.

To change, to stretch, to grow, we need to have hope, positive energy, and faith in ourselves. Imagine approaching yourself with warmth and support. Try telling yourself:

"This may be difficult, but with persistence I'm sure I can get it."

"While all is not as I would like it, I have been making efforts, and those efforts are important."

"I made a mistake, but everyone does. It's part of learning and growing."

"I've been having a hard time learning this because I'm so nervous about it. Let me just calm down some, and then I'll be able to grasp it."

"There are things I want to improve about being a mother/child/lover/spouse/worker, but there are also parts of these roles that I'm very good at."

"While I'm not as gorgeous as I would like to be, I have great eyes, good skin, and a winning smile. I really like the way I look."

"I'm a good person and deserve to be happy."

"I've been having a tough time and can use some tender loving care."

Sense how different these statements make you feel: **Experience the energy generated when you respect and encourage yourself.**

In order to become self-valuing successful adults, children need to be nurtured. Growing children need *compassion* for their feelings, *acceptance* of their individuality, *respect* for their worth, *encouragement* to strive, loving *support,* and physical and emotional *stroking.* These nurturing acts and attitudes are the growth conditions under which people flourish:

Compassion
Acceptance
Respect
Encouragement
Support
Stroking

Read down the left side of the list with me; the mnemonic acronym for happiness and self-esteem is: **CARESS**.

To be happy in life, you have to be able to CARESS yourself.

Take, for example, Diane, who learned to leave the failure cycle and enter the success cycle by nurturing herself.

When she first consulted me, Diane was struggling to be "someone," to fit in, to be liked, to be important, to be secure, to have a career and a family. At twenty-eight, she wondered why all these goals had eluded her. She came from a working-class family in Chicago, had gone on scholarship to a small college in Illinois, and then came to New York to make her way in the world. Despite being intelligent, attractive, personable, college-educated, and ambitious, she kept finding herself stuck in dead-end jobs where she felt different from her coworkers, neither liked nor appreciated. She was also unhappy with being single, but her experience with her father—who was alcoholic, self-involved, distant, condescending and rejecting—had left her mistrusting and fearful of men. She had had very little dating experience and despaired of ever being able to establish the family she desired.

In trying to cope with her problems, Diane alternated between blaming the world—for giving her such a bad start, for not rewarding her, for giving all the goodies to others—and blaming herself. Deep down she felt that there must be something terribly wrong with her that drove people away, and left her so alone and unfulfilled. She was constantly trying to figure out what this nameless thing was; at the same time she was terrified of finding out, believing that it was something that would be too dreadful to live with. So she picked at the things that she could grasp: too reticent, not assertive enough, sarcastic, self-centered, shy, clumsy, lacking in social grace. The list went on and on, with each added item making her feel worse about herself, more hopeless, more depressed. Though sometimes she felt sorry for herself, at no time did she have any real compassion for herself, nor did she give herself credit for trying to improve her life.

Diane kept beating herself up this way because she did not know how else to motivate herself to make changes. She thought the logical way to approach improving her life was to figure out what was wrong with her so she could set it right. In our work together Diane came to realize that, by tearing herself down, she was actually keeping herself stuck. She learned that people, like plants, need to be "watered" in order to grow and flourish; and that the water we need is the milk of human kindness: Compassion, Acceptance, Respect, Encouragement, Support, and Stroking. With time and effort she learned how to give herself this nurturance, this CARESS. She now feels good about the person she is, has a rewarding professional job, and a satisfying marriage. (You will find more specifics about the process she went through in learning to value herself in part 2.)

You too, can raise your self-esteem and move toward attaining your goals by learning to nurture yourself. Accepting yourself, having compassion for your inner pain, and regarding yourself as a person of innate worth produce high self-esteem. Encouragement and support help you to persist in the face of obstacles, be they inner or outer hindrances. Stroking, both physical and emotional, enhances your sense of yourself as worthy, capable, appealing, and lovable. CARESSing yourself equips you to find happiness and success in life. When you start to CARESS yourself, by following the ten steps in part 2, you give yourself the helping hand you need to get what you want. But first, let's examine the concept of CARESS in more detail.

CHAPTER 2

CARESS: Six Key Ways to Nurture Yourself

COMPASSION

Compassion is "sorrow for the sufferings or troubles of another, accompanied by an urge to help"; a sense of "I'm feeling for what you are going through, and I want to help you because I care about you." Has anyone ever said this to you? How did it affect you?

Compassion, when you believe it to be genuine and allow yourself to take it in, is like a healing potion that goes directly to where you're hurting, warming and sustaining you. Think of a time when you were very upset about something and someone responded compassionately. Maybe it was a problem you contributed to (like getting fired), or maybe your distress was about something completely beyond your control (such as a loved one dying). Remember how you felt when someone reached out to you with caring and compassion. It didn't make the problem go away (you still didn't have a job, or your loved one back), but most likely it helped. Perhaps you felt a little less alone, or your mood lifted some so that your problems did not seem quite so severe, and you felt less frozen in your attempts to deal with them.

Wouldn't it be wonderful to feel that warming compassion whenever you are hurting?!

Sometimes you can get it from other people, but perhaps you are too wary or too ashamed to share your troubles with others. Or you may not have compassionate people to whom you can turn. Fortunately you need not be solely dependent on others for compassion. You can learn to give it to yourself. You can learn how to develop an inner voice that is caring and loving, ready to cheer you and give you the courage to go on.

ACCEPTANCE

Compassion and acceptance go hand in hand. When we respond to ourselves with compassion—rather than by being angry at and disappointed with ourselves—we are accepting ourselves as the imperfect human beings that we are. If you were fired from your job, your automatic reaction might be to be angry at and disgusted with yourself. Imagine, instead, accepting that you have needs, or problems, or conflicts that made it hard for you to perform your job. Instead of berating yourself, it would be so much more helpful to try to find out what these are and to help yourself with them. You may also have been fired for reasons beyond your control (office politics, company-wide layoffs, discrimination, and so on). In any case, you're feeling rotten and you need someone to comfort and help you, someone who loves you even when you mess up. You need to learn how to accept yourself as you are and to be there for yourself.

We all have problems, and failings, and things we've bungled or haven't been able to secure for ourselves. But that doesn't make us undeserving of caring, empathy, and help. We can't always do things right. On the contrary, we need to accept and appreciate ourselves as we are, even as we strive to improve ourselves and our lives.

Everyone wants to be accepted and understood. Acceptance helps us to feel OK about ourselves. When a woman tells me, with great embarrassment and chagrin, that she acted mean, or felt jealous, or procrastinated, or failed to stand up for herself, or made an error, my usual response is: *Join the human race*. We humans are imperfect creatures. Once we can accept that it is par for the course to be ungenerous of spirit or to mess up at times, then we enter the emotional space where we can also recognize that we have strengths, and virtues, and unrealized potential. The healing and mobilizing effects of acceptance and compassion will be readily recognized by anyone who has ever been in an ongoing support group with people who share similar problems or challenges, such as gatherings of new mothers, women alone, job-seekers, rape victims, arthritis sufferers, hostages' spouses, senior citizens, writers, or consciousness-raising groups.

Many people fear accepting themselves because they believe self-acceptance will lead to stagnation and resignation. They erroneously believe that self-acceptance means giving up on themselves and their dreams. I want to stress that this is totally untrue. Accepting yourself does *not* mean adopting the attitude, "This is the way that I am and there is nothing I can do about it." Accepting yourself means recognizing and genuinely appreciating your positive attributes, and also seeing your faults and understanding that they are part of the human condition as well as a product of your individual experiences. Your faults do not make you worthless: they just make you human with strengths and shortcomings. In fact, not only does self-acceptance *not* lead to stagnation, but the very opposite is true:

Self-acceptance leads to change.

This is one of the great paradoxes of life. Facing yourself and accepting—in a nonjudgmental, nurturing way—the things you previously denied or hated about yourself helps you to change these "negatives" into positives; not accepting yourself keeps you stuck. In my work as a therapist I have seen this happen many times. Lydia is a good example.

Old Way: Lydia finds it hard to genuinely care about others, but does not admit this to herself because she thinks it is bad to be selfish. When she catches herself, or is caught by someone else, thinking only of herself, she thinks that she is a terrible person for being selfish, and resolves to be more generous. However, blaming herself for her self-centeredness makes her feel worse about herself and therefore more unhappy and in need of comfort. Her unhappiness upsets her still more. She asks herself, "What's wrong with me now?" And concludes, "Here I go again feeling sorry for myself." By refusing to deal with her neediness, at the same time that she adds to it by berating herself, Lydia becomes depressed and even more wrapped up in her own unmet needs, and thus less able than ever to respond to and give to others.

New Way: Lydia finds it hard to genuinely care about others. Rather than hating and blaming herself for being selfish, she *accepts* it as a human failing, at the same time desiring to be more caring and connected. Not being caught up in blaming herself, she is able to consider why she is selfish. She starts to get in touch with the child inside her whose needs were ignored by her emotionally unavailable parents, leaving Lydia feeling empty and deprived. To make up for her deprivation, she now wants to be the center of the universe and have everyone give to her.

When Lydia gets in touch with her inner pain and accepts the hurt child within her, something starts to melt inside her. The barriers she erected against feeling vulnerable, to keep herself from being further hurt and deprived, start to soften. She has given to herself by understanding and having compassion for herself, and this self-nurturing builds an inner reservoir of good feeling, so she feels less empty. She begins to experience that she can give without being totally depleted. Thus, accepting her selfishness and having compassion for the child within her leads to her becoming more giving.

This is real change, and is very different from the surface kind of change that comes from "trying to be generous and giving." These surface efforts, while well-intentioned, usually do not last long, because deeper feelings are pulling in the opposite direction. Until a woman accepts her inner feelings, she will remain in unconscious conflict, consciously wanting to be, for example, giving, but unconsciously feeling empty and craving the world.

When we accept ourselves, we start to be close to ourselves and to fill ourselves up. In so doing, we also become more able to accept what others have to offer. The more we are able to genuinely receive from ourselves and others, the more we have to give.

In order to fill up the emptiness inside, you have to let others in where it hurts. But you cannot let someone else in if you cannot let yourself in; and you will not, and should not, let yourself in to your deepest pain if your response will be to criticize and attack yourself where you are most vulnerable. As you learn to nurture yourself, you will become better able to open up to yourself and others—and will get the caring, acceptance, and approval that you need and deserve.

Of course, the above illustration of a self-involved woman becoming more caring is just one example of how self-acceptance leads to change. I do not mean to imply that most women with self-esteem problems are selfish, for the opposite is true. Women with low self-esteem by and large have great difficulty emphasizing their own needs and being assertive about getting these needs met.

Women generally are not taught to be assertive, and usually are not rewarded when they do act assertively. Men, through sports and military service, are taught to compete fiercely while also being team players. Women are taught to try their best, while being sensitive to others and making sure that there are no hurt feelings. Men are hardened to rejection by life's lessons: being put on the bench if they're not playing well, having to ask women out and being turned down, and being expected to "take it like a man" without crying. They usually inure themselves to such rejections by distancing themselves from their feelings. Thus, while they learn to assert themselves, they often are not in touch with their emotions.

We women, on the other hand, usually find it easy to make emotional connections, but have a much harder time asserting ourselves to get what we want and need, or even giving ourselves permission to focus on figuring out what it is that we need. Instead, we spend much of our time taking care of others, and find it difficult to balance satisfying the needs of others with satisfying ourselves. When we focus on our own needs, we may feel guilty and selfish. When we devote most of our time and energy to doing for others, we may feel depleted and inferior. The happy medium between the two is often very difficult to achieve.

Actually, this very hunt for the precise balance between meeting our own needs and those of others is an illusory search. What woman among us can perfectly combine duty to self with duty to others? The best we can hope for is to stay in touch with our needs and accept them as valid as we ebb and flow between these two polarities, sometimes swinging in one direction, and other times swinging in the opposite direction. If your life has no flow, if you are always other-directed (or, more rarely, always inner-directed), start by accepting that this is where you are without judging yourself. This very acceptance will help you start to change your focus.

Learning to accept yourself is something that happens bit by bit over time. As you move forward, there are bound to be old habits and patterns that cause you to step backward at times. Therefore, one of the first things you have to accept is that you are not going to change overnight. Change takes place slowly, and at each step along the way you need to give yourself credit for what you *are* doing, rather than focusing on what you are not doing.

RESPECT

Do you feel underrated and taken for granted? Do you long to be esteemed, appreciated, and valued? Is much of your inner energy spent railing against being put down or treated like you're not important? Are you always trying to please people so you'll get that regard you long for? Then you know just how important respect is: it gives a lift, promotes feelings of competence, and helps to harness inner strength.

However, women as a group are not respected in our society. Women's traditional roles—mother and homemaker—are not viewed as difficult, demanding, or impressive. Women themselves, used to being devalued, often say, "I'm just a housewife," in an apologetic tone.

When my children were young, my husband took care of them on the two or three days I worked, and I took care of them the rest of the time while he worked. We both agreed, hands down, that taking care of children and the house was twice as difficult and exhausting as working outside the home. This experience gave both of us new respect for anyone who is raising children.

Women who work outside the home also have a hard time receiving the respect they merit. If working women have children, it is often presupposed that by working they are neglecting their children. No one views men, even men who are single parents, as neglecting their children by working. And the argument that men's incomes are needed to support a family just sidetracks the real issue, because most women's earnings are also vital.

Women who are single (whether never married, divorced, or widowed) or childless fare no better. Unmarried women are usually viewed as society's rejects, childless women are considered selfish and unnatural, and lesbians are afforded even less respect. A widow is often seen as having outlived her usefulness, like the appendix (unless she redeems herself by remarrying).

Women have special difficulty gaining respect in the workplace itself, too. We have to walk a thin line between being too passive and too assertive. What is considered healthy competitiveness in a man may be viewed as shrill, abrasive, or—that catchall condemnation—"unfeminine" in a woman. (See chapter 17 for help in maintaining self-esteem at work). Women at work, moreover, do not have equal access to the symbols and rewards of respect (good salaries, promotions, bonuses, titles, raises). This applies even more to women of color, who bear the burden of being doubly devalued.

When society shows us so little respect, it is hard to respect ourselves. When we are told that our value lies either in our catering to men and children, or in being a beautiful accoutrement, a possession, it is hard to feel our own intrinsic worth. When society's treatment tells us that we are not as good as men, and that women of color have even less value, it is no wonder that we have to struggle so hard to respect ourselves. In our heads we may react with outrage to being devalued, but in our guts it is hard not to buy into the dominant message and feel that we are inferior. The more we assert ourselves without getting into power struggles, the better we feel. (Power struggles will be addressed in chapters 11 and 17). However, asserting ourselves on the outside is not enough: We also have to learn how to respect ourselves from within.

Can you remember a day when you were feeling really low, and then someone let you know that she or he really appreciated something about you? Maybe it was your smile . . . or the quality of your work . . . or your ability to play. Can you remember how that made you feel? Remember that good, glowing feeling radiating through your body, as you thought, "Yes, I do have a nice smile . . . or do good work . . . or am able to be fun-loving and spontaneous." Feel that glow of self-respect warming you, calming you, and energizing you. Wouldn't it be wonderful to always have that inner glow emanating from within? With it you could conquer the world!

Unfortunately you may find this glow elusive, or at best fleeting. Do you stop to take in these good feelings? Or do you push them away, telling yourself, "OK, so maybe I have a nice smile, or do good work, or enjoy playing—but, so what?! There is so much else wrong with me, and there are so many other people who do not respect me, and this person would not respect me either if she or he knew me better." Here you are following failure guideline #2 from the list in chapter 1 ("If people praise me, it's because they've been taken in by my 'surface' virtues—hard work, talent, pleasant manner, looks, etc.—but when they get to know me better, they will change their opinion"), which fosters low self-esteem, in turn producing feelings of helplessness. Fortunately, you are not stuck here. You *can* learn to respect yourself, so you will have the inner regard and centeredness that is vital to self-esteem.

ENCOURAGEMENT

We all need encouragement to stretch beyond where we are now, to reach for goals and to believe that we can attain them. When one baby starts walking, the proud parents reach out their arms and say, "Come here. You can do it." The baby, sensing their encouragement, takes another step. The parents gather her up, beaming proudly, and say, "You did it!" What a sense of accomplishment shared by all!

Another baby learning to walk is told, "Be careful, don't fall, don't try to come here. You might get hurt. I'll come and get you." This baby, too, learns to walk, but without the same inner sense of success. Despite the outer success, this baby is being taught to feel that she probably will not succeed, and should not take risks.

Women who were not sufficiently encouraged while growing up often find it difficult to encourage themselves. And all too frequently women are not encouraged. Society is full of messages suggesting to us that we be beautiful objects waiting to be judged and chosen, rather than encouraging us to be full human beings. When we have not been encouraged, it is hard to say to ourselves, "I can do it," because we feel as if we cannot. Better to stay safe and not try, than to try and fail. (Remember the failure guidelines:

"No points for trying," and, "Anything short of total success is failure.") We tell ourselves:

"Why ask for the raise? I know I won't get it."
"No sense going out, it'll only make me anxious and I won't be able to handle my anxiety."
"I'll never find a mate. There are no good ones left, and if there is one, he (or she) wouldn't want me."

Thus many of us deal with feeling discouraged by discouraging ourselves still more, and we do this at a point when we most need encouragement, when we need to believe that what we want is attainable and we can achieve our goals.

It is hard for many women to believe that something is within reach because we give ourselves no room or hope for progress. We have never learned that change usually takes place slowly and unevenly, and that most goals are only attained through a process of trial and error. A baby learns to walk by taking a step, falling down, picking herself up, taking a couple of steps, falling down again, and so on until eventually the baby walks mostly without falling. Imagine what would happen if, after a baby fell down three times, she said, "OK, three strikes and you're out. That's it. I'm just a failure. I guess I'll never learn to walk. But it seems to come so easily to other people."

Many women believe that, if they do not attain something on the first try, then it is beyond their grasp. They do not see that asking for a raise, even if turned down, may make a raise more likely the next time, and that even asking is an accomplishment for which they should take credit. Similarly, an anxious woman— who often feels alone, insecure, overwhelmed, and inadequate— very much needs encouragement to face and conquer the fears that provoke anxiety.

The woman who believes she will never meet the right partner seldom makes an effort to do so. If she does make the effort and does not meet "Mr. (or Ms.) Right," she concludes that she should not have made the effort in the first place. She does not give herself credit for trying and does not encourage herself to keep trying. Instead she goes home berating herself, and feels rejected and dejected. Think how much better she would feel if her inner voice said, "I know how you feel. It is terrible to want something so much and not find it, and it's so awkward standing around trying to strike the right air, and all the time feeling so rejected." (Compassion.) "I guess most women feel the same as you do." (Acceptance.) "But, you know, you really have a lot going for you. (Respect.) "It was really brave of you to go, especially feeling as vulnerable as you do. I think if you keep on trying, eventually you will meet someone. These things usually take time and effort and persistence. I really think you have a lot to offer the right person, and if you persist in looking, you will find him (or her)." (Encouragement.)

SUPPORT

Have you ever felt so bad that you just wanted to stay in bed and hide from the world for a few weeks, or months, or years— hoping that things would somehow magically improve in your absence? Inside you felt depleted and weak, and the world seemed so bleak. You longed for a shoulder to lean on—someone to love and support you, someone like a nurturing parent to take your hand and lift you out of your misery, someone to give you the courage to go on.

We all long for this kind of support, for the knowledge that we have a loving, caring, nurturing parent behind us: someone with whom to share our joys and sorrows, someone whom we can always count on to feel for us and be on our side; someone who lets us know that, whatever we are dealing with, we are not alone, because that person is there and cares about us.

When we support ourselves, we are being this kind of loving parent to ourselves, being the parent that we wish we had had— the sort of parent to whom we know we can turn, assuring us that no matter what happens, we can always come home and be loved. Supporting ourselves is letting ourselves know that no matter how bad things get, no matter what losses or disappointments we may suffer, we will still have ourselves in our corner loving us, and rooting for us, and being there for us.

Such support enables us to feel that we are standing on solid ground. We know that, even if we slip, we will not slide off the face of the Earth to float in space eternally alone and unanchored. Rather, we feel grounded and secure, with other people and within ourselves.

Children with supportive parents can explore and develop and grow confident in safety, secure in the knowledge that if things do not go well, they will not be left alone to pick up the pieces. As these children mature, they incorporate this supportive presence within themselves. They learn to believe in themselves and to be able to take risks because they will not make themselves feel like failures if these ventures aren't successful. Rather, they know how to support themselves through the bad times, while having faith in themselves and their future. Their having been supported by their parents has led to their being able to support themselves.

However, many of us were not supported as children. Now as adults we may long for and seek out support at the same time as we may mistrust and thwart it. We often are fearful of trusting anyone lest we be disappointed, betrayed, or abandoned. Despite our great desire for support, we may not be able to accept it because we do not feel grounded enough in ourselves, not confident enough of our ability to stand on our own two feet. We cannot risk letting anyone else be our "crutch" (except for very limited situations or periods), unless we believe that we will not fall down and be permanently injured if that crutch is suddenly taken away.

I have often encountered this in my therapeutic work. A woman will long to be helped, even rescued, at the same time as she will fend me off—not knowing how to be both independent and dependent, strong and needy, capable and vulnerable. Take, for example, Monica.

Monica, an executive who is now in a loving, supportive relationship, came into therapy in her early thirties after the breakup of a two-year relationship. This relationship had been characterized by frequent fighting and infrequent sex. As could be guessed from such a history, Monica had problems with intimacy. She longed to be guided and taken care of, and she also wanted to stand on her own two feet. She dealt with these contrasting needs as polarities, and feared that feeling dependent, needy, and vulnerable meant that she couldn't also be independent, strong, and capable. Consequently, she denied and suppressed feelings of "weakness" for fear of becoming overwhelmed and non-functioning.

This conflict was played out in sessions where she would tell me how important I was to her and give me more than my fair share of credit for her progress, rather than owning the important role she had in the changes she was making. At the same time she would maintain her distance, often find it difficult to talk about the things on her mind, sometimes become irrationally angry, stay away when she was most needy, and in general resort to various maneuvers to fend me off out of fear that her dependency needs would lead her to be a weakling and a nothing.

Monica, like many of us, had to learn that we are all filled with seemingly contradictory feelings: We want to be strong and we want to be taken care of. We want intimacy and we want to be left alone. We want excitement and we want peace and quiet. We want adventure and we want security. The secret lies not in trying to figure out what we really want, but in accepting the ebb and flow between polarities. **Letting ourselves be where we are leads us someplace new. Keeping ourselves locked where we wish we were, leads to stagnation.** When we need support, ask for it, and take it in, we feel better and stronger. When we need support, deny this need, and try to act strong without it, we become more isolated from ourselves and others and therefore even more needy. It is the truly independent person who finds it easiest to be dependent, and it is the one who can most readily allow her dependency needs to be satisfied who becomes really independent.

Some women struggling with conflicts around independence/ dependence go to the other extreme. Rather than, like Monica, living a life where they fend off people and their own dependency, they cling to their dependency for fear that, if they truly stand on their own two feet, no one will ever again take care of them. Consider, for example, Jackie.

> Jackie, a beautiful, intelligent, personable professional in her mid-thirties continually got into relationships where she was focused only on pleasing her man. Rather than say what she really thought and felt, she would say what she guessed he wanted to hear. After even a weekend of this masquerade, it would be such a strain that she couldn't wait to get away. But she would remain in the relationship, usually for years, for fear of being left alone. Eventually she would break away, after having first started another relationship.
>
> In the rest of her life she was also afraid to go after what she wanted. She lived in a small apartment, though she could afford better, waiting for marriage to move. At work, too, she opted for a mid-level position that did not require her to be competitive. She literally was afraid to put herself in the driver's seat, so had never learned to drive.

In our work together Jackie became aware of how she continually soft-pedaled her many strengths for fear that, if she took care of herself, no one else would ever do so. This is a common fear among women. We have been taught that men want a "total woman," a sexy, all-giving woman who cares only about pleasing them. A self-sufficient career woman is often pictured as cold, demanding, aloof, without needs beyond career. So Jackie attempted to protect herself from abandonment by hiding important parts of herself.

Jackie came to understand that, before she could be comfortably connected to a man, she had to feel free to be herself, and this freedom would come only when she was anchored enough in her ability to be independent that she was no longer terrified at the thought of being alone. For the first time in her life, she went through an extended time without a relationship, and during this period bought and furnished the kind of apartment that she had been wanting for so long, earned a promotion at work, and learned to drive a car. When she was secure in her ability to take care of herself, she then was able to enter into a relationship where she was no longer afraid to be herself for fear her man would leave, because she now knew she could stand alone.

Are you someone who was not supported when you were growing up? Then perhaps you feel, "Why depend on anyone? She or he will only let me down, or leave me, or not be enough for me." If so, you may have difficulty in relationships. Such difficulty can take quite different forms:

- You may approach on the one hand but avoid on the other by seeking out unsupportive people with whom you do not have to risk really opening yourself up.
- You may hide and deny your real strengths in order to cling to a loved one whom you believe is your only source of security, and in so doing create the distance that comes with denying a whole part of your personality.
- You may hold back from involvements rather than allow yourself to risk being let down or left.
- You may be in a relationship about which you perpetually feel ambivalent, and blame your partner as well as yourself for your discontent. Underneath you may long for support, but fear that if you allow yourself to depend on another, you will lose the capacity to stand on your own two feet. Thus, even when support is offered, it may be difficult to accept.

Whatever your coping strategy, before you can allow yourself to truly utilize support from others, you first need to feel confident that you won't undermine yourself in doing so. This confidence comes when you learn to support yourself. Supporting yourself builds inner strength and makes you less threatened by your vulnerabilities because you know that no matter how bad things get, you will be there for yourself like a nurturing parent, making yourself feel backed up and loved. The stronger you feel inside, the easier it becomes to accept support from others appropriately, because you need no longer fear losing your ability to take care of yourself. Then you will be in a support circle, where supporting yourself enables you to accept support from others, which strengthens your ability to support yourself.

STROKING

Have you ever petted a cat, gently stroking it all over? The cat luxuriated in your touch, stretching out or curling up and purring. **Can you remember being stroked yourself in this way? Maybe someone gently massaged your back or neck, or ran soothing fingers against your face or through your hair. Perhaps you can picture being a child rocked on your mother's lap, or swung in your father's arms. Let yourself luxuriate in these sensations—the feel of the fingers . . . the sound of loving words . . . the sight of your loved one's eyes smiling at you . . . the smell of his or her body. Now experience the feelings that these sensations evoke. You feel warm and alive and happy and very good about yourself. You feel wonderful and special to have inspired these loving strokes. You did not have to earn them, you merited them just by being you. You feel like the kind of person to whom good things happen, and you feel worthy of getting all the good things that life has to offer. It feels like the world is smiling at you and reveling at being with you, and you are reveling at being in the world, confident of yourself and expecting to succeed. With this kind of send-off, you're bound to find your heart's desire.**

Unfortunately some of us got a very different kind of send-off. We got little stroking in our growing-up years, and entered adulthood feeling as if the world were frowning at us and had no room for us. We feel like the poor kid with her face pressed against the candy store window staring at the goodies that are only for others, never for her. Life seems to us to be a constant uphill struggle, where we are condemned like Sisyphus to eternally push the boulder to the top of the mountain, only to have it roll down so that we have to begin again. We long for someone to rescue us, to give us hope, to pull us out of the morass— someone to change us from life's victims into happy, satisfied, successful people. However, we have little real hope of this happening. Our self-image alternates between Diana Prince/Wonder Woman–type fantasies (i.e., under this mild-mannered exterior lies a terrific, wonder woman) and feeling like a worthless, inadequate nothing. We do not really expect to be rescued, both because we feel deep down that we don't deserve it, and also because we do not see the world as a rescuing place, a place where we will be loved, and stroked, and nurtured.

We need to learn to rescue ourselves by stroking ourselves, by giving ourselves some of the love and appreciation and approval we long for. Then we, too, will be able to smile at the world and feel it smiling back—and will feel that nothing can stop us.

Some people stroke themselves physically when they need comforting. I often find myself gently rubbing my arm or stroking my cheek or my head without having made a conscious decision to do so. Other times, particularly when I am tired or stressed, I seek the comforting embrace of a hot bath. It always makes me feel peaceful and rejuvenated. Most often, I will stroke myself with words: words of comfort, words of hope, words of support, words of encouragement, and words of acceptance.

It may be hard for you to envision giving yourself Compassion, Acceptance, Respect, Encouragement, Support, and Stroking. For many people the very idea of nurturing themselves goes against the grain. The concept is easy enough to grasp:

> Attacking yourself produces decreased self-esteem and failure, while nurturing yourself produces growth, optimism, high self-esteem, and success.

However, in your heart and gut it may be hard to believe that CARESSing yourself is the true path to change.

Perhaps you view yourself as unworthy and inadequate, needing to be chastised and punished, or at least reformed, before you can approve of yourself. Maybe you believe that being nice to yourself will only spoil you and confirm you in your undesirable ways. Where did these negative self-appraisals come from, and what makes so many women adopt such draconian measures in dealing with ourselves?

CHAPTER 3

Why We Are the Way We Are

We devalue ourselves and treat ourselves in harsh, judgmental, overly critical ways because we have been taught to do so. In the previous chapters we looked at some of the general ways our culture undermines women's abilities to esteem ourselves. Now let's examine the influence of the first representatives of our society and transmitters of our culture that we came into contact with in our lives: our parents or parental figures.

Each of us comes into the world with her own personality and temperament traits. Some emerge from the womb as lusty babies who spend most of their time awake and intense; others are more placid, sleep a lot, and are easily comforted. From the moment of birth our temperament begins to interact with those of our family members—usually with Mother's first, and then with those of Father, siblings, and other household residents. Gradually the circle widens to include additional relatives, family friends, peers, siblings, friends, teachers, coaches, neighbors, camp counselors, clergy, and many others who touch our lives in some way. In each of these interactions there is the opportunity to be nurtured and CARESSed.

A noted longitudinal study of babies from the age of two months into adulthood shows that a crucial determinant in a child's emotional growth and development lies in how the parents respond to the child's temperament.[1] If the parents react to the child's personality with loving acceptance, the child grows up to feel good about herself, and capable of many things. If the parents react with annoyance, anger, distance, or by being overwhelmed, the child grows up feeling troubled and sometimes gets into trouble.

Some children are lucky enough to have parents whose personalities mesh well with theirs, or (even luckier) have parents who are able to appreciate their child's personality even though her temperament clashes with theirs. Others are not so lucky. They have parents who mainly disapprove of them, who constantly criticize them and demand that they be both different and better. Still others have parents who largely ignore them, parents who pay attention to their children only when their children are catering to their needs. The children of these critical, distant, or self-involved parents grow up feeling that they are not good enough to merit their parents' love, so they constantly criticize themselves, hoping to improve and thereby gain their parents' attention and approbation. The most unlucky of all are children whose parents seem to hate them—nothing these children do is ever right or can ever please. They get the message that they should never have been born and, in identification with their parents, hate themselves for being here and having needs. They spend their lives trying to make up for what they believe to be their badness.

Most people's experiences growing up were somewhat mixed. Perhaps one parent was nurturing and CARESSing, and the other was withdrawn . . . or critical . . . or absent. Perhaps both parents were sometimes overly critical, and sometimes caring and compassionate. Maybe one parent was both self-involved and critical or over-involved and critical. Perhaps your parents divorced and remarried, or only one remarried, and you grew up shuttling back and forth between two very different households. Maybe your parental figure(s) were not mother and father but mother alone, grandparents, an aunt, foster family, sibling, or a paid caretaker.

The possibilities for the kinds of parenting experiences are infinite, because each human being is unique, and each pair of parents is a unique pair, and each child born to a couple is also unique. Two children growing up in the same family, even two children close in age, often have very different parental and familial experiences. These differences may be due to the child's temperament or birth order or gender; or they may be due to how each of the parents is feeling about her- or himself, each other, having another child, other stresses in her or his life, or the color of the child's hair. Perhaps the parents desperately wanted a son, and got a daughter instead. Maybe daughter number two looks like Grandma, whom Mother adored . . . or hated. Maybe child number one was desired to prove Father's virility, and number two was excess baggage. Or maybe child number one completely disturbed the parents' lives and life-style, while number two entered into a family that had become more child-centered. Perhaps the parents put lots of energy into their first two children, and left the last two to be raised by their older siblings. Perhaps the parents were busy establishing their careers while the first two were small, and then poured their energies into the last one. The possibilities are endless.

To communicate clearly and coherently about our parental experiences, however, we need to make some generalizations, establish some categories, even as we recognize that these categories will not fit everyone, and will fit no one exactly. Let us consider, then, different styles of parenting and their effect on our ability to nurture and CARESS ourselves. For the sake of simplicity I will refer throughout to the primary caretaker as "Mother," and the secondary one as "Father," even though this is not always the case.

First, though, I want to make clear that we are examining these styles of parenting to help ourselves, not to blame our parents. I firmly believe that most parents, no matter how much they might not have met our needs, did the best they could at the time—and they too were once children and suffered the ravages of family and society. This doesn't mean, however, that we don't have a right to feel angry, sad, or hurt about many of the things that our parents did or didn't do. It is important to acknowledge these feelings and work them through, so that we are not burdened with them for life. We all know that "she who does not learn from history is bound to repeat it." Our history is important to each of us, so that we don't perpetuate what started in childhood. Some of the steps in part 2 are designed to help you stop destructive patterns that you learned while growing up.

THE GOOD-ENOUGH MOTHER

D.W. Winnicott, a British psychoanalyst, described the "good-enough mother" as a woman who, while far from perfect, is able to consistently enough respond appropriately to her child's needs so that the child grows up with the feeling that Mother is there when needed, and that the world is a good place where the child can be her authentic self and where her needs will be meet.[2] As the child moves through the different stages of growth and development from symbiotic bonding, through separation and individuation and going off into the world, Mother remains there when needed, setting appropriate limits, guiding and supporting, but also being able to let go—giving her child both roots and wings.

Sounds simple? It's easier said than done. I remember being a new and exhausted mother with a six-month-old infant. I struggled with whether to let her cry herself to sleep when she awoke at 2:00 A.M. after being asleep only two hours. Did she need me and would I make her feel rejected and abandoned if I did not go to her? Or, as my pediatrician maintained, was she developing bad sleep habits and should she be encouraged to sleep through the night by not picking her up? Steeped in psychoanalytic literature from my then recently completed analytic training, I desperately longed for a book that addressed the nuts and bolts of how to be a "good-enough mother"—a kind of psychoanalytic

Dr. Spock. By the time I had my second child, two years and eight months later, I had discovered that not everything I did was crucial. I had learned that no one everyday act of mine—like picking her up or not picking her up, like going out for the evening or not going out, or even yelling at her or not yelling at her—was going to ruin her for life. Rather, what was important was the overall quality of my mothering, a consistent loving presence despite my limitations. I had also learned that children are resilient (though some are more vulnerable than others), that they are born with strong biological processes that push them towards growth and development, and that it takes more than a sometimes-raised voice or an incorrect disciplinary measure to halt these processes.

THE OVER-INVOLVED PARENT

Some of us had a parent, usually Mother, who could not let go. As we left the warm snuggliness of early bonding and attempted to set off to see the world on toddler's feet, Mother was there over-protecting, longing to have her baby back in her arms and against her breast. As we grew, and persisted in our desire to find out what the world had to offer, Mother became angry and berated us, or tried to make us feel guilty for wanting to separate. At times she also may have thrown us out on our own too much (thus dealing with feeling rejected by "abandoning" us in return) but in the main she was pervasively intrusive—trying to pal around with our friends, reading our mail and diaries, dictating our dress and actions. When we tried to break away, Mother's constant message was that we were bad for leaving her. The more we persisted in breaking away and "abandoning" Mother, the more she assailed us.

Whether as children we responded to our over-involved mother with compliance or rebellion, or some of both—the end result was that we felt bad about ourselves. We (to our child's way of thinking) must be awful both to get Mother so enraged and to be so furious at Mother. Underneath our hurt, and rage, and guilt we felt alone . . . and filled with longing for the warm, loving, all-giving, and adoring mother of infancy. As adults we may search for this kind of closeness, but are doomed to be disappointed—for what is sought is not fully attainable in an adult relationship. Moreover, if we succeeded in separating from Mother (many of us don't, and remain tied to Mother in a love/hate relationship for life), we are often afraid to let anyone get really close for fear of losing our hard-won autonomy.

We also have great difficulty nurturing ourselves. We might feel sorry for ourselves for having had such a difficult childhood, but we find it difficult to be really compassionate towards ourselves. Instead, in our guts we experience ourselves through Mother's eyes as the "bad abandoner," and are plagued by guilt, which we try to assuage by berating ourselves as Mother did.

This is a common, but ineffective, way to deal with guilt. We try to make up for our guilt-invoking behavior by telling ourselves how terrible we are, and feel lousy. Our miserable feelings are meant both as an atonement for our guilt and as a spur to improved conduct. However, this just doesn't work. For instance, if we feel guilty for not wanting to visit our parents, berating ourselves may expiate our guilt, but it in no way helps us to come to grips with our ambivalence about visiting. As long as we blame ourselves, rather than accepting and working through our feelings, we will remain reluctant to visit, and feel guilty. Telling ourselves how bad we are does not help us to improve, it just keeps us stuck in a cycle of guilt and self-blame.

Those of us who had intrusive parents may have impressive accomplishments in the world—we developed a lot of strength in pulling away from Mother—but we are not impressed with ourselves and do not feel successful, because inside we feel bad and guilty. We hurt in a place where we cannot let others in, though we may feel that it is the others who are not there or will not enter. We do not realize that it is our own door that is not really open.

Consider Vivian, who at thirty seemed to have it all—a successful career, a loving husband, a house in the suburbs, and a baby. Her childhood was a different story. In adolescence she had had to fight tooth and nail in order to separate from a very intrusive, belittling, attacking, and irrational mother. She had not spoken to her mother in years. Vivian longed for the comforting mother of her infancy and grew increasingly despondent as she accepted this search as illusionary. She was deeply disappointed to discover that having a child, rather than making her feel fulfilled, only added to her neediness for what a mother could offer.

Vivian felt an emptiness that none of her relationships filled. Her husband, while loving and dutiful, looked to her to be the strong one and to be emotionally there for him. While this relationship felt safe in that it didn't threaten her autonomy, or make her fear abandonment, it also left her feeling isolated. She longed to be able to lean on her husband for empathy and support, yet feared opening herself up to him because she couldn't stand the pain and isolation she felt when she exposed her rawness and her neediness and he couldn't respond in the connected way she needed. Her friends, too, were disappointing, caught up in their own lives, concerned but not there like a grandmother would be to ease Vivian's burdens and adore her child.

Vivian longed to feel better . . . to have some hope . . . to ease the aching, lonely, emptiness inside of her, but she could not. She felt too depleted . . . and too angry at the world for not providing her with a good mother. When she learned to nurture herself and to CARESS the small child within her, she began to fill some of her inner emptiness and to feel more centered in herself and her life.

THE DISTANT PARENT

Some of us had a parent who was under-involved with us—a parent whose attention we never got nearly enough of, whose CARESS we longed for. This longing is poignantly expressed in the following poem by Rose, a young woman who entered treatment because she had intense anxiety:

Hearing your keys opening the locks wasn't always
an invitation to smile and say, "Dad's home!"
For when you walked into the house so many things
seemed to suddenly escape before you closed the door.
Knowing you were home meant that childish laughter
had to cease; playful sounds had to be muted;
And anything not related to putting your supper on
the table was simply of no interest to you.
Sometimes you'd stop off in my room on your way to
the kitchen to give me a bag of money to count out for
you, and that was fun and exciting for me.
But if there was no money to count, or no coupons
to add up, you had nothing to say to me and had no time
or patience for me to say anything to you.
That was OK—maybe you were really hungry and
just couldn't do anything until after you ate.
I could wait.

Hearing you get up from the table and leave the
kitchen meant that maybe now I could talk to you.
But that wasn't too likely to happen, for you
wanted to lie down in your bed and read the newspaper.
So many things were happening all around the
world—surely they were more important and more
interesting than what I might have had on my mind.
Besides, if I started to talk to you, you couldn't
hear the news reports on the radio.
That was OK—maybe after you finished reading
your paper and listening to the news you'd let me enter

your world—at least for a while.
I could wait.

Hearing you shut off the radio meant that you had
your fill of news for the day.
And that maybe now was the right time for me to
come and sit next to you for a while.
Maybe I could tell you about something that
happened to me today, or maybe I could listen about
something that happened to you.
But as I left my room and approached yours,
suddenly I heard you turn off the light on your night
table.
It was still so early—but then you always went to
sleep early.

I guess Mom was right when she said you worked
hard and got tired at night.
Funny thing, though: All of my friends' fathers
worked hard, but they didn't go to sleep so early.
Well, I guess it's OK—I didn't really have
anything special to say to you anyway.
Maybe you won't be so tired tomorrow night.
I could wait.

There are many reasons why parents are distant. Mother may
be seriously depressed and unavailable. Dad may have had distant
parents and never learned how to be close. Or he may be so
caught up in earning a living that he doesn't realize how distant
he is. Or maybe Mom feels so overwhelmed by all her responsibilities that she just wants to be left alone. Whatever the reasons,
the effect on the child is the same. The child sees and feels only
one thing, "I need Mommy and/or Daddy, and I don't have them."

When a child aches for a parent's love and attention and does
not receive it, she concludes that there is something wrong with
her—that she is missing something essential, something needed
to grab and maintain another's interest. If it was Mother who was

distant, the child grows up feeling unnurtured, insufficient, and deficient. If it was Father who was distant, the grown daughter often longs for a satisfying love relationship at the same time that she feels hopeless and inadequate.

Those of us who had a distant parent enter adulthood longing for closeness, while often afraid to be vulnerable. We search for the magic that will make us "like everyone else"—loved . . . accepted . . . valued. This becomes our holy grail, our golden fleece. Only instead of traveling the world searching, we search within ourselves—to figure out what is wrong, missing, lacking; what is off-putting about ourselves. If only we could find the magic key, we could turn it and make everything right.

THE NARCISSISTIC PARENT

"Mirror, mirror on the wall, who's the fairest of them all?" This was the query of Snow White's stepmother to her magic mirror. To stay on her good side and avoid her rage, the mirror had to answer, "You, you are the fairest of them all." Some of us were raised by this kind of parent, who related to us as though our reason for being was to be a mirror that would reflect our parent's greatness. We were treated as an extension of the parent, not as a separate person. We were encouraged, if not forced, to partic-ipate in the activities our parent was, or wished to be, good at—regardless of our interests or talents. We were expected to look the way our parent wanted us to look, and were often dressed up to fit our parent's image of the perfect child. Our narcissistic parents were too caught up in their own grandiosity and inner emptiness to see us clearly, or to consistently offer us compassion, acceptance, respect, encouragement, support, and stroking. In-stead their response to us hinged around how much we met *their needs* and fed their egos.

Those of us raised by narcissistic parents often have difficulty being empathically connected to others. We cannot give what we never received. Though we may have pleasant, charming person-alities, can be entertaining and erudite, and often have lots of people we call friends; underneath we feel empty. Our relationships usually lack real intimacy, and it is very difficult for us to CARESS and be CARESSed. As we head into mid-life we often become increasingly depressed, as our youthful good looks start to fade and people become less interested in playing mirror to our sparkling surfaces. We long to be seen . . . and appreciated . . . and loved—but have little idea how to let another human being get really close to us. Moreover, we usually are not aware that we are not close to the people in our lives. We just know that something seems to be driving us, and making us unhappy, and we easily feel picked on and not appreciated.

Ayanna was raised by a narcissistic mother and a distant stepfather. By age thirty-four she had made many unsuccessful attempts to please her mother. She tried to dress smartly, have a professional career, be independent and choose a man of whom her mother would approve. Nothing worked. If anything Mother seemed fearful of Ayanna outdoing her, and kept giving Ayanna the message that she expected her to mess up. So Ayanna tried messing up—flunking out of graduate school, getting fired, being evicted, and moving back in with Mama. This also didn't work, as Mother, in her typical martyred fashion, made Ayanna feel unwelcome.

When I started working with Ayanna she was always smiling, a really pleasant person, the kind of woman people always thought of as nice. Underneath she was a lost child who had locked away her feelings of neediness . . . and loneliness . . . and despair— locked away her authentic self—so she could keep herself safe from the pain of wanting and not having, the pain of needing and having no one there to meet those needs, the pain of being open and vulnerable and caring, and finding herself alone. These feelings are expressed in the following poem by Ayanna:

> *My smiling friendship*
> *Do not ask too much of me*

I want to be liked
Too much
To care about your tears
And pain.

Your tears and pain
They do not touch me
My armor is 100% steel
My smile dazzles
Blinds, seduces
There is emptiness
Behind the razzle-dazzle.
Do not ask me
To fill the void
Just ask me to smile
Do not ask me to dry your tears
With all this steel
I cannot hear you.

Deflect the pain
Behind the smile
Ask me about the weather
And about my job
About money and inflation
Do not ask me
Why I never married
Or if I ever loved
Or why I travel alone
With all this steel
I cannot hear you.

I disappoint her
Because I want
A smiling friendship
Not the kind that goes beneath the skin
Like seeds planted
Beneath the brown brown earth

But the smiling friendship
That hovers near the surface
Like oil in vinegar
Never mixing
Just being there
Never going behind the smile
To take a journey
Towards the sky
On my palomino.

Wind me up
I smile
Pleasantly
Never a bad word
To say about anyone
Don't take the chance
To remove the mask
And see the clouds
And rainbows
Just smile and bare
That ivory, enameled, gold-filled
Smile and build that wall
And smile.

Ayanna speaks for many of us when she says she is afraid to "remove the mask and see the clouds . . . and rainbows." We are afraid to remove our masks because we believe that it is our masks that keep us safe from our pain—the pain of not feeling lovable "just the way we are"—the pain of desperately wanting to be ourselves and get CARESSed instead of being ignored, rejected, or attacked. So we try to be what our parents want and what society wants, and we try not to want what we experience we cannot get. And after a while we forget what we really want, and we pursue what we know we can get—approval for our surface, our "false selves"—and we no longer know what is missing and why we feel so empty inside. We know only that something is lacking. If we try to delve into our emptiness, see what is behind it, we can become frightened—frightened of standing unmasked in an unnurturing world.

THE INSECURE PARENT

Some mothers or fathers are so insecure themselves that, despite their best intentions, they can model only insecurity to their children. This is the mother who continually feels and may often say, "I'm no good . . . I feel guilty . . . I never do enough." Or, the father who constantly conveys, "I'm weak . . . I'm a failure . . . I'm no good at anything." Their children sense these parents' insecurity and view the parents as weak and inadequate. These children are likely to regard themselves, too, as insubstantial, feeling "How can I be worthy when I'm the product of such an inferior being?"

In adulthood some of these children will identify with the stronger, perhaps bullying parent, while others will identify with the insecure parent and become insecure and overanxious to please. Insecure women tend to seek out authority figures (often mates) who seem sure of themselves, hoping to find a confident parent who will bestow on them the mantle of worth and adequacy. Unfortunately, all too often, insecure women choose mates (or other authority figures, such as bosses) whose aura of self-confidence proves to be ersatz: the mate who at first glance appeared to be self-assured, but at closer scrutiny proves to be merely opinionated, stubborn, and critical. The insecure woman usually then tries harder and harder to please this overcritical mate, but inevitably fails (because there is no pleasing overcritical people), blames herself for this failure, and thus increases her feelings of inadequacy. Over the years insecure women typically accumulate tremendous rage at their mates for being so denigrating, but they are unable to really assert themselves. They feel too insecure, too unworthy. They long to be affirmed—to be told that they are good, worthy, competent, and lovable, but they cannot affirm themselves. Consider Lois.

When Lois entered therapy she was forty-eight, had been married for twenty-two years, and had three teenage daughters. Her mother, Gertrude, had been an orphan who grew up in a group home. Gertrude married a sometimes benevolent, often tyrannical man and had four children, of whom Lois was the youngest. Gertrude deferred to her husband about everything, having little sense of her own worth or adequacy. Lois grew up with the model of her mother as a doormat. Gertrude paid scant heed to either her own or Lois's needs, and instead was totally focused on pleasing Lois's overcritical father.

In her own marriage Lois had duplicated much of her parents' union. She, too, married a sometimes benevolent, often tyrannical man whom Lois tried very hard to please at the same time that she felt enraged by him. She, too, acted like a doormat—and consequently her daughters, while loving her, had little respect for her. Lois was aware of this, and tried hard to be more assertive, but found it very difficult. She knew that her daughters' many insecurities were in part based on identification with her, and she very much wanted to be a model of security and self-confidence, but she could not. She felt too unworthy, too inadequate, too frightened of punishment and abandonment if she really stood up for herself. She longed to be CARESSed by her family, but she could not CARESS herself.

THE HIGHLY CRITICAL/ABUSIVE PARENT

Fairy tales are filled with stories of ogres and wicked witches and big bad wolves. For most of us these figures serve as stand-ins for the mean, angry, violent feelings that we harbor within us and that we fear in ourselves and in our parents. The wicked stepmother is both Mommy when she is angry and says "no," and a personification of our rage at Mommy for saying no to us. Similarly, the wolf who threatens to "huff and puff and blow your house down" is both how Daddy seems to us when he is angry, and how we feel when we are angry at Daddy for ordering us about.

Children who are reared in an accepting, nurturing atmosphere learn to put the good and bad aspects of their parents into one package. Mommy or Daddy can be strict, yell, get angry or preoccupied, but they are also responsive, involved, supportive, and loving. In the same manner, these children learn to put the good and bad aspects of themselves into one package. They can feel mean, spiteful, jealous, and hateful, as well as loving, warm, compassionate, and giving. The "bad" within thus becomes tolerable because it is not perceived as negating the good, rather it is acknowledged and accepted as part of the human condition. These children become adults who can love themselves, as they were loved by their parents, not only when being perfect, but all the time.

But what of those of us who grew up with a mother who generally (not just occasionally) really was a wicked witch? Or with a father who was a big bad wolf? We suffered the horrible continual trauma of being told that we were bad . . . willful . . . stupid . . . crazy. Nothing that we did was right. None of our efforts to make things better ever worked. Our attempts to feel loved, respected, valued, and supported were subverted. Instead, we were constantly berated and belittled . . . or worse. Some of us were beaten, or sexually abused. To make matters worse, we were told that we got this punishment because we were bad, and deserved it.

How can we possibly feel good about ourselves, and love ourselves "warts and all" when our warts feel like giant deformities, and our virtues a self-serving fantasy?! We know only how to attack ourselves, constantly criticizing, berating, and punishing ourselves in imitation of the twisted behavior that passed as nurturance at home. Rachel and Sharon grew up in different kinds of abusive homes.

Rachel, now a successful professional, originally consulted me shortly after graduation from college when she found herself depressed, and floundering, unable to find a direction in life and pursue it. The younger of two children, she grew up in a Jewish family that put great stress on education. Her sister was brilliant, the gem of the family and highly valued by her authoritarian father. Rachel, who has a learning disability that was not diagnosed until she was in her twenties, did poorly in school. She was scorned by her father who belittled and rejected her, refused to spend time with her, and called her "stupid," "lazy," and "retarded." Not surprisingly, Rachel left home in her teens, anxious to get away from this denigrating parent. After having some positive work experience, she entered college in her twenties, determined to prove that she was not stupid. Nevertheless she balked at actually completing her assignments, partly because she feared she would be found lacking, and partly because she did not want to give in to her teachers' demands, as previously she had resisted her father's orders. She got through college by beguiling her professors into giving her incompletes, playing out her need to feel special and cared about, while she slowly and laboriously wrote her papers. However, she could never feel special enough. Always around the corner lurked the possibility of being called on the carpet, berated, and flunked. No matter how much she proved her capabilities to others (and she eventually graduated with honors), inside she still felt her father was right—she was stupid, lazy, incompetent, a failure. On the one hand she was furious at her father for not CARESSing her. On the other hand, she could not CARESS herself.

Rachel's attitude towards herself mirrored her father's attitude towards her. Deep down she looked at herself through her father's eyes and regarded herself with disdain and contempt. She lived her life in fear that her "stupidity" would be discovered. Though she was constantly on guard with authorities and prepared to take the offensive at the slightest indication of her "rights" being infringed upon—determined never again to be her "father's" helpless victim—she could not fend off or defeat the critical father within herself. Consequently she frequently felt depressed and had a hard time mobilizing herself. In our work together she learned to replace her inner father with an inner nurturer, enabling her to be at peace with herself and to pursue her personal and professional goals with confidence and security.

Both of Sharon's middle-class, college-educated parents were physically and verbally abusive to her. The firstborn child, she was not wanted and barely tolerated. She was constantly yelled at, hit, made fun of, and told that she was ugly, bad, willful, and crazy. She remembers desperately trying to be good . . . trying not to do anything wrong . . . even afraid to leave her bed at night to use the bathroom for fear of being hit. She spent her childhood living in horror and dread of her parents' anger and attacks. As an adult she attacked herself in the same way. When I first met Sharon, she had little conscious anger towards her parents, though she had some intellectual awareness of the enormity of their cruelty, and instead had directed much of her anger towards herself, and feared that she really was bad and crazy. Though she had learned to assert herself, she remained overly fearful of all authorities and quasi-authorities, dreading that they would see how bad and crazy she really was and would then reject and abandon her.

Children of highly critical, abusive parents cannot help but feel that their parents are right and that they, themselves, are bad. The *reason* they cannot help but feel they are bad is that the alternative is even worse—to believe that Mommy and Daddy are bad. If Mommy and Daddy are bad, then there really is no hope . . . no escape . . . no salvation. An abused child, black and blue all over, scarred, burnt, still wants her mommy . . . still wants to be loved by the person who's supposed to love her . . . still wants to desperately cling to the possibility of being loved and CARESSed. So, if Mommy and Daddy aren't bad, then she must be bad. It must be all her fault. If only she could be good, be what they want, be what they need, be what they value. But no matter how hard she tries, she never succeeds. They keep on criticizing . . . and screaming . . . or maybe hitting. She must deserve it. She's just so bad, and they're so disappointed in her. She's such a failure.

Such feelings of inadequacy and failure, so drummed in during childhood, are hard to shake. Abused girls become women who are supersensitive to evidence of their faults, and largely disregard evidence of their assets. Others may see them as likable, attractive, and successful—but they, like Sharon, still feel rejectable, ugly, and a failure. They need to learn, as Sharon has, to recognize and value their true strengths, and to replace their abusive inner-critic with a compassionate and nurturing inner-caretaker. Sharon now has not only developed a positive sense of herself, but is also largely able to hold onto her own worth even in the face of criticism or other negative reactions.

What kind of parent(s) or parenting figure(s) did you have? Some of you may have had a parent that fitted neatly into one of these categories. Others may have had a parent that was more an amalgam, fitting two or more of the above descriptions. Perhaps your mother was both insecure and over-involved, or insecure and too distant. Perhaps your father was narcissistic and distant, or narcissistic and overcritical. Or perhaps you had a mother who was good enough . . . and then died when you were young—becoming instantly unavailable. Perhaps your father was good enough until you were seven, when he lost his job and became permanently depressed and distant. Maybe you were raised by your loving, good-enough grandmother and your abusive uncle. Maybe none of the above classifications is sufficient.

Human beings are complex, filled with conflicted feelings, highly capable of inconsistencies and of functioning on many different levels and in many different ways. They defy summing up into neat pigeonholes. Don't try to force your parents into one of these slots if they don't fit. Rather use this system of classification, as much as it is applicable, to understand some of how you were influenced by the styles of parenting with which you were raised. It is important to recognize the types of parenting your received because:

As you were parented, so you parent yourself.

As we saw earlier, some of us—in time of need—soothe, comfort, and encourage ourselves, while others of us kick ourselves. Some of us have an inner-caretaker who is compassionate and supportive, while others of us have an inner-critic who is disparaging and abusive. This is because our inner-caretaker is modeled after our actual parents and other authority figures. If our parents approached us with love and caring . . . if they nurtured and CARESSed us . . . we learned to love and nurture and CARESS ourselves. However, if our parents generally neglected us, or were angry or harsh; if they heaped upon us criticism and disapproval, we learned to hate and disparage ourselves, we learned to hold ourselves in contempt. If they modeled insecurity or guilt, we learned to hold ourselves responsible for all our difficulties and to blame ourselves for our inadequacy.

In our growing-up years some of us had important experiences with others, separate from our parents, that helped shape our lives and our attitudes towards ourselves. Some of us had a teacher who saw our potential and gave us special encouragement and support. Others had a Girl Scout leader, or family friend who became a kind of parent to us, giving us respect, and support, and guidance. Still others of us had a grandparent, aunt, or neighbor who loved and CARESSed us. Those of us who had one of these self-affirming relationships may have an inner-caretaker that is modeled, at least in part, after this nurturing person.

Others of us encountered authority figures who only made us feel worse about ourselves—teachers who made us feel stupid, coaches who made us feel incompetent, grandparents who told us we were naughty, peers who belittled and ostracized us. These negative experiences were mitigated if our parents were nurturing, but for those of us who were largely not CARESSed by our parents, these negative experiences only further confirmed our negative feelings towards ourselves, and became more fuel for the inner fires of self-hate.

Because our inner-caretaker is modeled on our actual care-takers, those of us that had the worst parenting, and therefore most need to be nurtured as adults, unfortunately stand the least chance of getting it. How can we feel nurtured when our inner-critic is constantly berating us? How can we be nourished if we are afraid to let people be close? How can we accept another's CARESS when our inner-caretaker tells us that we don't deserve it and that we should not feel good? Before we can be CARESSed by the world, we first need to learn how to CARESS ourselves.

PART II

Ten Steps to Liking the Person You Are

The ten steps that you are about to engage in are designed to teach you how to esteem yourself. Do them to the best of your ability, and you will learn how to truly value yourself. It is best to do the steps in the order presented, as each step builds on the previous one. However, as you read along, if you choose to try certain steps and not others, that's fine. Whatever steps you take towards raising your self-esteem will be beneficial. Even if you just read this book and try to apply the concepts in it without doing any of the exercises, you will be helping yourself.

Some of you may shy away from doing some of the steps because you feel silly, hokey, uptight, hopeless, or undeserving of nurturing. If you feel this way, stop now and give yourself the encouragement you need. Allow yourself to have hope and to do something different. You have nothing to lose (these exercises cannot hurt you in any way), and much to gain. Give yourself the helping hand you need.

There is nothing mysterious about the steps in this book. They are simple and straightforward and designed to teach you how to see yourself as worthwhile and deserving, how to stop holding yourself back by criticizing and belittling yourself, and how to CARESS yourself.

When you do these exercises, give yourself as much time as you need. Most people waste much more time with guilt, depression, and self-castigation than the amount of time these exercises will take, and the time you spend working on them will produce benefits that will enhance the rest of your life. Set aside a quiet time without interruptions, and choose a place where you feel comfortable and can write. For some of these exercises you will need pencil and paper. Unless otherwise noted, each step does not have to be completed at one sitting.

It is best not to do more than one step at a time. After you complete one step and before moving on to the next, you will need to give yourself time to absorb your feelings. These steps will be most helpful if you are committed to finishing them, but not at the expense of what feels right to you.

As you go through the exercises, remember that this is a manual for a lifetime. You don't have to rush through them, and some of them you may wish to repeat many times. Let your inner sense of what is best for you be your guide. If any one step seems particularly hard or starts to make you anxious, it is probably because it is touching a vulnerable place near feelings that are hard to face. That's good, because these are precisely the feelings that are most important to recognize, and facing them offers the greatest potential for change. If you are tempted to put off or skip a particular step—STOP! Then get in touch with what you are feeling. Ask yourself what you are afraid of, and keep asking yourself until the answer comes to you. Don't be concerned with whether your fears are rational. Often we are immobilized by fears that our heads say are baseless, but which terrify our guts. Once you know what you fear, you will most likely feel relieved enough to start engaging in the step. When you then start the step, it is very important for you to give yourself permission to stop when you want. Encourage yourself, rather than force yourself.

Some of you may be reluctant to go through these steps without first knowing what all of them are, and what their thrust is. If so, that's fine. Go ahead and read through this whole part first, or the whole book if you wish. When you're done, see how you feel. If you feel like the act of reading the book gave you enough, and you don't want to do the exercises, that's fine. The last thing you want to do is to make these steps a chore or a burden.

On the other hand, if in reading about the steps you feel any or all of them could be helpful to you, I urge you to try them. Nurturing yourself, like anything you learn, will be easier to integrate into your personality as you *actively* apply the concepts presented in this book. This is your opportunity to learn how to give to yourself, so that you will like yourself, feel good about yourself, and be successful. Take it!

As you participate in the different steps, be sure to support and encourage yourself, and don't expect instant change. Old habits die hard. If you are in the habit of berating rather than nurturing yourself, expect to invest considerable time and repeated conscious effort in replacing your old habit of criticizing and denigrating yourself with being able to CARESS yourself. This is not an easy change to make, but you can do it. Take this chance to change your life. Learn how to give yourself the Compassion, Acceptance, Respect, Encouragement, Support, and Stroking that are the keys to self-esteem.

CHAPTER 4

Step One: Recognizing Your Good Points and Believing in Yourself

RECOGNIZING YOUR GOOD POINTS

The first step in raising your self-esteem is learning to recognize and appreciate your abilities, capabilities, and personal qualities.

Make a list of what you like about yourself. Label it "WHAT I LIKE ABOUT MYSELF." State everything on this list in positive terms (e.g., "I'm generous," rather than "I'm not stingy") and precede each item with "I am."

You may find this a difficult exercise because you are not accustomed to thinking about what you like about yourself, but instead are usually busy focusing on what you don't like about yourself. If so, banish these critical thoughts for now (we will deal with them later on) and promise yourself to stay focused on your positives.

Begin by first writing down those positive attributes that pop immediately into your head. For Diane (the woman presented at the end of chapter 1) these were:

I have a good voice.
I am liked by children.

I'm on time.
I'm organized and efficient.*

Next reach for other good qualities that might not readily come to mind. Focus on the things that you like about yourself that you don't often think of, or take for granted. Diane, after some thought, was able to add:

I'm reliable and responsible.
I'm good with animals.
I keep my house neat.

Now think even more deeply about your good points. To get in touch with them, ask yourself the following questions:

What is it that others like in me?
What has helped me get through difficult times in the past?
What qualities do I have that enable me to have fun?
What qualities do I have that have enabled me to learn and to grow?
What qualities do I have that have enabled me to work?
What qualities do I have that have enabled me to raise children? (if applicable)
What qualities do I have that have enabled me to be in a relationship? (if applicable)
What do I like about my appearance?

After considering these questions Diane came up with the following positives.

I am a loyal friend.
I am a good listener.

*In various places I have used client material to illustrate to the reader how to do an exercise. Often in actual therapy sessions these exercises were done informally and verbally rather than in writing, as is possible in a one-to-one situation.

I come through for people when they need me.
I am willing to try new things.
I can enjoy being silly.
I am warm.
Even though I'm often depressed and despondent, I somehow
    keep going.
I have a dry sense of humor and can be witty.
I have the ability to learn.
I have an open mind, and consider other people's opinions
    before accepting or rejecting them.
I can conceptualize well and I'm good at details.
I have a nice smile.

**Once you've made your list as long as you possibly can
on your own, ask people who like you what they like about
you.** Perhaps they value qualities in you whose worth you never
previously realized, or skipped over. Diane's friends praised her
variety of interests, her creativity, her honesty, and her good looks.

Next, check over your list and see if there's anything missing.
**Take three SLOW deep breaths, and then ask yourself, "Is
there anything else that belongs on this list? Any other good
quality I have? Anything that seems missing?" Then pause
and wait quietly for a minute.** If something else comes to mind,
add it to the list. If something seems missing, but you don't know
what, try to get a sense of what that thing is. Then add it to your
list when it comes to you. Diane added, "I have a good heart."

Finally, as you go about your daily life, be conscious of trying
to recognize more of your positives. Be sure to note them and
add them to your list of things you like about yourself.

**Upon completion of this list, read it over slowly and out
loud. Really take in each positive attribute. Acknowledge that
each admirable characteristic is really true of you.** You *know*
that you have these qualities because you have repeatedly experienced them in your life. If you start to doubt that a good quality
is really yours (people who have trouble CARESSing themselves
are always doubting themselves), go back and remind yourself of

the process you went through in recognizing this positive attribute.

Read your list by saying "*I really*" before each description. For instance, for Diane:

I really have a good voice.
I really am liked by children.
I really am on time.
I really am organized and efficient.
I really am reliable.
I really am responsible.
I really am good with animals.
I really do keep my house neat.
I really am a loyal friend.
I really am a good listener.
I really do come through for people when they need me.
I really am willing to try new things.
I really can enjoy being silly.
I really am warm.
I really do manage to keep going, even though I'm often depressed and despondent.
I really do have a dry sense of humor.
I really can be witty.
I really do have the ability to learn.
I really do have an open mind and consider other people's opinions before accepting or rejecting them.
I really can conceptualize well.
I really am good at details.
I really do have a nice smile.
I really do have a lot of different interests.
I really am creative.
I really am honest.
I really am attractive.
I really do have a good heart.

Pay careful attention to how you feel when you've finished reading each attribute. After a lifetime of beating up on yourself, isn't it wonderful to finally recognize and appreciate how many good qualities and abilities you have?! It's like coming out of a chilly damp forest into the warm nurturing rays of the sun.

BELIEVING IN YOURSELF

Put your list of the things you like about yourself in some accessible place and read it over at least twice each day. Think of your twice-daily reading of your list as your time for warming and nurturing yourself. Take your time. *Don't rush through it.* Luxuriate in feeling good about yourself. Be careful not to let any negative thoughts intrude. Dismiss all your "yes, buts" as you focus on all the truly worthwhile qualities you possess.

At first you might feel a habitual pull to switch to criticizing yourself, such as: "Yeah, I'm liked by children, but who cares when I can't find a man?" Be aware of this habit and be ready to nip it in the bud. You learned to punish yourself and you can, with time and effort, learn to stop. By attacking yourself, you are robbing yourself of the opportunity to feel good. Stop depriving yourself this way. When you find yourself thinking in the old pattern, go back and slowly reread the list of what you like about yourself, but this time let yourself really take in each positive attribute. Allow yourself to feel the warm glow that comes when you feel good about yourself. With time and practice you will find it easier and easier to dismiss critical thoughts and to focus on that warm glow.

Remember to read your list at least twice each day. Many people find it helpful to read their lists at set times, usually once in the morning, and once in the early evening. You choose the times that are best for you. Make a copy of your list and carry it with you. Keep another copy at work. Whenever you start to feel bad about yourself, read over your list *slowly* and let yourself feel that this is really you. These admirable qualities really do belong to you. Take the time to feel warmed and nurtured.

CHAPTER 5

Step Two: Looking at How You Berate Yourself

$\mathcal{A}$s we saw previously, we all share the experience of having a part of ourselves, an inner voice, that can be hostile to us and seems to take over at times. This is the voice that tells us that we are bad, wrong, at fault, undeserving, and a failure. This is the critic in us, attacking and berating us. We need to rid ourselves of this inner-critic and to replace her with an inner-caretaker that, like a nurturing parent, is loving and supportive.

You are going to learn, in this and the next step, how to recognize the inner-critic in you. You will experience how this "bad parent" within keeps you from being able to attain your goals. And you will learn a new framework for approaching yourself and your problems with acceptance and compassion and respect.

Make a list of the things you do not like about yourself and label it "SELF-CRITICISMS."

This list will likely be easy to draw up. You probably, like most of us, have been writing it mentally for years. However, you may shrink from the act of putting it on paper because you are afraid to see and acknowledge your perceived faults and failings in black and white, even though you don't dare let yourself forget about them. If so, let yourself know that the process that you are about to go through in dealing with your self-criticisms will help you to feel better about yourself.

When writing down the things that you do not like about yourself, in order not to get caught up in the depression and hopelessness that these self-criticisms usually engender, imagine yourself to be describing another person who is just like you, and give this person a name. For instance, don't write, "Nobody wants me. I keep messing up at work and no one respects me. I'm never going to be able to have a relationship or have children. . . ." Instead, write, "Stephanie [or any other name that is not yours] can't get a man. Stephanie keeps messing up at work and no one respects her. Stephanie is never going to be able to get into a relationship or have children. . . ." This device will allow you to fully consider your perceived failings and problems while staying somewhat removed, so you will not feel overwhelmed or dejected.

Take your time and make your list as complete as possible. When your list is finished, make a copy of it and save both copies for future exercises.

Before moving on to the next step, let's first consider Diane's list of self-criticisms.

DIANE'S LIST OF SELF-CRITICISMS
1. Stephanie has something terribly wrong with her that makes people not like her.
2. Stephanie is not assertive enough.
3. Stephanie is shy.
4. Stephanie is oversensitive.
5. Stephanie is too sarcastic.
6. Stephanie is self-centered.
7. Stephanie is not giving enough.
8. Stephanie has to have everything her way.
9. Stephanie is too ambitious. She should stay in her place.

10. Stephanie is a failure at dating. She'll never get married or have children.
11. Stephanie is socially awkward.
12. Stephanie is too competitive.
13. Stephanie doesn't know how to deal with competition.
14. Stephanie is always feeling sorry for herself.
15. Stephanie is a big baby. She shouldn't let her problems bother her so much.
16. Stephanie is too often depressed.
17. Too many things make Stephanie anxious.
18. Stephanie makes too many mistakes at work.
19. Stephanie has a lot of problems getting along with people at work.
20. Stephanie's bosses don't respect her. This is because she really doesn't deserve respect.
21. Stephanie is ashamed of her family. It's not nice to be ashamed of your family.
22. Stephanie is such a jerk that she doesn't even know what she wants to do with her life.
23. To put it simply, Stephanie is just a big failure—a lousy job, no relationship, no children, no future. She's hopeless!!!

When we look at Diane's lists of assets and self-criticisms, it hardly seems that the person they refer to is one and the same. How can someone have so many wonderful qualities and be in such a mess all at once? It hardly seems possible. How can someone who is efficient, responsible, reliable, and creative not be respected at work? And how can someone who is warm and silly and funny and loyal and a good listener not get along with people? Sure it's possible to be so frightened and insecure in a dating situation that one freezes up. And lots of people have trouble finding a satisfying direction for their lives. But the rest of it? Something is wrong somewhere. It just doesn't add up. Maybe your two lists don't add up either. Let's see what the problem is.

Part of the problem is that Diane had not learned that it is both natural and human to have problems. We all have problems of one kind or another, and as we saw in chapter 3, the worse our childhood was, the more problems we're likely to have, and the worse we're likely to feel about ourselves. Of course, Diane knew this intellectually—she is very intelligent and well-read— but she did not accept it in her gut. In her gut she felt that her problems were the result of something intrinsically, basically, and unfixably wrong with her. She was sure that her lack of dates proved that she was a blob, not worth dating now or ever, and that she would remain alone. Similarly, at work, where Diane had management responsibilities with a secretarial title, she blamed herself for her lack of advancement in a small and demonstrably sexist company. She saw her condescending male boss being friendly to the women who were content with their clerical positions and willing to stroke his ego, and felt that there must be something terribly wrong with her, since he was not similarly friendly in her direction. Her friends had advised her to find another, more rewarding job, but Diane did not see other possible options. What's more, she felt determined to force her boss to like and respect her at the same time as she resented and bucked his condescending attitude. How did Diane get in such a mess, and what kept her in it?

The analytic explanation is that Diane had a "repetition compulsion"—a need to reenact the unhappy events of her childhood—causing her to seek a distant, narcissistic, condescending, and rejecting father figure against whom she would continually butt her head in a vain attempt to make things come out differently. In doing so she would be trying to get the recognition, respect, acceptance, and love that she had longed for all her life *from this kind of person.* However, by choosing someone so like her father (her boss), the only response she could get was what he was capable of giving, and this was a far cry from the CARESS she was looking for.

The analytic explanation is correct as far as it goes, and it is a helpful and vital part of understanding what was going on for Diane and in helping her come to terms with herself. However, it does not go far enough. *Diane was stuck because deep down she did not respect and like herself.* She kept looking for people who reminded her of her parents to affirm her worthiness because she did not feel worthy herself. This left her dependent on being accepted by the very people most likely to reject her, and most likely to reaffirm her own low opinion of herself.

Recognizing her assets had started to help her, but what she focused on most of the time was her mental list of self-criticisms. She was sure her faults constituted the real Diane and that any-body who got to know her would see her as she saw herself. She responded to her boss, as she had as a child to her father, with anger and frustration but most of all by blaming herself. She reasoned that something terribly wrong with her caused the boss to treat her coldly and critically, since he was friendly to other women in the office. She failed to see that he, like her father, was only nice to those he feared (his bosses) and those who were ready to feed his ego. The more she blamed herself for not getting the response she wanted from her boss, the harder she tried to figure out what she did that stopped her boss from liking her, and the more frustrated and depressed she became. Thus she continued to repeat the misery of her childhood.

In order to feel better and get unstuck, she had to stop blaming and criticizing herself in this way. She had to rid herself of her inner-critic, who was always knocking her down whenever she tried to forge ahead. She needed to learn how to deal with her list of self-criticisms in a way that would help her to change and free herself, rather than keeping her stuck. In the next steps, go through the process that Diane underwent, which enabled her to establish a professional career and a satisfying marriage.

CHAPTER 6

Step Three: Recognizing the Real You

TURNING ROCKS INTO GOLD

After Diane had completed her list of self-criticisms, I told her that she was going to learn how to turn these "rocks" into gold by using her self-criticisms to set goals for herself. To start with, I asked her to carefully reconsider each critique to make sure it really fit her. If a reproach wasn't accurate, I asked her to mark it F for false, and then next to it in parentheses to affirm the truth. Those self-criticisms that she still thought were accurate even upon reconsideration, she was to mark T, and then to restate them in a nurturing rather than an attacking way. I asked her to be as specific as possible in dealing with those reproaches she thought valid, stating under what circumstances she had this problem or evidenced this characteristic, and the kind of help she needed to overcome it. Diane then went through and redid her list.

Self-criticism #1:
Has something terribly wrong with her that makes people not like her.

Diane was sure this was true. I asked her to make a list of people who do not like her, and a separate list of those who do. To her surprise she ended up with a much longer group of people who liked her than of those who didn't. Her list of admirers included long-term friends, newer friends, and some people at work who—while not personal friends—were generally friendly, responsive, and supportive. Diane was surprised because she was usually so focused on the people who responded negatively to her that it seemed to her that she couldn't get along with anyone. However, with the evidence provided by her lists, Diane realized that her belief that she could not get along with people was unfounded. Despite her inner feeling of there being something terribly wrong with her, Diane realized that self-criticism #1 was not true. I then asked her if the people who disliked her had anything in common. Upon reflection she recognized that they were all competitive, self-absorbed, and condescending. She marked an F next to this self-criticism and in parentheses wrote: **"TRUTH: Many people like me and I get along well with them. Some people, especially people who are condescending, narcissistic, and competitive, I have a great deal of difficulty with."**

Self-criticism #2:
Not assertive enough.

Diane said this was definitely true. She could think of many times she had been afraid to speak up and had allowed others to have their way, and could recall only a few times when she had stood up for herself. I asked her to rewrite it in a nonjudgmental, nurturing way. She wrote: **"I need help to become more assertive."**

Self-criticism #3:
Shy.

Diane knew she was shy, but she also recognized that she was not as shy as she used to be. She marked this self-criticism true, and rewrote it: **"I am becoming less shy, but need further** acceptance and encouragement so I can feel more willing to put myself out there."

Self-criticism #4:
Oversensitive.

Diane wasn't sure about this self-criticism. She knew that she easily felt hurt, rejected, not liked. (Note: When people describe themselves as "sensitive," they generally mean that their feelings are easily hurt, not that they are acutely tuned in to other people's feelings.) However, she wasn't sure if she had good reason to feel hurt, or if she was always making a mountain out of a molehill. She decided to put a question mark next to it and return to it later.

Self-criticism #5:
Too sarcastic.

Diane thought this was sometimes true, but not always. She was also ambivalent about being sarcastic. On the positive side, she recognized that her flair for sarcasm was part of her dry wit, which she liked—as did others. On the other hand, she realized that sometimes her anger came out in the guise of sarcasm. After some thought she decided to mark this self-criticism as true, and rewrote it: **"I need help expressing my anger directly, rather than hiding it in sarcasm."**

Self-criticism #6:
Self-centered.

Diane felt this self-criticism was true. I asked her to give me examples of her self-centered behavior. She found it was difficult to come up with examples. I asked if, on the other hand, she could think of any times when she put others' feelings and needs before her own. She could think of numerous times. I then wondered what made her think she's self-centered. She said because she's always thinking about herself and wanting things for herself. Here Diane was confused between thinking and doing. Everyone has mean and selfish thoughts. This is very different from acting on them. There is a world of difference between feeling like blocking your friend's due promotion and actually doing it. When Diane realized this, she readily marked self-criticism #6 with an F. Then she wrote: "**TRUTH: I readily help others and am sensitive to their feelings.**"

Self-criticisms #7 and #8:
Not giving enough. Has to have everything her way.
    After the realizations she reached in considering whether she was self-centered, Diane quickly marked these two self-criticisms false. After #7 she wrote: "**TRUTH: I am giving. In fact I often give more than I get.**" After #8 she wrote: "**TRUTH: I tend to be very flexible when making plans with others, and rarely insist on doing what I want.**"

Self-criticism #9:
Overambitious, should stay in her place.
    Evaluating this self-criticism had Diane in a quandary. Her mother and brothers, who had low-status, poorly paid jobs, were constantly telling her that she had it much better than they did, and they didn't know why she was so unhappy with her life or her job. She wasn't sure if they were right, or she was. Though trying hard to advance herself, part of her felt that her family was right and she should stay in her place. Her head wanted to mark this one false, but her gut questioned whether it was true. She finally decided to mark it F and then wrote: "**TRUTH: I do want a better life than my family has and I need to be encouraged and supported in my desire to achieve and succeed.**"

Self-criticism #10:
A failure at dating. Will never get married or have children.
    This self-criticism particularly bothered Diane. She knew it was true that in dating situations she was frightened of being rejected or controlled, so froze up. This made her feel hopeless about ever getting married or having children. She marked it T and rewrote it: "**I need to accept myself more so that I will be**

less frightened of rejection. **I also need to understand and deal with my fear of being controlled so I won't have to avoid dating to protect myself. If I stop being so afraid, maybe I will be able to get married and have children, though it's hard to believe. I guess I also need a lot of encouragement."**

Self-criticism #11:
Socially awkward.

Diane realized she was awkward only in dating situations. She decided it was partially true and rewrote it: **"I need more practice and support in dating."**

Self-criticisms #12 and #13:
Too competitive. Doesn't know how to deal with competition.

Diane decided to consider these two self-criticisms together. In thinking about it she realized that she didn't know whether she was over-competitive or under-competitive. She did know that the whole situation scared her. After a lot of thinking and talking to her friends, she marked self-criticism #12 false, and self-criticism #13 true. After #12 she wrote: **"TRUTH: I am afraid to compete and think that if I compete at all I am overdoing it."** She rewrote #13: **"I need help becoming more comfortable with competition and in learning how to deal with it."**

Self-criticism #14:
Always feeling sorry for self.

Diane knew that she often felt sorry for herself, and by now she realized that it only made her feel worse and more stuck. She marked it true, but had a hard time knowing how to rewrite it. I suggested that, instead of feeling sorry for herself, she could try to have real compassion for herself. She looked first amazed, then delighted. She wrote, **"I need to have more compassion for myself,"** and underlined it.

Self-criticism #15:
Big baby, bothered too much by her problems.

Diane definitely thought that this self-criticism was correct. She was always being bothered by all kinds of things that other people seemed to be able to shrug off. I asked for examples. She gave examples of minor incidents at work that greatly upset her. I asked why they upset her so much, and she explained that they seemed symbolic to her of the negative view her bosses and colleagues had of her. I pointed out that most people feel badly at being disliked and disparaged, and that many of us tend to interpret others' reactions as proof of our own, already self-perceived, inadequacies. After some exploration Diane marked #15 true. She then rewrote it: **"I am not a big baby, but I do too easily interpret the actions of others as negative reactions to me. I also too easily accept other people's disapproving opinions of me, and assume they know 'the awful truth' about me. I need help to feel better about myself and to develop a system for evaluating myself that is not based on others' harsh judgments."**

Self-criticism #16:
Too often depressed.

Diane readily marked this as true, and rewrote it: **"I need to have more hope and to believe things can get better for me."**

Self-criticism #17:
Too many things make me anxious.

Diane marked this true and rewrote it: **"I need help feeling less frightened and overwhelmed so I will feel less anxious."**

Self-criticism #18:
Makes too many mistakes at work.

Diane knew she made mistakes when she was under a lot of stress. However, most of the time she was efficient, organized, and competent. This wasn't good enough, though, for Diane. She felt that if she wasn't perfect, then she was no good, deficient. I asked if her boss and other managers made mistakes. She said "sure," and that part of her job was to catch and correct their errors. "Why are they allowed and you're not?" I wanted to know. She began to accept that everyone makes mistakes, it's part of being human. Diane marked this self-criticism F and wrote: **"TRUTH: I make errors at work when under stress, but so does everyone. Most of the time I'm very good at my job."**

Self-criticism #19:
Lots of problems getting along with people at work.

Diane knew this to be true with her immediate boss, most of the other clerical staff (who were content with their positions, and interpreted Diane's ambition as meaning that she thought that she was better than they), and occasionally with other people in management. However, after drawing up the list of people who liked her (when she re-evaluated self-criticism #1), she now recognized that there were also some people at work on all levels that she got along quite well with, and occasionally she got on well with her boss, too. She decided this self-criticism was true in part, and rewrote it: **"I need to find a way to deal with feeling put down and rejected at work. I also need to develop more effective ways of handling distant, self-involved, and condescending authority figures."**

Self-criticism #20:
Bosses don't respect her/doesn't deserve respect.

This self-criticism was of particular importance to Diane. It galled her that despite her work's difficult, challenging, and specialized nature, her boss refused to give her the title and salary she merited. She wanted the respect and the recognition as much as she wanted the money. In the face of this lack of respect, Diane found it very hard to respect herself. She was always questioning herself and asking, "Is it me or is it them? Maybe they're right." However, she knew she did a good job and was more on the ball than her boss. She marked this self-criticism F and wrote:

"TRUTH: I do deserve respect and I am going to learn to give it to myself!"

Self-criticism #21:
Ashamed of her family.

Diane marked this as true. She rewrote it: "**I am ashamed of my family because I am ashamed of and afraid of being like them. I need help respecting myself. (I also have to realize that while it is not "nice," it is understandable to be ashamed of your family when they act like mine, and I don't have to feel so guilty for being ashamed.)**"

Self-criticism #22:
A jerk because doesn't know what she wants to do with her life.

Diane, by now, realized that she didn't have to hate herself for having difficulties. She marked #22 F and stated: "**TRUTH: Having trouble figuring out a career direction doesn't make me a jerk. How about some compassion for the hard time I am having?!**"

Self-criticism #23:
Lousy job, no relationship, no children, no future—a big failure.

Despite her by-now-positive mood, Diane instantly felt this self-criticism was valid. It certainly represented how she felt most of the time—like she was nothing and had nothing and never would. She quickly marked it true. I urged her to reconsider. Weren't there things that she had accomplished? Well, yes. She had gone away to college on scholarship. Afterwards she had come to a completely strange city and made a home for herself. She had managed to find ways to travel on little money. She had made her apartment into a cozy, comfortable home. She had established friendships, found several jobs despite no clear career path, wholly supported herself. She had pursued interests, taken courses, had fun. "But," Diane protested, "what does all that matter? That's just getting through life, that's not really accomplishing anything."

Here Diane was following the failure guidelines mentioned in chapter 1, specifically #3 ("Whatever I accomplish doesn't matter. What matters is what I have not accomplished.") and #5 ("If I am not a total success, then I am a failure. There is no middle ground, no so-so, no becoming, no points for effort.") I urged her to hold on to her goals (career, marriage, children) without condemning herself for not having yet achieved them, and encouraged her to CARESS herself. She decided to mark this self-criticism false and then wrote: **"TRUTH: I need to learn to accept myself and my shortcomings and have compassion for myself while giving myself the respect, support, encouragement, and stroking that I need to be able to pursue my goals with belief in myself."**

Having finished reconsidering all her self-criticisms, Diane then returned to #4 (oversensitive), which she had previously skipped because she had been uncertain how to evaluate it. After the self-evaluation process she had just gone through, she felt clearer. She decided that she was acutely sensitive to the possibility of being hurt in ways she had been hurt before—just as someone who has been in a bad fire is often acutely sensitive to the smell of smoke—and that she had good reason for this sensitivity even if sometimes it led her to expect fire when there wasn't any. She marked this self-criticism true, and rewrote it: **"I need to calm down when upset and then to evaluate just what is happening. Am I being attacked or not? If I could become less fearful of being criticized or rejected, I could learn not to overreact."**

Diane was now finished re-evaluating the things she disliked about herself, and her amended list of self-criticisms looked like this:

F   1.   Diane has something terribly wrong with her that makes people not like her. **(TRUTH: Many people like me and I get along well with them. Some people, especially people who are condescending, narcissistic, and/or competitive, I have a great deal of difficulty with.)**

T   2.   I need help to become more assertive.

T   3.   I am becoming less shy, but need further acceptance and encouragement so I can feel more willing to put myself out there.

T   4.   I need to calm down when upset and then to evaluate whether I am indeed being attacked or belittled or rejected. If I could become less fearful of being criticized or rejected, I could learn not to overreact.

T   5.   I need help expressing my anger directly, rather than hiding it in sarcasm.

F   6.   Diane is self-centered. **(TRUTH: I readily help others and am sensitive to their feelings.)**

F   7.   Diane is not giving enough. **(TRUTH: I am giving. In fact I often give more than I get.)**

F   8.   Diane has to have everything her way. **(TRUTH: I tend to be flexible when making plans with others, and rarely insist on doing what I want.)**

F   9.   Diane is overambitious. She should stay in her place. **(TRUTH: I do want a better life than my family has and I need to be encouraged and supported in my desire to achieve and succeed.)**

T 10.   I need more acceptance so I will be less frightened of rejection. I also need to understand and accept my fear of being controlled so that I don't have to avoid dating to protect myself. If I stop being so afraid, maybe I will be able to get married and have children, though it's hard to believe. I guess I also need a lot of encouragement.

T 11.   I need more practice and support in dating.

F   12.   Diane is too competitive. **(TRUTH: I am afraid to compete and think that if I compete at all I am overdoing it.)**

T   13.   I need help becoming more comfortable with competition and in learning how to deal with it.

T   14.   <u>I need to have more compassion for myself.</u>

T   15.   I am not a big baby, but I do too easily interpret the actions of others as negative reactions to me. I also too easily accept other people's negative opinions of me, and assume they know "the awful truth" about me. I need help to feel better about myself and to develop a system for evaluating myself that is not based on others' harsh judgments.

T   16.   I need to have more hope and to believe that things can get better for me.

T   17.   I need help feeling less frightened and overwhelmed, so I will feel less anxious.

F   18.   Diane makes too many mistakes at work. **(TRUTH: I make errors when under stress, but so does everyone. Most of the time I'm very good at my job.)**

T   19.   I need to find a way to deal with feeling put down and rejected at work. I also need to develop more effective ways of handling distant, self-involved, and condescending authority figures.

F   20.   Diane's bosses don't respect her, because she doesn't deserve respect. **(TRUTH: I do deserve respect and I'm going to learn to give it to myself.)**

T   21.   I am ashamed of my family because I am ashamed of and afraid of being like them. I need help respecting myself. (I also have to realize that while it is not "nice," it is understandable to be ashamed of your family when they act like mine, and I don't have to feel so guilty for being ashamed.)

F   22.   Diane is such a jerk that she doesn't even know what she wants to do with her life. **(TRUTH: I am having**

trouble figuring out a career direction, but that
doesn't make me a jerk! How about some compassion
for the hard time I'm having?!)

F   23.   To put it simply, Diane is just a big failure—a lousy
job, no relationship, no children, no future. (TRUTH:
**I need to learn to accept myself and my shortcomings
and have compassion for myself while giving myself
the respect, support, encouragement, and stroking
that I need to be able to pursue my goals with belief
in myself.**)

Diane now felt a lot better. Re-evaluating her self-criticisms
had taken a lot of thought, effort, and time, but it had been well
spent. She could see that, because she was so hard on herself,
many of what she had labeled "faults" were really misperceptions
with little basis in fact. She also felt better about the self-criticisms
she had decided were accurate: now they were stated in ways
that reached out for a solution. Her first list of self-criticisms had
made her feel like a failure. Now she felt like a flower that, once
given the right conditions, could blossom and thrive.

You can find the flower in yourself, just as Diane did, by re-
evaluating your self-criticisms. First, though, let's look at the
general principles to use in doing so.

1. *For a characteristic to be an accurate description of you, it has
to be generally true of your behavior.* I emphasize behavior because
this is the true test of character. Beware of condemning yourself
for your thoughts or feelings. It's natural to have thoughts and
feelings that are in conflict with how we want to act and be. Pay
them no heed when evaluating yourself, and judge yourself only
by your deeds. For instance if you think you're mean, forget about
your mean thoughts and see if you can readily think of *many* (not
just occasional) examples of your mean *behavior*. Also consider
whether you are ever kind. Think of as many of your acts of
kindness as you can. Take your time and don't gloss over or

discount any of them, no matter how trivial they may seem. (You know that you would never gloss over or discount your mean deeds.) Go slowly and really think about it rather than going with your first reaction. Unless you act mean a lot more than you are kind, chances are that you are mean only under certain circumstances. Figure out what these circumstances are, and write them down.

2. *Don't accept your self-criticisms as patently true.* Most of us are so used to criticizing ourselves that we often just assume that these criticisms are accurate without checking them out with other people or without objectively looking at our own behavior. For instance, you may be so used to thinking of yourself as "boring" or "dumb" that you just assume this to be the case. Actually, if you are self-critical, you are probably a very poor judge of whether you really are boring or dumb. So don't go by your feelings, but look for objective facts.

For instance, if you think that you are dumb, be sure to ask yourself: Can I learn? Can I figure things out that are important to me? When I am calm, can I analyze a situation and decide what needs to be done? Are there things that I have learned on my own? Can I understand this book?

If you think that you are boring, ask yourself if you are ever interesting. When you talk to people, do they usually try to move away? Are there people who not only don't move away, but who seek you out? Are you boring just some of the time? If so, under what set of circumstances?

3. *Be very wary in interpreting how others react to you.* If you're self-critical, you're likely to mistakenly interpret the actions of others as meaning that they have the same low opinion of you that your inner-critic does. A lack of response or a seemingly negative reaction from another person can be for a myriad of reasons that have little to do with you, and much to do with the other person. Perhaps a woman you would like to get to know better moves away from you at a party because she wants to approach a business contact, talk to a close friend, flirt with someone she's been eyeing for a while, or because she has indi-

gestion. Maybe she's concerned with some worry, and is incapable at the moment of listening to anybody, including you. The possibilities are endless, and most of them have nothing to do with you or with your being boring.

4. *Don't automatically accept the criticisms of others as valid.* When people are critical, they often have their own axe to grind or other agenda that cloud their perceptions. Some of you may be closely involved personally or professionally with someone who is perpetually demeaning. If so, it is especially important that you not accept his or her opinion as gospel. Look deeper and wider. Consider the opinions of people who like you and who are accepting in general. In learning to like and nurture yourself, beware of being sidetracked by those who are trying to keep you feeling inadequate.

5. *Be especially wary in assessing self-criticisms about your appearance.* We live in a society that puts a great premium on youth and good looks, especially for women. In the face of the unrealistic expectation that we should look like movie stars and stay perpetually young, we all fall short. Some of us (the fortunate few) have learned to live with our looks, appreciating our good points and accepting our imperfections. Most of us perpetually suffer from, at the very least, the desire to look different, and often we hate our looks—and ourselves alongside them.

If you have self-criticisms of your appearance ("ugly," "fat," "unattractive," etc.), evaluate very carefully the truth or falseness of your opinion. Be aware that there are very few really ugly people in this world, just as there are very few who are truly beautiful. Most of us fall somewhere in the middle. Many women, in our anguish at not being one of the few real knockouts, find endless fault with our facial features and our bodies, punishing ourselves relentlessly for what nature gave us. We tell ourselves that our noses are too big or too small, our ears too pointed or too flat, our eyes too small or too large, our lips too thin or too puffy, our cheekbones too pronounced or too understated, our necks too long or too short, our shoulders too round or too sloping, our breasts too large or too small, our legs too heavy or too spindly, and so on. In addition, most of us in this weight-phobic society don't know the difference between being full-bodied and obese. In fact, we don't even know when we're thin. How many slender women have you heard complaining about being fat?!

When I first became involved in the women's movement in 1967, I was astounded and relieved to sit in a consciousness-raising group and hear two beautiful, curvaceous women among us join in the group's talk about hating our looks; and not because they found their beauty to be a burden, but because they felt they were not attractive enough. They picked at flaws that only they could see. Truly, "beauty is in the eye of the beholder," and these women, like most of us, were blind to their real attractiveness.

While the women's movement is trying valiantly to redefine the way women are perceived and the way we perceive ourselves, is trying to help us to value ourselves for our personal attributes and strengths and not for our appearance, this has admittedly been an uphill struggle. The media (commercials, TV shows, movies, magazines) constantly bombards us with the importance of being beautiful; the message is that the worst thing a woman can be is a "dog." (I hate that label.) There is no similar way of describing an unattractive man. Men are condemned by calling them "losers" (i.e., unsuccessful), while women are condemned for not being beautiful. Ads aimed at women tell us not how to be powerful in our own right, but how we can get and please a man, if only we beautify ourselves properly. No wonder the most liberated among us struggle with feelings about our looks.

Not wishing to get a man does not get us off the auction block, either. Women who partner with other women are equally concerned with being physically attractive and desirable. No matter how much we might wish to de-emphasize the importance of our physical attractiveness, it's hard not to want to succeed at what society tells us is the most important game in town.

In thinking about your looks, don't measure yourself against celluloid perfection. (Have you ever seen a movie star without makeup? The difference is often amazing). Go to your local supermarket (unless you live in a very swanky area like Beverly Hills, then go to a supermarket in a neighborhood where people care about cost.) Spend some time there looking at other women. If you insist on comparing yourself, this is the place to do it—against real women of all ages.

How many women do you see with firm rounded breasts, small waists, thin thighs, shapely legs, and a face like Helen of Troy or Cleopatra? Not many, I'll bet. Likely you'll see many women either equally attractive or less attractive than you are. Let yourself know that this is what most women look like. Don't focus on the few women who may be stunning, and then compare yourself to them.

In life most characteristics, like beauty or intelligence, distribute themselves around a bell curve that looks like this:

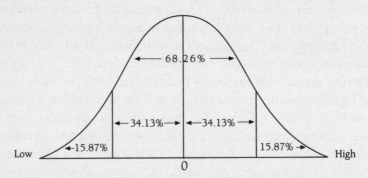

As you can see, a very small part of the population falls into the upper regions. Not being a genius doesn't mean that you're not smart enough for most practical purposes. And not being a beauty queen doesn't mean that you're not attractive enough to like yourself and get what you want. Most of those women in the supermarket are in relationships, raising families, working, or otherwise pursuing their goals.

If, after your supermarket trip, you still feel very critical about an aspect of your appearance, be sure to check it out with two or three truthful and supportive friends. Tell them why you are asking. If they tell you your nose is not too big, your eyes are not too narrow, and you don't look too fat—believe them! One friend might lie not to hurt your feelings, but not two or three. If your friends do confirm your own negative appraisal of your appearance, fine. This is your opportunity to make peace with this shortcoming without being consumed by it. Ask yourself how important this aspect of your appearance really is. Even if you do have wide thighs or a big nose, is it really that important? Can you think of these as minor imperfections that enhance the rest of your looks?

To make peace with your shortcomings you need to learn to take them out from under the magnifying glass through which you are used to regarding them, and to start recognizing and focusing on your good points. Often we are so overwhelmed by what we dislike about our looks that nothing else matters. We erroneously believe that others are also riveted on our big noses or fat thighs. In reality, only we are concerned with these things. Increase your awareness of your attractiveness by doing the following:

After reading this paragraph, close your eyes, take three slow deep breaths to relax yourself, and think about the ways in which you are attractive. (*Do not* stand in front of a mirror and examine yourself looking for your good points. At this stage you're far too likely to latch on to what you don't like and to gloss over everything else). Maybe you have nice hair, or soulful eyes, or a great mouth, or a wonderful smile. Perhaps you have a commanding walk, or a sexy air about you. Maybe you're soft and cuddly with a teddy-bear appeal. All of us have aspects of our physical appearance that are pleasing and enticing. Let yourself realize which you possess.

Take your time and really focus on your good points. Think of whatever physical attributes you possess that you have ever liked . . . remember what about your appearance has ever been praised by others. Let all your good points float into your awareness . . . savor them . . . and hold on to them. When you're ready, open your eyes and write them down. Label this list "BEAUTIFUL ME."

• • •

Those of you who are critical of your appearance may be wondering why Diane wasn't. In part she wasn't because she is quite attractive (though, as discussed above, this usually doesn't stop us women from being dissatisfied with our looks). Primarily, though, she wasn't because Diane wanted more than anything to be respected and appreciated for the competent, worthwhile person she is. She considered her looks to be a surface characteristic that served only to deflect men from taking her seriously—a problem attractive women often have, especially if they happen to be blond—and therefore to be a liability as much as an asset. She also was not worried about being able to attract a man, but rather about finding the kind of man who would value her as a whole person.

6. *Change your "rocks" into gold by turning your true self-criticisms into nurturing statements of your goals.* As we saw with Diane, there is a huge difference between recognizing what we need help with, and beating up on ourselves. To do so:

- **Say what you need help with, rather than what's wrong with you.**
- **Be factual, not judgmental. Recognize the problem you wish to correct, without blaming yourself for having it.**
- **Be as specific as possible. Define the conditions or circumstances under which you have this difficulty or exhibit this characteristic. For instance, if you often are overbearing, see if these acts have some common precipitating factor. Perhaps you are pushy when you feel attacked, or belittled, or threatened, or jealous, or anxious.**
- **Be fair to yourself. Don't leave out the times when you don't have this problem. (No one is always clumsy, graceless, boring, shy, unassertive, or mean.)**

For instance, Margaret wrote next to "mean": "T. When I feel I have been wronged I become enraged and vengeful and can be very mean. The rest of the time I am a sensitive and kind person. I need help to better evaluate whether I have truly been wronged, and to deal with my anger and hostility in a way that I approve of."

Another example is Teri who next to "boring" wrote: "T. I'm interesting when I'm relaxed, but most of the time I'm worried about being liked, so I clam up and have nothing to say and am too self-conscious to concentrate on listening to others, so I'm boring to be around. I need help liking myself, so that I will feel less worried about being liked by others and therefore more relaxed."

RE-EVALUATING YOUR SELF-CRITICISMS

Keeping all the above principles in mind, take out your list of self-criticisms that you wrote in Step Three and start re-evaluating them. Consider each one separately, and take as much time as you need. Think, feel, and rethink. Evaluate, restate, and correct until the results satisfy you. Go through the following process.

1. Ask yourself, "Is this quality that I dislike in myself a generally true description of me?"

2. If your self-criticism is not true, mark it F. Next to it, in parentheses, write what is true. Be sure to state the truth in a positive way, not only as a negation of the criticism. It is not helpful enough to write only, "I am not dumb" or "I am not crazy." For instance, Lois, whose very critical husband is always telling her how dumb she is, wrote next to "dumb": "F. I am a college graduate and I am fully capable of learning and understanding things. There are a lot of difficult things I have taught myself. I also love to read."

In dealing with your physical appearance, state in capital letters your pleasing or enticing physical attributes from your

BEAUTIFUL ME list next to your affirmation of the truth.

Next to "fat," Pat wrote: "F. I am not fat. I HAVE THE SHAPELY FULL BODY OF A REAL WOMAN. I ALSO HAVE PRETTY EYES, A SEXY MOUTH, AND GREAT LEGS."

3. If you are convinced that a self-criticism is true, mark it T and then restate it in a nurturing, rather than an attacking way. When rewriting your true self-criticisms, make them as specific as possible, stating under what circumstances you have this problem and the kind of help you need. Next to criticisms of your appearance, state the pleasing or enticing things about your appearance from your BEAU-TIFUL ME list, and write them in CAPITALS.

Next to "fat" on her list, Darlene wrote: "T. I am fifty pounds overweight, according to my doctor. I need help losing weight. I also need help feeling better about myself as I am now. I HAVE BEAUTIFUL EYES, A GREAT SMILE, AND I'M VERY SOFT AND CUDDLY."

On Barbara's list, next to "fat thighs," she wrote: "T. My thighs are heavier than the rest of me. I HAVE A THIN WAIST, FULL BREASTS, BEAUTIFUL EYES, CLEAR SKIN, AND A WONDER-FUL SMILE. Hey, maybe those thighs aren't so important after all."

When you have finished reevaluating your list of self-criticisms, stop and give yourself credit for all the effort you have put into this process. This is not an easy task, and you deserve respect and support for having entered into it and completing it. Give yourself a big pat on the back! Then immediately proceed to do the follow-up. It will take only a few minutes and will be well worth it.

FOLLOW-UP: FEELING BETTER ALREADY

1. **Read your original list of self-criticisms slowly and out loud, only this time say "I am" before each one.**

Take your time and see how you feel after each self-criticism.

2. **Now read your amended list of self-criticisms slowly and out loud. Take your time and see how you feel after each one.**

Can you feel the difference? As you read your original list, did you feel yourself cringe after each criticism as though you had been slapped? How did you feel after reading your amended list? Could you feel stirrings of hope and belief in yourself? Could you start to experience the enormous difference between attacking yourself and having *compassion* for yourself? Between *supporting* yourself and tearing yourself down? Did you experience how different you felt when, rather than seeing your difficulties as an unalterable given and the result of your innate deficiencies, you *accepted* your problems and focused on what you needed to overcome them? Wouldn't it be wonderful to treat yourself this way all the time? You've already started to learn how to nurture yourself! Let's move on to the next step.

Step Four: Finding Out Who Taught You to Feel Bad about Yourself

There's a song I like from the musical *South Pacific* that includes the lyrics: "I'm gonna wash that man right out of my hair and send him on his way." In the scene in which we hear this song, the woman singing is feeling assertive and good about herself. She is tired of wasting her energy, and wants to move on to pursuits that will be fulfilling. Identify, if you will, with that determination. Let yourself feel how good it will be to remove the voice of your inner-critic and get going on your way. The following exercises are designed to help you do just that.

Take your amended list of self-criticisms, from Step Three and break it into two groupings—with all the criticisms marked T in one group, and all the criticisms marked F in the other. Label the T grouping "GOALS." Label the F grouping "INNER-CRITIC." Then put your list of goals aside, for now. We are first going to focus on your INNER-CRITIC list.

For many of us, as for Diane, this is a long list. We have saddled ourselves with untrue self-criticisms and keep pounding away at ourselves. Trying to shape ourselves up, we keep digging ourselves further into the hole of low self-esteem. Where did we learn to treat ourselves like this? In chapter 3 we looked at how, in general, our growing-up experiences shaped the way we treat ourselves. Now discover the specifics of your own individual internal critic.

Read your INNER-CRITIC list over slowly, without the truths that you have written in parentheses. Start each criticism with "you." For instance, "You have something terribly wrong with you that makes people not like you . . . You are oversensitive . . . You are selfish and overconcerned with yourself" . . . and so on. **As you read this list over slowly, see if you can hear another voice besides your own.** Is it your mother's voice telling you that you are selfish and lazy, or jealous and greedy, or mean? Is it your father's voice telling you that you are dull and fat and will never amount to anything? Is it your aunt or grandfather saying that you are messy and wishy-washy? Is it your big brother or sister calling you dumb and hopeless? Maybe these things weren't directly said to you, but conveyed by an attitude. Perhaps your father sneered at you and ignored you, and you picked up the message that he thought you dull and contemptible. Perhaps your mother was depressed and withdrawn, and you picked up the message that you are dull and boring and can't hold anyone's attention.

Every item on your INNER-CRITIC list started with someone else's criticism, whether this criticism was implied or stated. No one is born being innately self-critical. This is something that has to be learned. It is very important that you figure out where these criticisms originated. Whose attitudes have you copied and made your own?

Some of you, the daughters of an insecure parent, may have learned to dislike yourself not by having accepted and internalized others' harsh judgments of you, but rather by having identified with a parent who felt inferior and inadequate. If so, it is important to realize that we all identify with our parental figures in many ways. Some of these identifications are very positive and make us feel good about ourselves (e.g., "I'm smart like Mommy and funny like Daddy"). Other identifications with these same parents may undermine our positive sense of self. Raised by a parent or parents who felt inadequate and unworthy, we may unconsciously identify and feel inadequate and unworthy ourselves. As you begin to recognize these unconscious identifications, you can start to separate yourself from them. (Step Eight will help you with this separation).

As you go through each item on your INNER-CRITIC list, close your eyes and imagine someone from your past stating or making this criticism of you. You don't have to decide who that person is. Just close your eyes and relax. . . . Then slowly state the criticism out loud, and ask yourself who in your past might say this to you . . . or think this of you or who might feel this way about him or herself . . . and wait for the image of someone you know to float before your eyes. . . . Stay relaxed . . . focus on the criticism . . . and the image will come.

When you discover where a criticism came from, mark the origin next to it. If it came from identifying with negative things about one of your parents or another role model, move it to a separate grouping labeled "MY NEGATIVE ROLE MODELS," and note who the role model was. Remember, the same parent can be a good role model in some ways, and a poor role model in others. Here we are focusing only on the identifications that cause us difficulty, but we are in no way blaming our parents for being the way they were or negating the help they gave us. When you finish, your INNER-CRITIC list may be smaller because some self-criticisms may have been moved to the grouping of MY NEGATIVE ROLE MODELS. If a self-criticism was taken both from a critic and a role model (a "double whammy"), put it on both lists.

Many of the origins of these self-criticisms will be easy to identify. Lois, for example (the woman married to a highly critical man), had no trouble figuring out where she got the idea that she was spoiled, selfish, and greedy—her older sisters had been telling her that all her life. What's more, they still were. She also had no problem figuring out why she thought she was dumb, mistaken, and wrong almost all of the time—her father had constantly belittled her whenever she differed with him, and her mother was self-abasing (the "double whammy").

If you have difficulty identifying the origins of a self-criticism, ask yourself the following questions:

1. **How old was I the first time I felt this way about myself? Can I remember the first time, or does it feel like I always felt this way? If I can remember the first time, what happened then to make me feel this bad about myself?**

2. **How did the important people in my childhood feel about me with regard to this facet of my personality? Did I feel that any one of them shared this negative opinion of me, even if they never actually said so?**

3. **Did one of the people who raised me feel this way about himself or herself?**

4. **What experiences have I had that made me feel this way about myself? Whom did I go through them with?**

Consider each item on your INNER-CRITIC list until you have identified all your original critics and negative models.

This step often is an emotional one. Your feelings may be stirred up as you recognize how much of other people's judgments and personalities you have swallowed whole. You may feel sad at how much was amiss in your growing-up years. Or you may be angry at having been burdened with such heavy and unfair baggage. Likely you will feel some relief at the prospect of ridding yourself of this weight.

Whatever you feel, *do not blame yourself*. It is not your fault that you accepted other people's judgments as true. Children always do. They are not yet able to think critically. Parental figures loom like infallible gods over young children, and it is at these vulnerable ages that the core of our self-image is formed. By the time people are grown, the concept of self has so solidified that generally they no longer think to question it. For instance, when

I was growing up, I was continually told that I was lazy because I did not like to do housework and typically procrastinated doing my chores. It took me many years to realize that I'm far from lazy. So again, *do not blame yourself.* Rather, when you are ready, continue on to the next step, which will show you how to unburden yourself of these unfair self-criticisms.

CHAPTER 8

Step Five: Letting Go and Liking Yourself

*T*ake out your INNER-CRITIC list. You are now going to continue the process of silencing your inner-critic. You began this process when you recognized that you had swallowed whole other people's negative judgments rather than recognizing the real you. Now you are going to increase your ability to view yourself accurately and positively, and to stand by your positive self-assessments.

Before starting, remember that—while the steps in this book are designed to take you through a whole process— any one of them can benefit you. Encourage yourself to do as much as you feel ready for, and don't think less of yourself if you don't do everything. Let yourself know that whatever steps you do take will help you to like and value yourself.

Make sure you have uninterrupted time, with the phone off the hook. This is an important and emotional exercise, and you won't want to be distracted. Start with the first self-criticism on your list. You may want to deal with only one self-criticism today, or you may want to deal with more. See how you feel as you engage in this step. It's important not to rush through this experience. Give yourself time to feel and absorb what is happening.

Imagine that your original critic(s) is (are) there in front of you, delivering the criticism. Then imagine yourself as you are today confronting this original critic. Picture yourself stating the truth (which you've written in parentheses) to this critic. Aim to make this an emotional experience, not just an intellectual exercise. The more you are able to feel what you are saying, the more benefit you will get from this process. Repeat this exercise every so often, and watch for changes in how you feel during and after it. If you have difficulty getting to your feelings, don't worry. That's just a sign that they are strong and you fear being overwhelmed by them. Just stay with it, and your feelings will come with time, and in a way that you can manage.

Before you start, consider how Diane did this exercise, beginning with her critic articulating a perceived shortcoming, followed by a statement of the truth:

1. DIANE HAS SOMETHING TERRIBLY WRONG WITH HER THAT MAKES PEOPLE NOT LIKE HER. (TRUTH: Many people like me and I get along well with them. Some people, especially people who are condescending, narcissistic, and/or competitive, I have a great deal of difficulty with.)

Diane imagined her father ignoring her . . . not listening to her . . . belittling her . . . condescending to her . . . ordering her about . . . taking her for granted. She thought of all the times she wished she had a "good daddy," the kind of father who would pay attention to her and appreciate her. Instead everything her father did gave her the message that there was nothing worthwhile or likable about her.

Then Diane imagined herself next to her father, looking at him. She saw him sitting there impassively, looking distracted and annoyed that she was bothering him, just as he always looked when not angry about something. She pictured him sitting in his chair while she stood above him, looking down on him, and realized that she was big and he was scaled down to life-size. She felt her feelings well up inside her: hurt, rage and longing fed by a lifetime of needing and not getting. Then she started to tell him how she felt about herself—how she had always felt like a nothing and a fraud, experiencing herself in his reflection of her as inept, incompetent, unworthy, unlikable, and unlovable. As she expressed her feelings, she felt her anger growing and herself feeling stronger. She looked her father in the eye and told him that she was through letting him be the mirror by which she saw herself and that instead she had been recognizing and owning all her positive qualities and that she was going to continue to do so. She told him, "You know, Dad, I really am a likable person, and there are a lot of people who like me. It's only people similar to you, who are condescending, self-centered, and competitive, that I have trouble with. I'm really angry at you for never respecting or appreciating me . . . and I'm filled with sadness that you can never truly see me and love me . . . but I'm beyond seeing myself through your eyes. I have my own eyes and from now on I'm going to use them whenever I look at myself!"

Then Diane saw herself walk away from her father. She did not wait for a response. She did not need one. She knew her father would never understand her feelings or be able to give her what she wanted, but that seemed less important to her. She was beginning to feel likable and lovable without her father responding to her; she was learning how to love and nurture herself.

Then Diane thought of the other people in her life who had made her feel unworthy and unlikable. First her mother, who—while more connected and caring than her father—resented Diane's attempts at separation and independence, and became angry and rejecting. Her mother viewed Diane as a disloyal daughter for spending the little spare money she had to go on vacation, rather than to fly home to visit. Her mother's attitude had always made Diane feel guilty, as though she were a bad person for upsetting her mother.

Diane pictured herself sitting with her mother, who was hurt and angry. She imagined looking her mother in the eye and saying in an assertive, though tender, voice, "I really am a good and worthwhile person, and most people who know me like me. It's not bad of me to want to be my own person, and it doesn't mean that I don't love you—but I have to love you by being me and loving you. I want to be connected to you, and I also want to go off on my own and have fun, and learn things, and make my own life. I know that you don't understand my desire for independence—that you think you ask little of me and that I refuse to give it to you . . . and I know that you will never understand why I keep my distance . . . and this saddens me a lot. I'm also angry at you for not seeing me and accepting me as I am, but I'm through seeing myself through your eyes. I have my own eyes and I'm going to use them from now on whenever I look at myself."

Next Diane thought of all the other people in her life who had ever made her feel unworthy and unlikable. She pictured them all together—brothers, teachers, peers, bosses, aunts, cousins—sitting down in a group, while she stood over them. Then she imagined telling them all to take their criticisms of her and get out—that she didn't need their messages inside of her putting her down—that she was through berating herself, so no longer needed their help to do it. If they refused to recognize her worth, so be it. She would deal with them in the real world, but she would no longer carry their voices around inside her head. Then she stood there quietly as she watched them file out.

As she saw them trail off, Diane felt strong and calm. But then she looked around, saw that she was alone, and started to feel panicky, wanting to yell, "Come back! Maybe I made a mistake. Maybe being berated is better than being alone." But she didn't. She remembered a saying she had read somewhere and liked: "When you learn something new, it feels at first as if you've lost something." She reminded herself how miserable she had been seeing herself through her inner-critics' eyes. She had also begun to believe that she could replace her evicted inner-critics with an inner nurturer. (You will learn how to do this in steps seven through ten).

After this Diane stopped for then working on dealing with her inner-critics; she felt that she had had enough for one day. She returned to do more two days later, at which time she began work on inner-criticism #2.

2. DIANE IS OVERCONCERNED WITH HERSELF. (**TRUTH: I readily help others and am sensitive to their feelings**.)

Diane pictured being a child with her parents, and being upset and crying at the constant fighting. She saw her mother looking critical and saying, "Don't be such a baby. You're just too sensitive." Then she saw and heard her father join in, "Yeah, stop making a fuss over nothing!" She saw the six-year-old Diane wanting to go out and play and her mother sarcastically saying "Play, baby, play," as if this were a bad thing to want. She saw the twenty-one-year-old Diane moving to a faraway city, and her mother crying at being left and getting angry at Diane for "only thinking of yourself."

Next she became her adult self, looked her parents in their eyes, and said, "Of course I'm concerned with myself and what I'm feeling. I have reason to be. This is a very upsetting house to live in. You're always attacking each other and trying to get me to take sides, and I'm terrified of being attacked and rejected by both of you, but especially by you, Dad. And you're both so preoccupied with your eternal warfare that you never stop to wonder how I'm feeling or how things are affecting me. You know, **I really am a sensitive and helpful person**, but neither of you knows that because you feel given to only when I allow you to control me and I do whatever you want! Well, I'm through viewing myself through your eyes as a selfish, self-involved person. I have my own eyes and I'm going to use them from now on. And I'm not selfish! I'm a caring, giving person!"

3. DIANE IS NOT GIVING ENOUGH. (**TRUTH: I am giving. In fact, I often give more than I get.**)

Diane imagined her mother and brothers constantly telling her (in childhood and now) that she's overly concerned with herself and takes things to heart too much. She heard them saying, "You wouldn't be so upset if you could think about other people and not only about what you want. You've got nothing to be upset about." She saw herself as a five-year-old crying from hurt feelings and her mother mocking her, saying "poor baby" in a sarcastic tone.

Diane then saw herself answering them: "It's true that I am often preoccupied with my problems, but I certainly have real concerns. The fact that the five of you aren't interested in hearing about my problems and rarely support me is part of what I'm upset about. You leave me alone to take care of myself, and then you wonder why I'm preoccupied with myself! With my friends I am sensitive to people's feelings and they find me really helpful."

In going through the rest of her INNER-CRITIC list, Diane conjured up many images from her childhood. She recaptured frequent scenes where she was told that she should stay in her place . . . that it was wrong to reach for more . . . that she should be humble and self-effacing. Her mother taught her by example, as well as told her, that it's fine to be angry at men, but it is not OK to be assertive, or to get out of a bad situation—that a woman's lot was to stay and be angry and suffer. Her father taught her that the only way for her to make her presence known at all was to wait on him or to fight with him, and yet either response brought only his contempt. With her brothers, she learned that she could keep them as allies as long as she avoided competing with them. Teachers at school taught her to be quiet and sub-missive. Her aunts told her that she was klutzy and socially awkward, while her parents preferred she not date. Her uncle molested her, teaching her again that men are dangerous and not to be trusted. At scattered times through her childhood there were some self-affirming experiences with adults—a few teachers who took a special interest in her, a friend's parents who were fond of her and welcomed her into their home—but not nearly enough to counteract the overwhelming messages at home. It's no wonder that, by the time Diane was ready for college, despite good grades, high intelligence, a pleasing manner, and an attractive appearance, she felt like a nothing and a nobody!

In doing this exercise, Diane experienced a strong catharsis, as she faced her old critics and stood up to them. As Diane went through each inner criticism, she saw how she had swallowed whole all the bad things her family and those around her had fed her. Now, as an adult who was daily reading her list of WHAT I LIKE ABOUT MYSELF, and taking in all her good points, she could start to separate her self-perceptions from those of her attackers, and experience how wrong all these people had been about her—how their criticisms had not been based on her at all, but had come out of each of her original critics' own history and problems. Her father rejected her not because she was unworthy and unlovable, but because he was incapable of connection and empathy. Her mother didn't have compassion for Diane's feelings, and didn't support and encourage her to reach, and strive, and separate and grow not because Diane was bad and unworthy but because Mother had not been nurtured herself, so did not know how to CARESS Diane. Instead she wanted Diane to be her mother and take care of her.

Diane felt a surge of freedom as she told her original critics that she wasn't going to swallow their messages anymore . . . that she no longer needed to prove anything to them (or to people she had "chosen" as stand-ins for them) . . . that she approved of herself and that was good enough. She could look at herself and see the truth about herself—that she is a warm, loving, giving, intelligent, perceptive, creative, talented, organized, responsible, attractive woman. She knew her original critics would never recognize her worth—they didn't have it within themselves to do so—but she could recognize her own worth and by so doing free herself from the tyranny of needing their approval.

Diane began to feel the power of being separate—no longer vulnerable to being dashed and depressed each time someone looked at her with disapproval. For the first time she felt she could start to disengage from the power struggle with her boss without feeling as if she had lost in giving up the attempt to win. She actually could feel (as opposed to knowing in her head) that trying to get her boss's (father's) respect and approbation was both futile and unnecessary. She now knew that she deserved respect and praise, and that she could get it from the person she needed it from the most—herself! She also began to believe that there are better bosses out there who would recognize her worth, and that she didn't have to force it from those least capable of giving it.

Diane was able to achieve this inner separation without confronting her parents in real life with what she had been learning about herself or realizing about them. She stood up to her inner-critics, not to real family. I emphasize this because I do not believe that blaming your parents is the path to either true separation or self-esteem. In fact, the need to argue with your parents, in futile attempts to change them, is often a sign that you are tied in to needing their validation. True separation comes about when you can feel good about yourself even without your parents' approval, acceptance, understanding, or respect.

This doesn't mean that I don't believe in working things out with your parents and siblings if possible, because I certainly do. Emotional connectedness to her family is a big help to any woman. I encourage the women in my practice to work on fostering such connections if feasible, and many significantly improve their relationships with their first families during the course of therapy. As a woman increases her self-esteem, she becomes less reactive to her family's manipulations and failings and better able to maintain her equilibrium and connectedness to her family in the face of them. With time and effort you can learn to do this too. Start now to confront your inner-critics.

Be sure to take your time with this exercise—it's not one to rush through. Perhaps one criticism at a time is all you might want to focus on. Maybe you will feel comfortable doing more. Either way, be sure to take the time to recapture scenes . . . and images . . . and feelings . . . and thoughts . . . and sensations from your growing-up years. As you go through each INNER-CRITIC criticism, go back in time and first observe, then confront, your original inner-critic. Give yourself the opportunity to experience the good feeling of standing up to a previously feared bully . . . and see the bully shrink as you grow . . . see the bully lose his or her hold over you as you assert yourself and affirm yourself . . . tell that critic that you are no longer going to see yourself through his or her eyes . . . that you have your own eyes and are going to use them. Tell the critics in your life that you know they are not going to change their opinions of you, and that while that saddens and angers you, you can live without it. You no longer need their approval, because you approve of yourself!

As you take this step, you might experience some separation anxiety. Change is frequently scary because it entails letting go of familiar, albeit unhelpful, ways of being. Just as a woman who gives up smoking may feel that she is losing her best friend— even though she knows that this "friend" is slowly killing her— so may letting go of your inner-critic feel like a loss. If it does feel that way, remind yourself that, by getting rid of your inner-critic, you are making room for your inner-caretaker, who will be with you as an internal nurturing presence for the rest of your life.

When you have finished this step, or as much of it as you are doing at this sitting, stop and see how you feel. Perhaps you feel strong and powerful at affirming yourself. Perhaps you feel lonely and scared, that an inner-critic is better than being empty inside. Many people feel a combination of both. Whatever you feel, be sure to give yourself credit for taking this step. This is a really tough one. How many people have had the courage to stand up to feared critics as you have? This is a very important process and one for which you surely deserve credit. It doesn't matter if you weren't as assertive as you would have liked to be. What matters is that you have begun the process—you have started to rid yourself of your inner-critics. Of course this, like all change, will not happen overnight. This is an exercise that you will probably need to repeat, in part or in whole, many times. Encourage yourself to keep at it, at the same time that you expect some backsliding. Remember that all change takes place with two steps forward and one step back. Give yourself the support you need to persevere, and be sure to give yourself credit for trying.

In your daily life, work on recognizing when you are criticizing yourself, and realize that this is the voice of your inner-critic attacking you. Don't let your inner-critic get away with it! Do this exercise instead. Stop yourself and identify which original critic is speaking, and then imagine yourself facing this critic and affirming your worth as you did in the above exercise. With practice you will become better and better at recognizing your inner-critic and cutting her off before she has a chance to do much damage.

Be particularly on the lookout for your inner-critic when you are feeling upset or depressed. (See chapters 13 and 14 for more help in dealing with anxiety and depression.) Often the reason you are upset is that your inner-critic is making you feel bad about yourself. Check it out. Ask yourself, "Am I upset with myself right now?" Or, "Am I down on myself right now?" Take the time to find out. If your inner-critic is giving you the business, cut the bully off and replace her with your inner-caretaker. Start to CA-RESS yourself, which you will learn more about how to do in steps seven through ten. First, though, let us deal with your negative role models.

CHAPTER 9

Step Six: You Be You and I'll Be Me

*T*ake out the list of NEGATIVE ROLE MODELS that you made in Step Four, when you recognized which of your untrue self-criticisms were based on identifications with poor role models. (If you don't have any negative models, you can skip this section and go on to the next chapter.) **Make a heading for each of your poor role models** (Mother, Father, Aunt Ethel, and so on), **then list under each model the negative ways you identified with each of them.** (This just entails rearranging your list into these different headings.) If you identified in the same way with more than one person, list the trait under each corresponding name.

To increase your self-esteem, it is important for you to differentiate yourself from these poor role models. Of course, you may also be identified with these same people in other ways that are healthy and beneficial. There is no need to change those positive identifications. Here we are focusing only on the critical and inaccurate ways you feel about yourself that are modeled on others.

First, go through each item on this list and consider if it is true for your role model. If so, mark it "True for Model." If false, then mark it "False for Model" and write down what is accurate.

For instance, Lois had one negative role model: her mother. She had identified with her mother in a number of detrimental and untrue ways, the first three of which were:

1. I'M DUMB, MISTAKEN, WRONG. (TRUTH: I'm smart and have learned and taught myself many things.) Partially modeled on mother.
2. I'M INADEQUATE. (TRUTH: I have overcome many things in my life, and coped with many difficult situations. I have problems, but I am not inadequate. I'm a planner and a coper.) Partially modeled on mother.
3. I'M UNWORTHY AND UNDESERVING. (TRUTH: I'm a valuable person and deserve to be happy.) Partially modeled on mother.

Lois considered whether any of these three statements were accurate descriptions of her mother. Lois knew that her mother had *felt* dumb, inadequate, and undeserving, but was she? Despite her mother's self-effacing manner and lack of confidence in her own judgment, Lois knew that her mother had had a quick mind, so she marked #1 "False for Model," and wrote, **"Mom was not dumb. She just thought she was."**

When Lois considered whether her mother had been inadequate, it was another story. Lois thought of the many ways her mother hadn't been there for her—all the times Lois had wanted to be CARESSed and instead was met with coldness and criticism. She remembered her mother's inability to make decisions, her breaking into tears at the slightest stress, her depressed withdrawal when action was called for; and she decided that her mother had indeed been inadequate in many ways. She marked this "True for Model."

Lois had no trouble evaluating the third detrimental and inaccurate way in which she had identified with her mother. She knew, after our many discussions about what makes a person worthy, that her mother, like people in general, was worthy and deserving just by virtue of being human and attempting to be moral. She quickly marked #3 "False for Model."

Lois then went through the rest of the items on her NEGATIVE ROLE MODELS list. When she finished, Lois could see that she had formed her own negative self-image based partly on what her mother had really been like, and partly on how her mother had felt about herself—that is, on the image her mother projected to the world. Lois found it helpful to realize that some of the things she most disliked about herself not only weren't inborn, but were only a copy of a false image.

Now start to differentiate yourself from your negative role models. (Note: You need to keep your eyes closed while taking this step. Either tape-record the instructions slowly, pausing to give yourself time to complete each instruction, or memorize the instructions.)

Close your eyes and take three slow deep breaths, and with each exhalation allow yourself to become more and more relaxed. Slowly inhale . . . then slowly exhale . . . allowing yourself to become relaxed. . . . Then choose one of the role models you have pinpointed. See yourself sitting next to this model, and let yourself experience your reaction to being like this model in the detrimental ways that you have identified. Experience how much you don't want to be like and feel like your model in these negative ways. . . . Then imagine gathering up all those negative ways of feeling about yourself that you have modeled after this person and ejecting them. See them rising up and out of you like a cyclone, twisting and turning and exiting you in a gush. Then face your model and say that you took this turmoil from her or him, and you don't want it anymore. . . . It's become an albatross around your neck, so you're giving it back. If your model doesn't want

these bad feelings, she or he doesn't have to accept them, and they will blow away into outer space, but not back to you. Just imagine those bad feelings going out of you and back to your model or into outer space . . . and in their place is a great, calm, clear place where you can hold good feelings about yourself. . . . Let yourself do that now. Clear out the bad and fill that space with what is genuinely good about you, the things you like about yourself, and the truths about yourself that you earlier identified. . . . All the good things about yourself that are really you. . . . Take your time. . . . Fill in that calm clear place with your self-affirmations. . . . Then, when you're ready, open your eyes, and come back to the room.

How do you feel? Could you take in that good feeling of knowing that you no longer have to blindly model yourself after past figures . . . that you can be yourself? If so, you undoubtedly felt a sense of freedom. If not, don't worry. Negative identifications are hard to get rid of, and it's common to have to repeat this exercise many times for it to have a lasting impact. Whenever your old bad feelings based on these identifications arise, do this exercise again. Visualize yourself sitting next to your model and returning these negative self-concepts to her or him. Eventually they will learn that you are no longer a friendly host, and will stay away. It will also be easier to let go of these detrimental identifications as you take the next three steps, which will teach you how to CARESS yourself.

When you're ready, not necessarily today, move on to your other negative role models—until you've returned all your inaccurate and damaging identifications to each of them. Some of you may have only one negative role model, while others will have several. However many, the important thing is to return to them the untrue ways of viewing yourself that have been undermining your self-esteem. Then you will be able to appreciate and love yourself as you truly are.

Step Seven: Learning What You Need to Feel Nurtured and Step Eight: Opening Your Heart to Your Inner-Child

In the last five steps you met and confronted the critic within you. You stood up to this disparager and said, "I'm not going to let you put me down like that anymore." You may have felt good, but you may also have felt alone and abandoned without your inner-critic to keep an eye on you. In the next four steps you are going to learn how to fill this void with an internal nurturing caretaker.

We all have at least the rudiments of an inner nurturer. Occasionally we are compassionate towards and accepting of ourselves. Sometimes we give ourselves support and encouragement. However, your inner nurturer may have only a small voice that is seldom heard and easily outshouted by your inner-critic. When you challenged your original critics and negative role models, your inner-caretaker's voice grew louder; but, it is not enough to assert yourself in opposition and defiance. You need to learn to love and CARESS yourself.

It's your inner-caretaker's job to keep you safe and foster your development. In part this means seeing that you get adequate food, clothing, and shelter, act responsibly and decently, pay your bills, and in general live your life according to your values. Equally important, your inner-caretaker also needs to attend to your emotional requirements—needs to give you the Compassion, Acceptance, Respect, Encouragement, Support, and Stroking that you, and all people, need to flourish.

> Your inner-caretaker's job is to nurture your inner-child as a good parent would.

Your inner-child is fun-loving, curious, adventuresome, creative, but she may be hiding her true self, and conforming and pretending in order to be loved; or she may act rebellious: angry at being overcontrolled and denied, so refusing to go along in any way, defining herself in opposition to demands and therefore not free to be genuine. Whatever her style, your inner-child wants to get her needs met but may not know how. Like a real child she requires your loving care and guidance—your physical and emotional succor—to be, to grow, and to flourish.

Children need to be loved freely and unconditionally. "Mr. Rogers," a popular educational TV program for preschoolers, ends each show with Mr. Rogers (a social worker by training) saying to the child at home, "I like you just the way you are." Isn't this what we all want? To be liked "just the way we are"? Child rearing books caution parents, when disciplining children, to always distinguish the bad act from the essence of the child. For instance, they instruct parents to tell a child that "writing on the walls is bad," but not that "you are bad." If a child acts up a lot, enlightened parents assume that something is troubling their child and they will try to find out what is wrong.

Those of us who are mothers want our children to grow up

feeling good about themselves and loved, *unconditionally loved.* Yes (let's admit it), we want our children to get A's on their report cards and to have good manners—but we don't want them to feel unloved or unlovable if they don't.

The same way parents strive to accept and unconditionally love their real children, so you need to strive to unconditionally love your inner-child. If your inner-child acts up, you need to talk to your child and try to find out what's wrong, instead of hating her for causing trouble.

Nurturing, however, does not mean that you should be all-giving. It is important to set appropriate limits to protect your child, as well as to teach frustration tolerance. Your child, when her desires are blocked, must learn when to persist, when to wait for another time, and when to desist. A wise parent distinguishes between what is genuine need, and what is impulse—and knows it is important to satisfy the first, but not necessarily the second. Every whim and desire need not be gratified.

Many women, not having learned how to identify and meet their genuine needs, instead give themselves pseudo-nurturing. Examples of pseudo-nurturing include: binging on food or using drugs or alcohol to fill inner emptiness and to cover up painful feelings; going on an ill-affordable spending spree; and compulsive sex. These are pseudo-nurturers because, despite an immediate effect of making a person feel good, they don't give her what she needs over the long run. She may feel "filled up" in the moment, but as soon as the food—or drugs—or alcohol—or sex—or spending spree—is gone, she is left feeling empty, unhappy, and disappointed, and even worse about herself because of the binge.

If you habitually use a pseudo-nurturer, it is a sign that you haven't yet learned what it is that you really need, and that instead you have latched on to something that will give you a quick high and a long letdown. You can change that. If you are addicted to alcohol or drugs, give yourself the help you need by joining Alcoholics Anonymous, Narcotics Anonymous, or other recovery program. You will not be able to truly esteem yourself if you cannot get through your days without these crutches. Also, take special advantage of the following step to discover what real nurturance is.

STEP SEVEN: LEARNING WHAT YOU NEED TO FEEL NURTURED

In my experience what makes most people feel nurtured is subsumed within CARESS (Compassion, Acceptance, Respect, Encouragement, Support, and Stroking). However, this need not be true for you. Perhaps there is a different kind of giving that nurtures you. In the following exercise, let yourself discover the kind of nurturance you need. (Note: You need to do this step with your eyes closed. Either tape-record the instructions, pausing to give yourself time to complete each instruction, or memorize them).

Close your eyes . . . let yourself sink into the chair or couch or whatever you are sitting on, and take a deep breath. When you exhale, exhale all the tension out of your body so you become relaxed. Do this three times and with each exhalation let yourself become more and more relaxed. . . . Then imagine a scene where you are being nurtured. . . . This scene can be something you have actually experienced or it can be something made-up. It doesn't matter which . . . just let yourself relax and visualize a situation where you are nurtured. . . . Perhaps you are with a nurturing person . . . or you might be alone . . . Just take your time . . . and wait to get an image. Don't force it. Let it come to you. . . . Relax and ask yourself, "Being nurtured, what's that like for me?" . . . and wait for a scene to float before your eyes. . . . Stay relaxed and give it time, and repeat to yourself the question, "Being nurtured, what's that like for me?" . . . An image or feeling will come. When it does, take it in, and savor that good feeling of getting what you need and want. . . . Take as much time as you need . . . luxuriate in being nurtured. . . . And then let your-

self know what it is about this scene that feels so good to
you . . . what it is that makes it so nurturing. When you
know, hold it close to you so you won't forget it. . . . Then,
when you are ready, open your eyes and come back to the
room.

**Now write down the elements that went into your feeling
nurtured.** Maybe you pictured being held and stroked, or imagined discussing a problem with a friend who understood and
supported you. Perhaps you pictured someone dropping everything to come over and help you hang wallpaper, or imagined
someone praising you and encouraging you to do more. Maybe
you pictured someone smiling at you with love and tenderness,
or envisioned someone important to you respecting your opinion
and feelings. Perhaps you imagined relaxing in a hot bath or
listening to beautiful music. Whatever you pictured, write down
what it was about that situation that made you feel nurtured.
Label this list "MY NURTURERS."
        For instance, in the examples above:

Being *stroked* (held).
Being *understood* and *supported* by a *compassionate* friend.
Being *supported* (hanging wallpaper).
Being *encouraged* and *supported* (praised).
Being *stroked* and *respected* and *accepted* and *loved* (smiling at
        you with love and tenderness).
Being *respected* by someone important to you.
Being *stroked* (hot bath and music).

**Then repeat the exercise, only this time imagine a different
nurturing situation. Take your time and enjoy this experience.
When you're ready, return to the room and write down what
it was about this situation that made it nurturing.**
        **Then repeat the exercise again, and keep repeating it until
you've identified all the different elements that go into making
you feel nurtured. Make sure you've added all these elements**

to your list of MY NURTURERS. Then set this list aside for now. We'll come back to it in steps nine and ten.

How do you feel? As you imagined being nurtured, did you take in that good feeling? Did you experience how wonderful it is to be given to? Did it leave you with a longing to really receive all that you pictured? Do you already feel a little filled up? For many of us imagining something, if we really put ourselves into it, is a little like having it for the moment. That is why we like to daydream about things like winning the lottery or being famous.

I once heard Elie Wiesel, the Holocaust survivor and Nobel prize–winning writer, tell of first discovering his literary talent as a teenager by participating in a storytelling contest with fellow concentration camp prisoners. Wiesel's strong, detailed, loving description of a Sabbath meal left those starved, emaciated souls spellbound. Hearing about the meal, rather than making them feel hungrier, served a need. For a moment they lost themselves in memories of happier days. They felt "fed" and more hopeful. The story made them prize themselves.

Recognizing our genuine needs and imagining having them met is an important step, giving direction and temporary comfort. Satisfying those needs, however, entails more than just imagining them being fulfilled. In order for us to get the spiritual and psychological nourishment we need, our inner-caretaker has to learn not only what our inner-child needs, but also to be willing and able to meet those needs in a warm and responsible way; and our inner-child has to be open and responsive to our inner-caretaker and respectful of her morals and values. Then we will have inner harmony, with our inner-child happy and able to enjoy who she is and what she is doing because our inner-caretaker is accepting and approving.

However, this is usually not the case. Many a woman is beset by constant conflict between her inner-caretaker and her inner-child. Commonly, her inner-caretaker wants to get ahead in the world and thinks the inner-child is holding her back by being lazy, self-indulgent, recalcitrant, anxious, depressed, inept, timid, or too needy—caring only about her own needs, impervious to the inner-caretaker's wishes. On the other hand, her inner-child may experience the inner-caretaker as cold, critical, and rejecting—caught up in her own program and ignoring the child's very real feelings and needs. Consider the following poem by Rose, who entered treatment because of pervasive anxiety and whose poem about her distant father appeared in chapter 3:

> There's a little kid deep inside me,
> only sometimes it comes too close to the surface.
> When it does, I become fearful and insecure, and I don't
> know what to do about it.
> These are the times when I feel most removed from myself,
> and a certain type of sadness flows within me.
> It's a quiet and passive sadness, not a depression filled
> with anger or hostility like I feel at other times.
> Nevertheless, I want to free myself of this child in me, for
> it's tiring to recognize its presence.
> It asks for too much attention from me, and I don't have the
> strength to deal with it.
> I experience its presence in me as a burden, and now I
> realize that I am becoming angry toward it.
> It's like a despairing type of anger, and I hear myself
> saying, "Please leave me alone—I don't have anything
> to give you—let go of me."

Rose feels burdened by and angry toward the child in her. She is aware that her child feels fearful and insecure, but she doesn't know what to do about it, and feels helpless and tired. She wishes her child would just go away. At another moment Rose, identifying more with the child in her, wrote:

> I want to be free. Free of myself.
> Free from the me that obsesses over what is the "right"
>   thing to do.

Free from the domineering "shoulds" that seem to forever
    resonate in my mind.
Free from the fear that if I don't achieve "greatness" my
    life would be meaningless and wasteful.
For as long as I can remember, I've felt an urgent need to
    be more than I am.
I've never been satisfied with myself, though I've never
    been able to find out why.
It's a feeling of wanting something very specific, and yet
    I'm ignorant of what that something might be.
It's an unreal feeling that it's "out there" somewhere,
    while at the same time I think it's very deep within me.
Sometimes I get the feeling that it's right in front of me,
    staring me in the face.
But I remain blind to it.

Like Rose, many women are torn between their inner-critic's rage at and resentment of the kid within them, and their inner-child's fear of and resentment towards their inner-critic. Is this familiar to you? Do you feel that there are things that you want to accomplish, but some part of you is holding you back or undermining your attempts? Do you feel in conflict? Perhaps part of you feels that you have what it takes, while another part is not at all sure and doesn't want to take a chance. If so, pay particular attention to the process that Rose went through:

Rose came into treatment in her mid-twenties suffering from crippling anxiety that had lasted several years. The frightening and overwhelming symptoms of anxiety (heart palpitations, trembling, profuse sweating, dizziness) came upon her most often in public places, so she had ceased going to department stores, movies, concerts, restaurants, any space from which she could not instantly escape. In an early therapy session she was stuck in silence—unable to talk or reach out for help. I asked her to visually represent the feelings she was having at the moment. The image that came to her was of a part of her sitting at her desk, feet up, calm, and in charge.

She imagined another part of her cringing in a corner. I suggested she stay with this image and "see" how her two parts acted and spoke with each other. At home, later that day, Rose described this session in her journal:

The "in-control me" was angry at the "frightened me," for being fearful. I didn't understand why it was fearful. The "in-control me" wanted to shut out the "frightened me," to push away and deny its existence. I couldn't be giving to that "me," although towards anyone else who was scared I would be understanding and supportive. The "frightened me," however, didn't want to be pushed away. In fact, she wanted very much to become a greater part of the "in-control me." But the "in-control me" wouldn't allow her in. I wouldn't allow all the negativeness and weakness of the "frightened me" to be accepted by the "in-control me."

At home Rose continued to explore this inner conflict, and then described it in her journal:

When I got home right after the session, I wanted to "play out" the rest of the fantasy to see where it would go. I sat at my desk, with my feet up, and chair tilted back, as usual. For a minute or two I just sat there, and then I looked over into the corner, until I could somewhat visualize the "frightened me." When I did, I immediately said aloud, "You son-of-a-bitch!" Silence took over for about a minute. Then I saw the "frightened me" look up at the "in-control me," with saddened eyes, saddened face, and she sadly said, "I'm sorry." I could tell that the "frightened me" was hurt by the "in-control me" calling her an S.O.B. But the "in-control me" got angry. I thought, "Here I called you a son-of-a-bitch and *you* apologize??! Why don't you get angry at me for calling you that?" I saw the "in-control me" go over to the "frightened me," and I took her by the shoulders and shook her hard and banged her against the wall and shouted, "What the hell is *wrong* with you? What the hell are you afraid of?"

The "frightened me" started to cry, tears rolled down her cheek, and she answered, crying, "I don't know—I don't know." There was despair and helplessness in her voice. Although the "in-control me" was still angry, she started to feel sorry for the "frightened me," so took the "frightened me" into her arms, held her close, and let her cry on her shoulder for a minute till she stopped crying. Even though the "in-control me" was trying to show the "frightened me" some warmth and reassurance, which the "frightened me" appreciated, the "in-control me" felt phony and frustrated. She felt that the "frightened me" hadn't changed at all—she was still standing in the corner. The "in-control me" walked away, and was about to go out of the room, but first I turned around to look back at the "frightened me," who was now collapsed on the floor in the corner, and said, "Look, if you can't stop being fearful, okay—but don't drag me down by making *me* fearful. I may have to put up with your presence in me, but I will push you aside as much as I can. You're no good to me the way you are—why can't you see that? If you must be that way, be that way in silence. I don't want to know about you anymore. I want you to leave me alone. Your weakness is getting to me and I won't let that happen. Since you can't seem to change, then I'm the one who has to change. I'm the one who has to push your presence out of my mind and try to go ahead with the business of living."

Rose ended this journal entry with the following note:

This about winds up the fantasy. The end was obvious, and perplexing. I wound up at the end of the fantasy exactly where I am today: Unable to understand the fearful part of me, I shut it out and don't allow it to be felt; I try to cover it up and go on with my life. But clearly, that's not easy and it's no adequate solution. But the fantasy is exactly my life!

Many women spend their lives caught up in inner turmoil and conflict. Like Rose, they try to push away the fearful parts of themselves, ferociously trying to stem feelings that will not be denied. Rose's inner-child collapses exhausted in her corner—abandoned, depleted, more hopeless than ever. Rose's inner-critic feels frustrated and discouraged. She fails to understand why a show of phony warmth has not been sufficient to change her inner-child. She feels burdened by this coward and wishes she would just go away.

Do you ever feel angry at and resentful towards the child within you? Do you blame all your troubles on your inner-child and despair of ever getting her on the right course? Do you wish she would just go away and leave you alone?

If so, like Rose, you need to learn that, in order to be happy and successful, you must first accept that your inner-child is here for life. There is no way to get rid of the angry, frightened, sullen, or hurting child within except by helping her to develop and become happy. To get what you desire in life you need to stop rejecting your inner-child, and learn to nurture her instead. If not, if you continue to resent your inner-child, she will resent you back and you will remain at odds with yourself, pushing forward at the same time as you hold back. Let's see how Rose learned to accept her inner-child and move forward.

After some exploration in therapy Rose started to understand that her "frightened me" was really the child within her—container of her hurts and fears and longings . . . and also of her wit and humor and creativity. Intellectually she began to accept that the child in her was a really good kid: bright, curious, earnest, warm, dependable, and creative—needing only love to blossom and grow. But Rose still needed to accept her inner-child emotionally, in her gut. With encouragement, she went back to her inner dialogue, which was presented above, picking it up after her "in-control me" called her "frightened me" an S.O.B., and the "frightened me" started to cry. Here it is as recorded in her journal:

As the "frightened me" continued to cry, the "in-control me" noticed how tightly she was holding on to the "in-control me"—as if she were holding on with every ounce of strength she had. The "in-control me" forgot about her anger, at least in this moment, and instead of closing off to the "frightened me," she held her tightly in return. I watched this for a while—somehow it felt good to me to see the "frightened me" and the "in-control me" holding each other that way. It made me realize how needy the "frightened me" was, but not all in a bad way. I guess I saw how much love and also how much emptiness there was in the heart of the "frightened me," and suddenly my heart felt like it opened up to her. Picturing this, tears rolled down my face. Something was happening—something was moving in me.

The "frightened me" and "in-control me" stood there, crying together, holding each other, and the "in-control me" began to gently smooth her arm up and down the back of the "frightened me." The "in-control me" spoke softly to the "frightened me," whispering to her, saying, "I'm here. It's all right. Let yourself cry—I'm here. I'm with you." The "frightened me" drank in those words as if they were breathing life into her. After a couple of minutes the "frightened me" loosened her hold on the "in-control me" and pulled back a little, just enough so she could look into the eyes of the "in-control me." The "frightened me" saw warmth and comfort in the "in-control me." And the "in-control me" saw innocence and longing in the "frightened me." As the "in-control me" gazed at the "frightened me," she saw, perhaps for the first time, the child within her and she wanted to protect her.

As she told me later in a therapy session, Rose ended this journal entry with the following note:

For the first time I felt loving towards the "frightened me." I could *feel* that she wasn't some alien creature that just appeared at different times to torment me, but the lonely,

scared part of me that needed my understanding and help—
and that I needed her help too, that the only way I could
stop fearing and hurting and pulling myself down was by
understanding and helping myself with her pain, which is
really my pain.

This self-acceptance represented a breakthrough in Rose's
treatment. While we worked together long and hard to understand
and work through her many insecurities, the real breakthrough
was Rose's acceptance of and commitment to the "child" in her.
Then Rose was able to regard and help herself in ways she never
could before. Instead of thinking that there was something wrong
with her and indirectly keeping herself stuck, she accepted her
child and learned to nurture her.

This shift from self-hate to self-acceptance and self-love is very
moving to witness and remarkable to experience. Sometimes it
comes about in a dramatic way, as in Rose's case. Other times it
occurs in a more gradual way, as for Ayanna.

Ayanna (whose poem "My Smiling Friendship" appears
in chapter 3) spent her twenties and early thirties getting
heavily into debt, being fired from jobs, getting involved with
the wrong men, and flunking out of graduate school. This
behavior, while self-defeating, was really an attempt to get
nurturing. Ayanna felt, on some level, that if she messed up
enough, then her cold and distant mother would be forced
to come through and rescue her. She was threatened by success or independence because she felt that, if she could stand
on her own two feet, then no one would ever take care of her
again. And yet, through it all, she really was standing on her
own two feet—supporting herself, being creative, establishing
friendships, obtaining a series of jobs, slowly bettering her
relationships with men. Only she never really acknowledged
this to herself, or accepted taking care of her inner-child as

her responsibility. She kept looking for people to bail her out and rescue her. At one point she got evicted from her apartment, and her mother reluctantly took her in. This became Ayanna's last-ditch attempt to get nurtured by her mother. By the time Ayanna moved out months later, she was convinced that her mother never could or would give her what she wanted and needed emotionally. She now knew that it was up to her. Ayanna worked hard to get to know, as well as to accept and love, her inner-child. As a sign of her commitment to continue nurturing herself, Ayanna even decided to formally adopt her inner-child. She drew up papers, and we had a ceremony and celebration together.

Ayanna experienced many changes in herself after the adoption, which took place over ten years ago. The most notable shift was her accepting responsibility for her inner-child, which she continues to do to this day. As she nurtured her inner-child and met many of her emotional needs, she felt better about herself and less needy. After a while Ayanna even felt that she had filled herself with enough inner supplies that she wanted to share some of them with another, so became a "big sister" to a needy teenager, offering this girl the nurturance Ayanna had learned to give to her own inner-child. Ayanna also changed the quality of her relationships with men. While in the past she had been attracted to men who were self-centered and ungiving, she now began to seek out men who could CARESS her. In time she established a relationship with a man who loves her and cares about her happiness. Ayanna continues to be accountable for her inner-child and resists the temptation to surrender all responsibility for her to her husband. He loves and nurtures her inner-child along with, but not instead of, Ayanna.

Both Rose and Ayanna in their separate ways grew close to the child within them, instead of struggling to cast her out. Their lives were enriched and made more content and fulfilling by this touching and moving contact with themselves.

You, too, can learn to nourish yourself. Can you picture nurturing and loving your inner-child in this way? Can you imagine wanting to adopt yourself, so that you will have a nurturing parent for life? Can you start to sense how good that would feel? The following step is designed to help you open your heart to the child within you.

STEP EIGHT: OPENING YOUR HEART TO YOUR INNER-CHILD

(Note: You need to keep your eyes closed during this step. Either tape-record the instructions slowly, pausing to give yourself time to complete each instruction, or memorize the instructions.)

Take three deep breaths, and with each exhalation release the tension in your body and let yourself become relaxed . . . . Then close your eyes and imagine your inner-child and inner-caretaker sitting next to each other hand in hand . . . or perhaps your inner-child is snuggling on your inner-caretaker's lap . . . or being held in her arms. See them together . . . looking into each other's eyes with love . . . . Let yourself sense how good this feels, how much you want it for yourself. . . . And let yourself know that you can have this mutual love, by doing what you are picturing here—by being with and loving your inner-child.

Then in your mind's eye go back in time and remember or imagine a time before you started to doubt yourself. Perhaps you were a small child, or even a newborn. Allow yourself to experience your innocence and your promise. Visualize that small child that was you, come into the world with personality and the drive to grow and flourish . . . Now project the rest of your life before you, like a movie, and watch what went right and what went wrong—what was good and what was harmful—what nourished you and what was lacking. . . .

Even if you don't know exactly what went amiss, let yourself know there was a time when everything was fine, and that something must have happened to cause the insecurities you're now experiencing. . . . Then quickly rewind the movie of your life and return to that small child that once was you, eager to be in the world and unaware of what lay ahead. . . . And let your heart go out to that child—innocent and expecting, so strong and so vulnerable, so lovable and loving . . . Extend to that small child the love you know she so urgently longs for. . . . It's not too late. . . . That child is still within you, and desperately needs your love. Embrace your child and tell her that you'll always be there to love and guide and help. . . . Then be that child and take in this love. . . . Really take it in. . . . Don't rush. . . . Just be that child and take in that love. . . . Then, when you're ready, come back to the present.

How do you feel? Were you able to offer yourself love and take it in? Are you starting to feel differently towards your inner-child? Do you feel that you really do want to be there for her? It's a wonderful feeling when you can accept and value your inner-child. You've already started to do that by opening your heart to her.

Now you need to become better acquainted with her, to discover her needs and desires, her hopes and fears, what she's angry at, aspires to, enjoys. You may have spent years disliking and attacking her without really knowing her at all. Maybe you have no idea how to contact the "child" in you. The next steps will teach you how to reach her.

Step Nine: How to Listen with Your Heart and Talk so You'll Be Heard: Learning Empathic Communication

*T*his step is different from the previous ones, because it does not revolve around a structured exercise. Instead you will learn important principles for communicating effectively with your inner-child. These principles will give you vital tools that you will utilize in Step Ten.

You've already started to get to know your inner-child. When in Step Eight you imagined being nurtured, your inner-child introduced herself and told you a lot about her needs and longings. It is important for you to be attuned to these communications.

Take out your list of MY NURTURERS now and reacquaint yourself with your inner-child. Read your list over slowly and let yourself know that this is your inner-child speaking, asking for what she needs.

However, your inner-child does not always express her feelings and needs directly. She may be afraid to expose vulnerable feelings, or believe that attempting to get her needs met by asking outright would not only be futile, but would invite criticism. Instead, your inner-child may find subterranean ways of expression, acting out emotions by passively resisting your inner-caretaker's agenda. Rose's "in-control me"/ "frightened me" conflict in chapter 10 is one example of this. Here is another.

Laura, a professional, is job-hunting. Her last employer moved out of state, and Laura used her liberal severance pay to take three months off and relax. Now she is facing re-entering the work world and is filled with anticipation and trepidation. Her inner-caretaker is eager to go back to work because she believes it is important to be responsible, independent, and challenged.

Her inner-child is creative and curious and likes the idea of learning new things and being challenged by interesting work, yet she is also afraid. She fears that Laura will take an overly taxing job and then slave away at it to prove what a good worker she is, so that what started out as interesting and creative work turns into sheer drudgery. This happened at Laura's last job, and Laura's inner-child is very afraid it will happen again. Her misgivings are intensified by knowing that Laura's inner-caretaker doesn't take her fears seriously, and tends to pooh-pooh them or to hate her for being afraid.

Laura's inner-caretaker, on the other hand, fears her inner-child will drag her feet forever, and not like any job. She is aware that her inner-child sabotages her job-hunting efforts by feeling too depressed or sick to get up and start job-seeking activities, or by putting off thanking people with whom she is networking. Laura's inner-caretaker is enraged at being undermined like this, and despises her inner-child for doing it. Her inner-child, however, is scared to death of being "sold down the river" and is dragging her heels as her only defense. She is mad that her caretaker doesn't understand her fears about going back to work, and feels isolated, lonely, sad, and depressed.

All of this is going on below the surface. Laura is only aware that she is in turmoil, and can't seem to get much done, but she doesn't know why. She reacts to her inner conflict with self-abuse:

> "I ended up sleeping the morning away instead of working on my cover letter. I hate myself when I do that."
> "I feel really disgusted with myself. I want and need to get a job, but I can't seem to get organized."
> "I dread making those phone calls, and put them off as long as possible. Then it's too late in the day to call. I can't stand it when I do that."
> "I had set this past weekend aside to develop a job-hunting campaign—but the weather was so beautiful, I ended up going to the country with Larry. It was a lot of fun, but now I wish I hadn't done it. I'm really upset with myself for playing when I should have been working."

Although Laura recognizes that she's having difficulty carrying through on her job-hunting plans, and that something is making her drag her feet, she doesn't stop to ask herself, "What's making this happen? What's going on for me? What is this conflict about?" Instead she blames herself for having this problem and berates herself.

Laura needs some way to get inside herself, to contact her inner-child and find out what's wrong. One way to do this is to pretend that her inner-child and inner-caretaker are two real people and to have a dialogue between them.

Whenever we have a decision to make, we ponder what to do and argue it back and forth in our heads. Whenever we are feeling down on ourselves, there is an inner voice berating us. And when we feel good about ourselves, we have an inner voice praising us. Having a dialogue between your inner-caretaker and your inner-child is simply a way of taking what is already happening and making it more explicit so you can look at it, deal with it, and work it through. Let's see what happens when Laura tries to contact her inner-child:

CARETAKER: Listen, I really want to get a good job and to continue to grow and develop in my profession. I wish you weren't always dragging your feet. What's with you anyway? Why are you doing this to me?

"CHILD": I'm afraid, and I don't want what you want. You're all into your career, and being a success, and proving yourself. I want time to be with Larry and our friends, and to have fun, and to play the piano, and go to the country. And I know how you are. It's so important to you to be respected and recognized that on a new job you'll just throw yourself into it, and work a zillion hours, and lose track of everything else. That would make me miserable.

CARETAKER: I know that you don't want to work hard! All you want to do is stay home and indulge yourself! I tried being good to you. I took three months off work, and let you go to a masseuse and be pampered. But there's no end to your neediness. The more I give you, the more you want. Nothing's ever enough! If I didn't push you, you would never do anything. You'd probably spend the whole day sleeping and watching TV. As it is, even when I do push you, you barely move. I'm really sick of you and your neediness! It's time we did something—time we got back to work.

"CHILD": I'm trying. But I feel so tired and depressed. I need to relax and be taken care of.

CARETAKER: I've spent enough time taking care of you. Now it's my turn. I want to go back to work, and we're going to. I'm in charge and what I say goes!

"CHILD" (defiantly, but silently): We'll see.

The conflict between Laura's inner-caretaker and inner-child ends in an impasse. Neither side listened to the other with empathy and caring. Rather each side listened to rebut. Listening to rebut is what lawyers do in court. Their aim in trials is to overpower and win. They are not trying to open up communication. We are, though. We need to find a way for our inner-caretaker and inner-child to work together, to problem-solve together, and to give and get from each other. For positive change to take place, our inner-caretaker and inner-child need to realize their inter-dependence and to help each other to achieve agreed-upon goals.

The kind of communication that went on between Laura's inner-caretaker and inner-child in the above dialogue—locking heads together, attacking each other without any acceptance of the other's feelings—is called a *power struggle,* and always ends in a deadlock.

There is no winning in a power struggle.

Yes, the "parent" can push the "child" around and bully her, but this will never get the child's cooperation, acceptance, or re-spect—or vice versa—and this is what each desires and needs. To work together productively, both sides need to be able to share *feelings,* as well as thoughts, and to do so in an atmosphere of acceptance and respect. I emphasize *feelings,* because this is the area where real change takes place.

It is relatively easy to change someone's ideas; that is, if you have persuasive facts. It is much harder to change someone's feelings about something. That is why for many people positive feedback helps only for the moment. Later they are still left with their ingrained negative *feelings* about themselves. For instance, if your inner feeling is that you are dumb, lazy, ugly, fat, incom-petent, clumsy, selfish, or mean—other people telling you that you are smart, industrious, attractive, slender, competent, grace-ful, generous, or kind feels good, but usually doesn't last long. You may think that others are only trying to cheer you up, or that they don't know the truth about you. You cling to your own perceptions of yourself as though they were facts—learned at an early age and accepted as "God-given" truths that are eternal and inalterable.

These are the *feelings* about yourself that you need to change if you are to like yourself; but before you can transform your feelings, you first have to bring them out into the open, like exposing an infected wound so it can be cleansed and healed. However, you are not going to expose your vulnerability (even to yourself) unless you feel safe.

In order for you to feel safe, there has to be an atmosphere of mutual acceptance and respect. No one wants to express her innermost feelings if she expects to be attacked and belittled. You can establish this atmosphere of acceptance and respect by learning to communicate in a way that I call empathic communication.

Empathic communication is talking and listening with respect, acceptance, and caring about the feelings of the other person in a conversation. The aim of empathic communication is to draw the other person out, and particularly to draw her feelings out, so that you can better understand her. You can learn to communicate this way by using the techniques of empathic communication. Let's look at them.

TECHNIQUES OF EMPATHIC COMMUNICATION
Reflecting Feelings Back
Asking for Clarification
Encouraging Further Expression of Feeling ("Tell me more.")
Stating One's Own Feelings (especially important for the inner-caretaker)

Reflecting feelings back: This is an important way to let people know that you understand what they are feeling. When you reflect feelings back with acceptance and compassion in your voice and attitude, it encourages others to go on and express more of their feelings. This simple but powerful technique is used by a majority of therapists since it is so effective. It greatly facilitates communication whether you are having a dialogue with yourself or talking to other people, and is an instantaneous way of turning an argument into a dialogue.

"Reflecting feelings back" is the opposite of "listening to rebut." It's easy to learn, and gets easier and easier with practice. All you have to do is: **Listen for the *feelings* in what the other person is saying, and then state those feelings back in slightly different words.**

Your aim in reflecting feelings back is to convey understanding and acceptance of the feelings that the person you're talking with has just expressed. Acceptance means that you accept and respect that he or she feels that way—it does not mean that you necessarily share those feelings.

Suppose, for example, a husband wants his mother to move in with his family, and his wife doesn't get along with her mother-in-law. If this couple listens to rebut, the conversation might go like this (H is the husband, W is the wife):

H: Mom can't manage on her own anymore, and I can't stand the idea of her in a home. We owe it to her to take her in.

W: But you know she drives me crazy, what about your obligation to me?

H: There you go, always thinking of yourself. She's an old lady.

W: And I'll be old before my time if I have to live with your mother! You call me selfish, you're the one who's thinking only about what he wants.

H: What do you want me to do? Let her live in the street? Put her in a home? You're so unreasonable!

W: Now you're trying to make me feel guilty, like I'm an evil monster for not wanting your mother to live here. You never care about what I feel.

H: And you care only about what you feel! [Storms out of the room. Wife sits and cries].

Now consider how the conversation could have gone if this couple knew how to reflect back feelings.

H: Mom can't manage on her own anymore and I can't stand the idea of her in a home. We owe it to her to take her in.

W: You feel obligated to her.

H: Of course, she's my mother.

W: Tell me more about what you feel.

H: I feel awful. I hate seeing her so old and sick. And I wonder if our kids will feel burdened by us someday.

W: You feel burdened by Mom and worried about being a similar burden when you get old?

H: Well, yeah. Look, I know it's not going to be any picnic having Mom here. She's always been a martyr and that's really grating. I wish just once when I ask her what she wants to do, she would tell me, rather than her usual, "Whatever you want is fine." I hate having to second-guess her, and always ending up feeling like I guessed wrong. I really don't look forward to having her here, but I know it's the right thing to do.

W: You're really torn. You want to do the right thing, but you really wish there were some other way without Mom having to live here.

H: That's right. And I'm worried about you too. I know what a pain you find her, and I don't want to overburden you, either.

W: So, that's another pressure on you.

H: Yes, how *do* you feel about her living with us?

If this couple is taking turns exploring each other's feelings, as many couples who communicate empathically do, they will now switch roles and the wife will share her feelings while the husband reflects back.

w: I dread the prospect. She's always criticizing everything I do, and if I react to it, she gets all hurt, like I'm picking on her.

H: You dread having to live with that constant criticism.

w: I really do. And I hate the way she plays up to the kids and you, like everyone's golden and I'm clay.

H: How does that make you feel?

w: Like I'm a nothing and a nobody. Then I get very angry and feel like punching her out! Of course, I wouldn't. So then I feel like running out of the house or locking myself in my room. But then she starts up again with, "Where are you going at this hour?" or "Does Jim know that you spend so much time brooding in your room?"

H: It sounds like you feel trapped and angry.

w: That's right. Then after a time, I start feeling real down. I'm afraid that if Mom lived here, I might be depressed all the time. On the other hand, I know she's an old woman and needs a place to stay, and I don't want you to feel that you can't ask your own mother to live with us.

H: So you're really torn. You can't stand the idea of having her here, but you think it's the decent thing to do, and you're also concerned about how I feel.

w: That's right. I also feel guilty about not wanting her. It makes me feel like I'm a bad person, like I'm mean and selfish.

H: Not wanting Mom to live here makes you feel bad about yourself.

w: Yes. But it helps a lot knowing that you're not thrilled about it either and that you care about how difficult it would be for me. It makes me feel that if we do take her in, I would really have your support. Before I was worried that you would side with her and blame me if she's not happy, and I know she won't be happy because she's so hard to please.

Observe what's happened here. In the first dialogue the husband and wife took turns rebutting and attacking each other, and it led to anger, hurt, and distance. In the second they took turns listening to and accepting each other's feelings. After this sharing they felt closer. Moreover, and equally important, when the husband and wife no longer had to be constantly defending themselves against the other's attacks, each was able to discover and express his and her own ambivalent feelings about his mother living with them. This is always the case with human behavior. I call it:

The Golden Rule of Ambivalence
If you agree with one side of a person's ambivalence, she or he will take the opposite side. If you remain neutral and encourage a person to express feelings, you will hear both sides.

If you doubt the validity of this, just think of the last time you were ambivalent about anything, trivial or important: "Should I stay up and keep reading, or go to bed?" "Should I buy this house, or stay where I am?" Whatever the significance of the decision is, the process is still the same. If someone tells you to go to bed, you say, "But this is such a good book, I don't want to put it down." If someone tells you to keep reading, you say, "But I'll be tired in the morning and all day tomorrow." The same with buying a house. If someone tells you to get the house, you'll respond with your worry about not being able to afford the mortgage payments. If someone tells you then to wait on buying the house, you'll respond with what a great house it is and how much you want it.

We respond this way to advice, because that is the nature of ambivalence. It means that we are torn two ways, and therefore find it hard to make a decision either way. Advice becomes a tug in one direction, so we tug in the opposite direction in order to maintain our middle position. The harder someone tugs us in one direction, the harder we pull in the opposite direction. When this happens, it looks like we aren't ambivalent (like the couple in the first dialogue), but (as demonstrated in the second dialogue) this may often be far from true.

In dealing with ourselves, our ambivalence is generally voiced by the differences between our inner-caretaker and our inner-child. The "child" wants to stay up reading, or wants to buy the house. The caretaker, on the other hand, is worried about being tired the next day or paying the bills. What is needed to resolve this conflict is not outside advice, but empathic communication between inner-caretaker and inner-child until they find enough common ground so that they can reach a joint decision, or until the inner-caretaker can set limits in an empathic way.

When you talk with your inner-child, it is vital to reflect back feelings, rather than listening for the sake of rebutting and attacking. Just remember what happened with the husband and wife above. Each encouraged the other to express his or her feelings by listening with acceptance, compassion, and respect. Without fear of being attacked, neither needed to become defensive, so each was able to express both sides of their ambivalence. They ended up feeling in the same boat and supportive of and supported by each other.

This sharing brought them closer together. After more of this kind of sharing, they decided to ask his mother to live with them. The wife felt better about doing this because she felt she really had her husband's support, and didn't have to pretend that it was just great. Most important of all, she accepted her own feelings of not wanting Mom there, rather than feeling like a bad person for resenting an old woman. They both agreed, too, that if it got really bad, they would consider other options, so neither felt trapped for life. This helped them feel that they could more readily welcome Mom into their home.

I've used an example, here, between two adults—rather than

between a parent and a child, which would seem more appropriate to our subject matter—because your inner-child is not a real child. Your inner-child has had as much school as you have had, and is as smart as you are. We would not expect a real child to reflect back feelings, but your inner-child can do this as well as your inner-caretaker. Maybe even better. In talking to your inner-child, however, beware of using too many big words, because this is usually a sign that you're being too intellectual and getting away from feelings.

Asking for clarification: This means asking questions so you can learn more about what the other person, or other part of you, is *feeling*. Sample questions for clarification are:

What are you scared of?
What about that makes you angry?
What about what I said made you feel hurt?
What are you longing for?
What do you feel you're needing right now?

Avoid, if at all possible, asking "why?" questions. "Why?" asks people to figure something out, usually putting them into their heads and away from their feelings. Asking for clarification helps us to find out what is going on in the other person, and it also communicates our desire to know the other's feelings. It is important to ask these questions in a nonjudgmental way. "What's the matter with you?!" is not a real question. It is not part of an attempt to understand another person, rather it is really a critical statement ("There's something wrong with you!") disguised as a question. Beware of statements disguised as questions.

Encouraging further expression of feeling ("Tell me more."): This technique is very easy to learn. You simply encourage the person to amplify on feelings already stated, often by saying, "Tell me more about what you're feeling." For example, if your inner-child says, "I don't like talking to you because you make me so nervous," your inner-caretaker could respond with, "Tell me more about feeling nervous when you talk to me."

Most of us hesitate to talk about our feelings because doing so makes us feel vulnerable. We feel freer to express our innermost thoughts and emotions when we believe that the other person really wants to know how we feel, and that she or he will be accepting and nonjudgmental. In the example above, saying nonjudgmentally, "Tell me more about feeling nervous when you talk to me," encourages the inner-child to keep talking. Consider how different this is from the inner-caretaker saying, "I don't know why you feel nervous. I just want to know what you're feeling." Here, while the inner-caretaker is ostensibly expressing interest in the inner-child's feelings, she is really being judgmental, implying in words and tone that there is something wrong with the inner-child for being nervous—that the inner-child is *at fault* for being nervous. Feeling blamed and criticized, the inner-child is likely to clam up and feel bad.

Stating one's own feelings: In empathic communication the dialogue must represent a sharing of experiences, where each participant not only states his or her own feelings but has those feelings accepted by the other, as the husband and wife did above. In stating your feelings, be sure to start your sentences with "I." A statement that starts with "you" is likely to be critical and attacking. In internal dialogues the inner-child usually is eager to express feelings, while the inner-caretaker often hides feelings under judgmental statements. Familiar examples of such judgmental statements include:

> "You're a big drag!" (Instead of "I feel afraid of being dragged down by you.")
> "All you do is feel sorry for yourself!" (Instead of "I want to make changes, and I wish I had your help to do so.")

If your inner-child is rebellious (rather than compliant) she too may attack and be judgmental, saying such things as:

"You're a bully."
"You're an old fuddy-duddy."
"You're a selfish controller."

Then you're well on your way to a power struggle.

If in your inner dialogues, you find yourself in a power struggle—
STOP! Take a break and figure out what's wrong. Chances are
your inner-caretaker and inner-child have been attacking each
other, rather than using the techniques of empathic communication.

Let's see the power of empathic communication in action by
observing Laura, the woman who was struggling over returning
to work, and seeing what happens when her inner-caretaker and
inner-child communicate empathically:

CARETAKER: Listen, I really want to get a good job and to continue
to grow and develop in my profession. I wish you weren't
always dragging your feet. What's with you anyway? Why are
you doing this to me?

"CHILD": I'm afraid, and I don't want what you want. You're all
into your career, and being a success, and proving yourself. I
want time to be with Larry and our friends and to have fun
and to play the piano and go to the country. And I know how
you are. It's so important to you to be respected and recognized
that on a new job you'll just throw yourself into it and work
a zillion hours and lose track of everything else. That would
make me miserable.

CARETAKER: You're afraid that when we go back to work we'll be
swamped with work, and never have any fun.

"CHILD": Well, not exactly. I know that we'll have some fun, but
it'll just be squeezed into everything else that needs doing. I
want time to relax, and just be with Larry. I feel so good when

Larry and I have time around the house together without a lot of outside pressures. I love it when we can just hold each other, and talk, and laugh. I also like having time to myself.

CARETAKER: You don't want to go back to work if it means giving all that up.

"CHILD": Well, I don't mind giving some of it up. I like to work too. It's interesting learning new things and meeting new people. But that's another thing I'm afraid of. Maybe I won't do well on the new job. Maybe the boss will end up thinking I'm a nothing. Maybe I'll be fired.

CARETAKER: I'm afraid of that too. That's why I work so hard, so it won't happen.

"CHILD": Tell me more what you feel about that.

CARETAKER: I want to prove once and for all that I really am capable and talented and smart. I hated it when our father constantly condescended to me and patronized me, insinuating that because I'm a woman I couldn't be really intelligent.

"CHILD": It's really important to you to prove him wrong.

CARETAKER: Yes. But, I'm not really sure that I can. Then, when you start dragging your heels, I'm sure that I can't. I wish you would help me, rather than work against me.

"CHILD": I'd like to help you. I can feel how upset you are. But, I'm upset too.

CARETAKER: Tell me what you're upset about.

"CHILD": I just want to feel loved, and taken care of, and safe. I don't want you to devote yourself to proving how smart and competent you are at the expense of everything else. I've always felt so lonely and bereft, and always had to do for myself and others. Mom was too depressed to take care of us, and then she died and that was so much worse. I've felt so alone ever since. I'm tired of struggling—tired of having to act grown-up—and I'm also afraid that if we take a job, I'll just prove how inadequate I am.

CARETAKER: I want to be safe too. That's why I've been working so hard. When we have prestige, and security, and money—when we're very self-sufficient—then we'll be safe.

"CHILD": Those things don't make me feel safe. What makes me feel safe is love, and understanding, and compassion, and support. When you're working, you totally ignore me like Mom did when she was depressed, and I feel abandoned and lonely and sad. Then if I try to get your attention, you get angry at me. I wish you would pay more attention to me and care about what I feel.

CARETAKER: I do care about you. That's why I've been working so hard, so that I can take care of us. But you seem to have so many needs. I wish you could be alright and not need me so much.

"CHILD": But I do need you. I need you very much.

CARETAKER: Tell me more about needing me.

"CHILD": My whole life I've felt I had to be good, and not make demands, and not ask for too much, and always think of others first, and be grown-up. Now I want to be taken care of, and I want you to take care of me. I don't just want it. I really need it. I feel so terrible when you don't pay attention to me—sad and lonely and depressed. Then when you get angry at me for feeling this way, I feel even worse—angry and defeated and worthless all at once.

CARETAKER: You're really unhappy when I push you away.

"CHILD": I am! I'm so glad you understand that. I've been wanting you to understand that for so long!

CARETAKER: I'm starting to understand it now. And I want to be there for you. I hate to see you so unhappy. But I'm not sure how to give to you, and not be overwhelmed by your needs.

"CHILD": How would you be overwhelmed?

CARETAKER: You just seem so needy. I've always felt that the more I give you, the more you want, and there's no end to it.

"CHILD": I do feel needy like that a lot, but there are also a lot of times that I feel up and want to have fun. I feel more needy when you don't listen to me or accept my feelings. I don't like spending the morning brooding in bed, either. It's no fun staying home and being depressed! But I don't know any other way to get you to pay attention to me. I feel a lot better now, though, because you're listening and seem to care.

CARETAKER: I do care. I never realized that you were acting that way because you needed something from me. This talking together really helps.

"CHILD": It helps me too.

CARETAKER: Let's talk again soon.

"CHILD": Fine.

Something very important happened in this dialogue between Laura's inner-caretaker and inner-child. *They began to listen to and understand and accept each other's feelings,* despite the fact that each of them started off feeling angry and defensive. Feeling heard and accepted allowed them to let down their angry guard and start to really talk to each other. They discovered that they weren't as far apart as they thought; that they were struggling with the same feelings, though each had a different solution in mind. They began to support each other, rather than attack and sabotage each other.

After this initial dialogue Laura started to feel better. Now she knew what was upsetting her, and what her internal conflict was about. She also experienced hope. She could see that, through continuing communication between her inner-caretaker and inner-child, it would be possible to find a resolution.

Over the next weeks Laura encouraged problem-solving by initiating a series of inner dialogues. With each dialogue she could feel more and more love for her inner-child, as she grew to accept, respect, care about, and feel compassion for her "child's" feelings. As she CARESSed her inner-child, her inner-child began to feel safe, and nurtured, and loved. Laura's inner-child no longer needed to act up to be heard. They began to work together.

In this process Laura realized that her inner-child's fears and needs were her responsibility, and that she had to deal with them or she would never be happy. She empathized with the fears of her "child," at the same time as she encouraged and supported her inner-child to believe in herself and push forward. She promised that she wouldn't take a job that was so demanding as to make them both miserable. Her inner-child then cooperated with job-hunting, despite her fears, trusting that Laura would not ignore her needs.

Laura was now in the success cycle. By CARESSing her inner-child, her inner-child became happier, more confident, cooperative, and hopeful. In response to her inner-child's new attitude, Laura's inner-caretaker no longer felt angry. Instead she wanted to give to and CARESS her "child"—which made her inner-child still happier. In the end Laura found a job that she likes very much, which requires limited overtime (a rarity in her profession). Thus the success cycle goes:

CARESS leads to success leads to CARESS.

You can learn to be in the success cycle, too.

CHAPTER 12

Step Ten: Giving Yourself the Nurturance You Need

*M*aybe there is something particular bothering you: perhaps you are in a troubled relationship . . . or are facing a stressful situation at work . . . or have a difficult problem with a child . . . or are consumed with feelings of emptiness, worthlessness, depression, or anxiety. Or maybe there is nothing extraordinary bothering you, but you feel tired, worn out, unappreciated, or bored. However you feel, in this step you are going to learn how to help yourself feel better. Not how to magically solve your problems overnight, but how to give to yourself while you're striving to change and to grow. You are going to learn how to figure out what's wrong, and how to make yourself feel better.

As you engage in the process described in this chapter, I urge you to be patient with yourself. Remember, change takes time. You are not going to become self-nurturing overnight. Each small step you take is important and you deserve credit for each one. Keep in mind the Chinese adage, "A journey of a thousand miles starts with a single step," and give yourself credit for every step you take. Don't be discouraged if you see yourself taking two steps forward and one step back. Progress is never steady. It is always like the baby learning to walk who takes a step, falls, takes two steps, falls again. It is only in retrospect that change seems easy and quick, not while you're going through it. Remember, it is common for people to feel most stuck just before they take a big step forward.

Focus on what is changing and give yourself the encouragement and support you need to keep changing. Take a minute now to review the progress you have already made. Have you started to value things about yourself that you previously disregarded or took for granted? Can you recognize that you have many pluses, and not just minuses? Have you begun to like yourself, even a little bit more? Do you feel some hope where previously you felt only despair? Have you started to be able to stand up to your inner-critic and to assert your self-worth? Take stock of the ways in which you have already changed and give yourself credit for them. Let what hasn't changed stay in the background, something to be dealt with later when you are better at nurturing yourself. What is important now is that you are willing to learn how to nurture yourself, you have already taken many important steps in being able to nurture yourself, and you are going to persist. TAKE TIME EACH DAY TO GIVE YOURSELF CREDIT FOR TRYING. And remember to read your list of positive attributes at least twice each day.

Now, take out the list of goals that you wrote in chapter 7. Each goal represents something you are working on, or want to work on; and each goal states something about what you need to change to attain that goal. You are going to learn how to establish internal nurturing dialogues—in which your inner-caretaker and inner-child work together allowing you to understand what's going on inside of you, reach a forward moving resolution, and make your goals a reality. First, though, you must decide how you want to contact your inner-child.

There are three ways to have dialogues with yourself: in your head, in writing, or out loud. For now it is most helpful to talk with your inner-child either out loud or in writing. After you have more experience communicating positively with your inner-child, you can have dialogues in your head. I, myself, prefer to speak with my "child" out loud. I find it faster and easier than writing and more immediate and emotional. However, some of you may prefer writing down your dialogues. You might find the slower pace gives you more time to think and feel, and you may also like having what you wrote available for future reference. It doesn't matter which method you use. Choose whichever you are most comfortable with. If you're not sure which you prefer, try both and see which works better for you. It's fine to use one method for all your dialogues, or to switch and use one method for some dialogues and the other method for others. The important thing is not the method, but that you actually experience the dialogue going on. Let me explain how to do this using each method.

Out loud: This method is something like acting out a scene from a play that has two characters, where you're the only actress and are playing both roles. When you're talking as your inner-child, sit in one place and imagine that you are facing your inner-caretaker, just as you did in Step Seven when you spoke to your inner-critic. Observe how your inner-caretaker is sitting and what expression is on her face. For most of you, your inner-caretaker will look as you do now. However, if you get another image of your inner-caretaker, go with it. Images are powerful messages from our feelings, and always bear exploration. Frequently they are a rich source of information.

When your inner-child is finished with what she is saying, change seats to where your inner-caretaker was seated. Now become your inner-caretaker and face your inner-child. See how old she looks, what expression she has on her face, how she is sitting. Let her really come alive for you.

Your inner-child can appear at any age before adulthood. Do not decide ahead of time what age you want her to be. Just start talking and see what emerges. Your inner-child might be at a different age for each dialogue, may always stay the same age, can be an indeterminate age, or even a conglomeration of ages. It doesn't matter. Allow whatever happens to happen. You don't have to control it. Accept it, and go with it.

When your inner-caretaker finishes responding to your inner-child, switch seats again. Return to where your inner-child is seated, take this position, and respond as your inner-child would. Continue this throughout the dialogue, changing seats whenever you change roles. In each role let yourself experience the feelings that go with the role, like an actor getting into a part.

In writing: Imagine that a conversation is taking place, and it's your job to record it. You are like a court stenographer who writes everything down without interjecting anything of her own. You are able to see in your mind's eye both parties—where they are sitting, the looks on their faces, their ages, their postures—all this without having to look up from the paper you are writing on. The dialogue starts with your inner-child talking. The stenographer writes the "child's" words down. Then the stenographer waits to hear how the inner-caretaker responds and records that. Back and forth the dialogue goes. The stenographer invents nothing, but records everything. The inner-child and inner-caretaker speak for themselves.

Out loud or in writing: Let both sides express what is on their minds and in their hearts and guts. Use the techniques of empathic communication. Avoid name-calling, belittlement, and other kinds of attacks. End your dialogue with an agreement to talk again.

In your inner dialogues, be honest. Don't feign compassion or acceptance or support. If you don't trust the other side, say it openly. True communication is based on honesty. You don't have to and should not pretend to feel something that you do not feel.

Be as forthright as you can be about your feelings, but don't let one side attack the other side. If that starts to happen, catch it and stop it. Replace habitual destructive inner dialogues with empathic communication. It is this kind of communication that is nurturing and produces growth. Let's see, by example, how this works by considering Diane's first dialogue.

"CHILD": I need help to become more assertive.

CARETAKER: Tell me more.

"CHILD": I don't stand up for myself enough, and then later I feel walked over and taken advantage of.

CARETAKER: What is it that makes it hard for you to stand up for yourself?

"CHILD": I feel afraid to.

CARETAKER: Tell me more about feeling afraid.

"CHILD": I don't know . . . I guess I'm afraid of the other person getting angry at me and not wanting to have anything to do with me.

CARETAKER: You're afraid that asserting yourself will lead to the relationship getting worse and falling apart?

"CHILD": That's right.

CARETAKER: Is that what happens?

"CHILD": I'm not sure. I don't often assert myself. I know that's what happened with our family. If I stood up for myself, I was considered selfish and everyone got angry and withdrew.

CARETAKER: You're afraid that if you assert yourself the same thing will happen now that happened in our family?

"CHILD": That's right. I'm afraid that if I try to stand up for myself, I'll fail and be more alone and feel even worse.

CARETAKER: Putting up with being dumped on seems better than not being liked and being left.

"CHILD": I don't like the way that sounds, but I guess it's true.

CARETAKER: Hearing you say that really gets me upset. I want us to get someplace in the world. I want to accomplish things. And I want to be happy. I don't want to put up with being dumped on, and when you accept it, I get really angry at you.

"CHILD": You're angry at me for being afraid to stand up to people?

CARETAKER: I sure am. I feel so held back by you and your fears! I hate the idea of being taken advantage of.

"CHILD": You're angry at me for holding you back and letting you be mistreated.

CARETAKER: That's right. Look, I understand that you're afraid of being rejected and alone. I don't want that either. But I don't think we're going to get anywhere hiding out. We've got to go after what we want.

"CHILD": I agree. That's what I started out saying—that I need help to become more assertive.

CARETAKER: What kind of help do you need?

"CHILD": I'm not sure . . . I think I need someone in my corner supporting me, telling me I'm right. I think if I had that, I wouldn't be so afraid.

CARETAKER: You wish you had someone on your side.

"CHILD": That's right. And I also would like more success. I'd like to ask for a raise and get it.

CARETAKER: You need someone to believe in you and you want to be rewarded for your efforts.

"CHILD": Yes. That would be great! Then I think I could assert myself. . . . But [getting discouraged] that all feels so far off.

CARETAKER: You don't believe you can get that?

"CHILD": It's hard to believe I could. I've been trying so hard to get ahead, and haven't made much progress.

CARETAKER: That's not true. We haven't gotten as far as I would like, but we have done a lot of things. We moved away from home, got a nice apartment, made friends, traveled some, had our share of good times. I wish you didn't get so easily discouraged and depressed.

"CHILD": Well . . . we have done those things. I guess I take them for granted, and forget that they really weren't so easy to do. Realizing that makes me feel a little better, a little more hopeful. I'm really glad you pointed that out. It cheers me up some.

CARETAKER: I want to cheer you up. I want you to be hopeful and to work with me. There's so much I want for myself, so much I want to accomplish.

"CHILD": Do you really think we can do it?

CARETAKER: Well, I have my own doubts about that sometimes, particularly when you're submissive. Then I feel like I'm fighting a battle on two fronts: in the world and within myself. I really wish I had your help.

"CHILD": I want to help you, but I need your help too.

CARETAKER: What do you mean?

"CHILD": Before I can be hopeful or take chances I need you to support me and cheer me up, like you did today. I felt so much better after you pointed out what I had accomplished. And I was really surprised when you did it. Most of the time you just tell me how worthless I am.

CARETAKER: I'm sorry about that. I know that I'm angry at you a lot, but it's not because I'm against you. It's because I need your help and I get so angry at being dragged down.

"CHILD": I can understand your being angry. But, I feel so awful when you belittle me. I just want to run and hide. And I also feel furious with you.

CARETAKER: You feel furious with me?

"CHILD": Yes! I feel enraged. And I want to get even with you— do whatever I can to mess up your plans. But, today I feel so different. Today I feel that you like me and want to help me and want me to help you.

CARETAKER: I do. When I felt how much you were hurting, I wanted to cheer you up. I didn't do it to get you to help me, and I was really surprised when you said you wanted to. I feel better than I have in a long time.

"CHILD": Me too. Let's talk again soon.

CARETAKER: Great!

Observe what happened in Diane's dialogue. By using the techniques of empathic communication, both sides moved from adversarial positions to working together. They accepted each other's feelings with compassion, and started to support and encourage each other. Together they expressed respect for what they had accomplished and felt happier and more optimistic. Each side CARESSed the other, and each side felt buoyed up by that loving CARESS.

Does this sound too simple? Try it. You'll be surprised by how much better you'll feel when you start to CARESS yourself. You'll discover that you have the power to make yourself feel lovable and valuable.

Before starting your first dialogue, **take out your MY NURTURERS list that you prepared in Step Seven and read it out loud.** It will help your inner-child and inner-caretaker to know what they need to feel better. When you start your dialogue, let it flow, using the techniques of empathic communication. If your dialogue gets deadlocked, first make sure that you are communicating empathically. Then check your MY NURTURERS list to see if there is something you need that you are not giving to yourself. By communicating empathically with yourself and nurturing yourself in the ways that you need, you will find yourself moving out of power struggles and the failure cycle into feeling whole, integrated, lovable, and capable—able to esteem yourself.

If you are going to have a written dialogue, have paper and pencil handy. **It is important to complete a dialogue in one sitting, so make sure you have uninterrupted time in which to do so.** Keep your GOALS list and the techniques of *empathic communication* from page 146 written down nearby for handy reference.

YOUR FIRST DIALOGUE: NURTURING YOURSELF

Now get started. First take three slow deep breaths, and when you exhale, exhale all the tension out of your body and let your body become very relaxed. If you are writing, imagine your inner-child stating one of the goals from your GOALS list, and write it down. If you are doing the dialogue out loud, be your inner-child and say out loud what you need. If your inner-child feels like saying more than that, that's fine. If not, switch roles (and seats if you are acting out the dialogue) and let your inner-caretaker respond. Now your dialogue has begun. Let it unfold according to its own rhythms, which might be very different from Diane's. Remember to use the techniques of empathic communication, and not to belittle, berate, or attack. Keep going until the dialogue feels finished for now, or at a point where both sides wish to rest. *End by promising to talk again.* Then put the dialogue aside and come back to yourself.

How do you feel? Pay attention to what you experience. Have you started to feel the magic of CARESSing yourself? If you haven't yet, you will as you continue the dialogues. **Give yourself credit** for sharing your feelings (this always involves taking a risk) and for having the courage to delve into yourself. Whatever you experienced, praise yourself for trying and let yourself know that communicating with yourself, like most things, gets easier with practice. With time and repetition empathic communication will become easier and easier for you, and as it does it will become almost automatic for you to CARESS and nurture yourself.

ONGOING DIALOGUES: KEEP CARESSING YOURSELF

Keep communicating with your inner-child. It is helpful at this stage to talk with your inner-child frequently. You may wish to pick up where you left off in your last dialogue, or you may be ready to go on to another of your goals. Go at your own pace, but be sure to get through your entire list of GOALS so that your inner-caretaker and inner-child will be working together on all of them. Always start with your inner-child stating the goal. When discussing a new goal, you may include previously discussed material, just as you would in an ongoing dialogue with another person. However, raise only one new goal on any given day. Each time begin by relaxing, then read slowly your list of what makes you feel nurtured. After the dialogue, notice what went on between your inner-caretaker and inner-child and how you feel. Each time be sure to give yourself credit for the time, effort, and feeling that you have put into helping yourself.

Let these internal discussions of your goals be the jumping-off point for deep and continual communication between your inner-caretaker and inner-child. Help each side to express her feelings: fear, anger, anxiety, desire, guilt, shame; and hope, cheer, delight, and love in an atmosphere of acceptance, respect, and compassion. Remember, these two sides are both part of you, and for you to feel good about yourself and be ready to meet the world they have to be working in concert, supporting and encouraging each other.

It may take some time to get through your list of goals, depending on the size of your GOALS list and the frequency of your dialogues. That's fine. Don't rush it. This is not a prescription to rush through after which you'll be all better. This is a way of being with yourself as a nurturing presence that you are learning; a way of bringing yourself understanding, caring, hope, and comfort that you will want to continue for the rest of your life.

Once you've gone through your entire GOALS list, you are ready to incorporate all that you have learned about nurturing yourself. You now know a lot about your inner concerns, and understand why they are important to you. You're developing compassionate acceptance of yourself, and have started to respect yourself for the person you are. You've learned to support yourself by believing in yourself, and to stroke yourself by giving yourself credit for all your efforts. You've been reading your WHAT I LIKE ABOUT MYSELF list twice daily and feeling better and better about yourself. When you start to berate yourself, you know how to nip this destructive process in the bud by stopping yourself and then replacing your harsh judgments with words of understanding and encouragement. Now you're ready to dialogue informally.

INFORMAL DIALOGUES: LIKING YOURSELF FOR THE REST OF YOUR LIFE

Having informal dialogues means having them in your head, like you've been doing all your life. Only now, instead of using these dialogues to berate yourself—as you used to do—you are going to use these dialogues to support yourself and to problem-solve. The process is exactly the same as you have been using in your written or spoken dialogues, except that from now on you can dispense with talking out loud and changing places, or writing down what each side is saying, except at those times when you are having a particularly difficult time and desire the added clarity of doing dialogues out loud or in writing.

Dialogue frequently, preferably several times a week. Be on the lookout for signs that something is bothering you. Common signs are boredom, anxiety, restlessness, and depression. Have your inner-caretaker and inner-child explore what's going on that's creating these feelings. Once you know what's wrong, see if your inner-child and inner-caretaker can work together on finding a mutually acceptable solution.

When something upsetting happens, give your inner-child permission to feel whatever she is feeling, while your inner-caretaker CARESSes her. Keep reading your list of MY NURTURERS to remind yourself what makes you feel better. Be sure to give yourself the support and encouragement that you and all people require before they can make changes. Feel the flow from accepting yourself where you are, giving yourself permission to be there, and—in so doing—becoming ready to move on.

A familiar example of the flow from self-acceptance to change can be found in how people deal with death. Before someone can get over the loss of a loved one, she first has to acknowledge feelings of pain, loss, grief, anger, and abandonment. People who deny or repress these feelings cannot finish mourning and move on to other relationships, nor are they able to put more into their remaining relationships. They remain forever tied to an illusion ("I'm not upset, I'm fine.") that leaves them isolated from themselves and others, and therefore incapable of being satisfied. On the other hand, bereaved people who are able to acknowledge their inner pain and accept these feelings can with time accept the reality of their loss and are able to take in solace from themselves and others. The caring is able to get to where the pain is, so that in time the mourner starts to heal and to move on.

Remember, in order to change you have to let yourself into where the trouble is, and that means letting yourself in

on your most painful feelings, and meeting those feelings with the healing balm of acceptance and compassion.

For instance, let's say you made an important error at work, or mishandled something at home, or presented yourself poorly on a date—an old dialogue in its essence would be:

"CHILD": I messed up.

INNER-CRITIC: You certainly did. You're really worthless.

"CHILD": I am.

Now you're ready to talk to yourself in an entirely different way. You have learned to love your inner-child and to respect her feelings, even if you don't always approve of the actions that emanate out of these feelings; and your inner-child has learned to respect and value you. Most important of all, you have learned that *change is brought about by empathy and support and talking through feelings, not by criticizing and belittling.* Try imagining your own nurturing response to having made an important error, before you read the following sample.

"CHILD": I messed up.

CARETAKER: What was going on for you that made you do that?

"CHILD": I was feeling anxious and flustered, so couldn't think straight.

CARETAKER: And now you're really upset.

"CHILD": Yes. I feel so stupid and bad.

CARETAKER: I understand you're feeling down now; anyone would, but remember this is just one incident, and it's not really representative of you. That's not what you're really like.

"CHILD": Yes it is. And even if it's not, I still feel terrible.

CARETAKER: Come on now, you know that you really can do a lot of things well. And of course you feel terrible. You're disappointed that things didn't work out better. That's real upsetting for anyone. Let's see what we do to make things better.

Inner-caretaker and inner-child next engage in a problem-solving session in which energy is put into deciding how to repair the present problem or make things come out better next time. There is plenty of energy available for envisioning solutions, because it is not being wasted in futile self-reproach.

Let yourself use your energy to grow and change and flourish! Give yourself the nurturing you need, the CARESS you need, to feel like and become a success!

You now know the fundamentals of how to nurture yourself, but like any skill it requires practice. With enough practice it will become habitual for you to treat yourself with compassion, acceptance, and respect. After a while your first impulse will be to give yourself encouragement and support and stroking. But within the next year these skills can be easily lost without frequent application. You have already started to feel much better about yourself. These good feelings will greatly increase, the more you CARESS yourself. Remind yourself how good it feels to be nurtured, and accept this as your responsibility. **Adopt your inner-child and nurture her for the rest of your life.**

PART III

Nurturing Yourself in Difficult Situations

There are certain situations in which it is particularly hard to affirm and nurture yourself, such as when anxious, depressed, raising children, making love, and at work. All of these situations can be undermining to your self-esteem. Women who are anxious typically denigrate themselves for being anxious. Those who are depressed are usually even more down on themselves. Raising children can be very stressful (in fact, having young children is one of the factors cited by the American Psychological Association study as accounting for the prevalence of depression among women).[3] Sexual encounters offer all kinds of opportunities to feel inadequate, while work is a place where women have been traditionally devalued. In the following chapters you are going to learn special techniques for fostering and maintaining your self-esteem in each of these problematical situations.

CHAPTER 13

Nurturing Yourself When Anxious

*A*nxiety is something that all of us experience some of the time. It is a natural response to perceived physical or psychic danger—a warning signal to tell us to be careful. Walking alone late at night on a deserted city street makes us a little anxious and therefore properly wary, helping us to be on the lookout for danger. Similarly, if you promised your demanding, irritable boss to have a report ready by the end of the day and you're finding it slow going, you might start to feel a little anxious in anticipation of being yelled at and chastised. Here your anxiety is telling you to be careful, so you can take steps to avoid being chewed out.

Anxiety can run the gamut from mild situational anxiety to generalized anxiety, phobias, panic attacks, agoraphobia, and post-traumatic disorder.

SITUATIONAL ANXIETY

This is anxiety that occurs when a particular situation is perceived as being dangerous. Some situations that commonly provoke anxiety are:

Making a speech or presentation (the perceived danger is
making a fool of oneself).
A job interview (the perceived danger is not getting it and
feeling unworthy).
A blind date (the perceived danger is being rejected and feeling
undesirable).

In these kinds of situations, usually once a person actually
gets into the feared situation and starts feeling more confident,
the jitters go away. Here a little anxiety can help a woman to be
prepared to put her best foot forward. However, too much anxiety—rather than being a helpful warning—is undermining. It is
hard to seem confident, poised, and competent if your hands are
trembling and your voice is quaking. For instance, consider Nadia.

Nadia, twenty-eight, had a job that required her to make
periodic oral reports to her large department. While she loved
her job and was very good at it, she dreaded this aspect of
it. The night before she would hardly be able to sleep, awak-
ening many times. (Troubled sleep is a frequent concomitant
of anxiety.) When the time came to give her presentation,
she'd be drenched with perspiration, have to hold her hands
to keep them still, and use deep breathing techniques to keep
her voice steady. Her anxiety was based on her belief that, if
she messed up in front of her colleagues, they would never
respect her again. Past success at these presentations did not
lessen her anxiety, because each time she anticipated anew
that she might fail and be totally humiliated.

When people feel considerable situational anxiety it is usually
because they, like Nadia, imagine the situation going badly and
then exaggerate the meaning and consequences of the anticipated
negative outcome. For instance, in Nadia's case, if her presentation
did not go well her colleagues would probably just think she was
having an off day. It certainly isn't true that they would never
respect her again. Nadia doesn't recognize that she is exaggerating

the negative consequences of giving a substandard presentation because she expects the world to judge her with the same harsh, perfectionistic standards that her inner-critic uses. Nadia also increases her tension by taking any negative reaction from others, or any belief on her own part that she did not do as well as she could have, as "objective confirmation" of her inadequacy. In so doing, she is setting herself up to be anxious. How could she not be anxious when she is letting her whole sense of competence, worth, and adequacy ride on this one event?!

This is a common occurrence. For instance, if—prior to a job interview—a woman is thinking about how awful it would be not to be hired and that this rejection would prove (as she already believes) that she isn't capable or worthy, no wonder she becomes anxious.

Similarly, if before a blind date you're thinking that your thighs are too big, your hair unmanageable, and that you're going to be found boring and unexciting—of course you will feel anxious. If you then add on to this anticipation of rejection by exaggerating its significance—telling yourself that you don't know why you bother going on blind dates anyway because no one will ever like you—naturally your anxiety will increase. Whose anxiety wouldn't, if she viewed her whole sense of desirability as riding on the response of this one unknown person?

If you become anxious in a particular type of situation, you can learn to calm yourself and reduce your anxiety by holding on to your positive sense of self. Focus on your assets, soothe the worried child within you by helping her to view the situation more realistically, and commit yourself to continuing to like yourself, whatever happens. The following process will help you to do so.

1. **Read your list of WHAT I LIKE ABOUT MYSELF from Step One aloud.**

2. **Connect these assets to the anxiety-provoking situation that you are facing. For example, before a job interview you might remind yourself that you are bright, responsible, reli-**

able, creative, and work well with people—qualities that make you highly desirable to your prospective employer. Or before a blind date, focus on what you like about your appearance and your personality, and remind yourself that these are likely to be qualities valued by your date.

3. (Note: Memorize or tape-record these instructions, as they need to be followed with your eyes closed.) **Sit or lie down, close your eyes, and relax yourself by taking three very slow deep breaths. Next, alternately tense then relax each part of your body separately: toes, feet, lower legs, upper legs, stomach, buttocks, pelvis, diaphragm, back, chest, shoulders, arms, hands, fingers, neck, jaw, face, head. Then relax even more by imagining yourself in a very peaceful and pleasant setting, such as at the beach or in the country, or whatever place you prefer. Let this be your relaxation spot. Stay there in your imagination, taking in the feel, smells, sights, and sounds of your special spot until you feel very peaceful.**

Then envision yourself in the anxiety-provoking situation and imagine it going very well. See yourself being poised, relaxed, and self-confident. Imagine a positive outcome—getting the job, or being asked out again, or delivering a well-received speech. . . . Take your time and relax as these positive images fill your mind. . . . Take them in . . . . Then return to your relaxation spot and enjoy the peacefulness you feel there. When you're ready, open your eyes and come back to the room.

How do you feel? Are you more confident and less anxious? *Imagining a positive outcome diminishes anxiety, while imagining a negative outcome increases anxiety.* This is only common sense—seeing a situation as dangerous triggers anxiety, while seeing a situation as safe allows us to relax, and the more relaxed we feel, the easier it is to present ourselves at our best.

But, you might wonder, why should I imagine my date, or presentation, or interview going well, when it may not? Aren't I only deluding myself? Shouldn't I be preparing myself for the worst? No, you shouldn't be, because by expecting the worst you are courting failure. By going into an important encounter in a tense, anxious state you are inviting difficulty. The more anxious you are, the harder it is to concentrate, making it difficult to present yourself at your best. In an anxious state you may also miss signs of positive response, or be unable to follow up on them. A much better way to prepare for possible disappointment is to address your fears and soothe your inner-child.

4. To soothe your inner-child, first ask her how she feels. If, after the above relaxation experience she is still worried, find out what she is worried about, and then reassure her. Likely she fears that, if she doesn't succeed, you'll be disappointed in her . . . and angry at her . . . and see her as a failure. If so, assure her that you'll keep on liking and respecting her whether or not she gets the job, or is asked out again by her blind date, or does well on the speech. Let her know that there are all kinds of factors that are beyond your control that may influence the outcome, such as another applicant's having more relevant work experience or important connections, the personality or availability of your date, and the receptivity of the audience. Tell her that you know that she is going to do her best, and that's all that counts, and you don't expect her to be perfect.

In the case of a blind date or a job interview, stress that this is not just a question of being rejected or accepted by the other person. You are also the chooser, and you want to be sure that this is the right person or job for you. The date and employer have to sell themselves to you, too. Hold on to this power!

Promise your inner-child that, even if things don't turn out as you wish, you will not react by criticizing her and by telling her she's inadequate and hopeless. Give her and yourself the support, compassion, and encouragement that you so need when dealing with a disappointment. Accept her sadness and hurt, and assure her that there will be other opportunities and you will help her to find them.

You can communicate this in the form of a dialogue, or you

can sense your "child's" fears and speak comfortingly to her—
just be sure you don't lecture, threaten, or criticize. Imagine you
are talking to a friend who is worried and anxious, and soothe
yourself as you would her.

**5. As close to the time of the anxiety-producing event as
possible, once again get in a comfortable position, shut your
eyes, relax yourself by taking three very slow deep breaths,
slowly in and slowly out, and again first relax yourself by
alternately tensing and relaxing your muscles and then visualize yourself first in your relaxation place, and then going
into the situation in a calm, poised, self-confident manner.
See the positive outcome. If you start to feel anxious, return
to your relaxation spot and become peaceful again. Then once
more go back to the tense situation and see yourself handling
yourself well, and getting what you want. Take in the good
feelings. When you are ready, return first to your relaxation
place, and then to the room you're in. Experience how wonderful it is to give yourself this positive send-off.**

The above steps will not only help you to diminish your
situational anxiety, they will also help you to improve the outcome, for incredible as it may seem, there is a correlation between
imagining things going well, and their actually going well.

GENERALIZED ANXIETY

This is the everyday kind of anxiety that many women experience
and suffer from. Sometimes a woman may know what is making
her anxious, but can't get her anxiety to go away. Other times
she has no idea why she is anxious. She just finds herself jumpy,
nervous, unable to concentrate or sit still, and unable to sleep
well.

Jackie, a thirty-five-year-old, single, attractive professional, suffered from recurrent anxiety. Sometimes it took the

form of troubled sleep. She would fall asleep with difficulty, only to reawaken several times during the night. Other times her anxiety took the form of a general restlessness and edginess that interfered with her concentrating on anything or being able to enjoy what she was doing. When I met her she had no idea why she would start to feel anxious. She was similarly in the dark about why her anxiety would go away. She would go through periods where she was anxious for weeks at a time, and other periods that were anxiety-free.

In learning to handle her anxiety, the first important principle that Jackie needed to learn is that there is always a *trigger*—some thought, feeling, association, or event that makes a person anticipate a dangerous or unhappy outcome. Anticipating that things will go badly, she then starts to become anxious. (She might also start to feel depressed. We will deal with depression in the next chapter.) Underlying her anxiety is an imagined scenario of how events will go badly. What makes her anxious is that her imagined scenario sets off one of her basic fears. Common basic fears are:

Fear of Loss (this is a very important and very common trigger. It will be examined in detail later.)

Fear of Abandonment

Fear of Being Alone

Fear of Being Humiliated

Fear of Failure

Fear of Success (usually because outward success is perceived as being accompanied by some kind of loss. For instance, believing that, if you're successful, no one will ever again take care of you or want you.)

Fear of Rejection

Fear of Domination .

Fear of Harm Attack or Retaliation

Fear of Intrusion, Invasion, and Engulfment

Fear of Being Controlled

Fear of Withdrawal of Love and Approval

Fear of Loss of Respect
Fear of Illness and Death
Fear of Criticism
Fear of Betrayal
Fear of Being Out of Control
Fear of Going Crazy
Fear of Anger (yours or others')
Fear of Being Unworthy
Fear of Annihilation
Fear of Loss of Status
Fear of Intimacy (lest you open yourself to betrayal, aban-
donment, or being intruded upon and controlled)
Fear of Being Vulnerable (lest you be abandoned, hurt, be-
trayed, dominated, controlled, or abused)
Fear of Trusting Another (for the same reasons basic to fear
of vulnerability)
Fear of Being Overwhelmed

The kind of underlying fears a woman has are related to the
kinds of parenting she received and other important life experiences. If she had a distant parent, her major fears are likely to
center around fear of abandonment, loss, withdrawal of love,
being alone, anger (especially her own anger, lest it drive her
loved ones even further away), and rejection. If she had an over-
involved parent, her fears probably center around invasion, engulfment, and abandonment. If she had a self-involved parent,
major fears for her are likely to be loss, abandonment, rejection,
withdrawal of love and approval, loss of respect, and criticism.
If she had an overly critical parent, she may have almost all of
the above fears, with her major fears being of loss, abandonment,
criticism, attack, loss of approval, anger, humiliation, and annihilation.

The things that a woman fears do not have to actually happen
to make her feel anxious. Just the thought that they *might* occur
is enough to create anxiety. Take, for example, a woman who is
over-charged at a store and anticipates that her complaint will be

answered with surliness and anger. If she is afraid of anger, she's likely to become anxious even though it might turn out that the salesclerk is courteous and apologetic. Similarly, in anticipating a blind date, a woman's anxiety is a product of what is happening in her head and feelings, not of her unmet date's actual behavior.

Often the specific trigger that sets off an underlying fear is very hard to put your finger on, as we saw for Jackie above, especially if your anxiety doesn't seem to be linked to any particular event in your life. You may feel tense, jittery, unable to sit still or concentrate, but don't know what you're worried about. When these feelings occur, it is very important to take time to explore them. See if you can get some sense of what might be troubling you. This may be hard to do, because *often we hide our feelings from ourselves.*

Hiding your feelings from yourself may sound strange, but it is a very common experience. We try to hide our feelings from ourselves when *we don't approve of how we feel,* when our feelings clash with our idea of how we are or would like to be. For instance, if you want to think you're brave and courageous, you might not want to admit that you're afraid to take an unpopular stand. If you wish to think that you can deal with your parents, you might not want to admit that visiting them makes you anxious. If you like to think of yourself as independent, you may not want to admit to yourself that you feel shaky at the thought of your relationship ending. If it's important to you to think of yourself as secure, you may not want to acknowledge that your partner's impending business trip is triggering fears of abandonment and loss.

If you try hard to figure out what's triggering your anxiety, and just can't get to it, don't be surprised or discouraged. This is a common experience, and you'll get much better at it with practice.

In searching for the fears and feelings that underlie your anxiety, it is helpful to know that the most common fear that produces anxiety is fear of loss, which is also sometimes called "separation anxiety." This fear has its roots in childhood. As babies our very survival depended on an adult being there to feed and clothe us, and protect us from harm. We also needed an adult to give us the emotional connection and physical touching that stimulates growth. Babies raised in hospitals with almost no touching or consistent caretaker fail to thrive physically, cognitively, and emotionally.[4] Beyond this, our healthy emotional development requires a constancy of care and affection.

By "constancy" I don't mean that each and every time we needed our caretaking adults (usually our parents) they were there for us. This is clearly impossible for any parent to do. Rather, I mean that we had an overall sense that our parents loved and cared about us and approved of us, and that we could get their positive attention when we really needed it.

Many of us just did not get that constant care and affection. Our primary caretakers may have been inconsistently connected to us, at times nurturing and other times depressed and unavailable, or angry and withdrawn, or self-involved and distant, or intrusive and critical. This kind of intermittent reinforcement leaves us hooked on trying to get care, at the same time that we are fearful of abandonment, loss, and rejection. Perhaps these feelings were mitigated by the presence of other caring adults, or perhaps they were worsened by other uncaring, abusive, or inconsistent adults.

Others of us suffered major losses in childhood: a parent who died, or had a prolonged or degenerative illness; a primary caretaker who was a paid employee, who subsequently left or was let go; a grandmother who raised us until she died or Mother remarried and took us far away; a father who was distant or unavailable after a divorce. Whatever the loss, it deeply affected us and left us fearful of future losses. Again, if there were other loving, consistent adults in our lives, it helped—but not enough to totally make up for the loss of such a loved one.

Any woman who suffered loss in childhood, whether it be absolute loss through death or separation or the on-again, off-again experience of inconsistent parenting, is particularly vulnerable to anxiety. All human beings have a need for independence and connection. If either is missing, we suffer. The very thought of losing one or the other can make us anxious. What we have experienced in the past makes us anticipate similar experiences in the present and future. Thus, if our childhood was filled with loss or the threat of loss, we feel apprehension as adults at the slightest hint, or even thought, that loss could occur. Or we are afraid to connect at all for fear of loss.

Melissa, whose beloved father deserted the family when she was a child, got anxious whenever her husband left the house. It's not that she consciously believed that he was not coming back—she just felt anxious. When she learned to identify the source of her anxiety, by realizing that it was her inner-child experiencing the loss of her father, she still felt scared, but her anxiety lessened. With time, by acknowledging her scared feelings and talking with her inner-child whenever needed about them, she became less anxious as she learned to be more there for herself.

Monica's mother, who was her dominant parent, was connected and helpful in a crisis, but the rest of the time was generally either preoccupied with her own concerns, or depressed and unavailable. She also favored Monica's older sister, whom she constantly praised and boasted about. Monica grew up feeling insufficient, and uncertain of Mother's love. Monica's adult life was plagued with anxiety and indecision as she was pulled between her strong desire for connection and even greater fear of loss. She was reluctant to make any kind of commitment, because to commit herself wholeheartedly to anything or anyone felt to her as if she were opening herself to the disappointment that the relationship, job, hobby, or vacation would inevitably bring. To guard against disappointment, and the feelings of abandonment and loss that it engendered, she would get involved to an extent, while feeling perpetually ambivalent about whatever or whomever she chose.

When Monica entered treatment she was plagued with anxiety, often spending sleepless nights and anxious days. Most of the time she had no idea what was making her anxious. In treatment she learned to identify her underlying fears (primarily loss and abandonment, but also invasion and humiliation), and then to recognize the many things that triggered her fears. Often the triggers were seemingly very small things, such as thinking about leaving her job, for instance, or thinking about staying, or thinking of taking any course of action. Nothing bad had to happen to trigger her anxiety. In fact, when real loss occurred, she handled it well. It was the anticipation that made her anxious.

In our work together, by accepting and CARESSing her inner-child, Monica strengthened her belief in herself. The more she felt able to take care of her own emotional needs, the less she felt she would wither and die without Mother to sustain her. Knowing that she could care for herself, she also became less fearful that—if she depended on others—she would fall apart or go crazy when this "crutch" disappeared. She learned that she herself could support and soothe her scared and worried inner-child. It's not that now she never becomes anxious, but her intense bouts of anxiety that used to be frequent have become rare, and when they do occur she knows how to figure out what's scaring her and how to calm her inner-child.

Jackie, the professional woman we considered earlier in the chapter, also discovered with exploration, the triggers to her anxiety. She would begin to feel anxious when she invested herself in a relationship with a man. The better things were going, and the more she cared about him and therefore about losing him, the more anxious she became. Then she would add to this anxiety by imagining that he was dating others, or would want to do so, or that he would pull out of the relationship for some other reason. Her anxiety was exacerbated by choosing men who were ambivalent about commitment.

When Jackie was able to recognize this trigger, she learned to soothe the frightened child within her by reminding her that they could and had managed fine on their own without a man, and that the actual loss of a relationship would not be the disaster that it felt like emotionally. This reassurance allowed other of her inner-child's feelings to emerge, particularly her fear that being married would mean having to constantly please her husband (lest he leave) and thereby losing her own autonomy.

The more Jackie became aware of the triggers to her anxiety, the less anxious she became. This doesn't mean that she completely solved her ambivalence about relationships—this took a lot of long hard work in therapy—but it did mean that she was a lot less anxious as she worked her ambivalence through.

In helping yourself to deal with anxiety, it is important to recognize what your basic fears are. Start by considering those on pages 181 and 182. Put a check next to those fears that you have to any degree. Then ask your inner-child to go over the same list and ask her to check the ones she has. If she says that she's afraid of something—accept it and add it to your list (if it's not already there). Don't try to talk her out of it. If you feel like telling her, "You're not really afraid of that," note it. Your reaction is an important clue that this is a fear that you are trying to hide from yourself. It is particularly important and helpful to acknowledge your hidden fears. Then ask your inner-child if she has any other fears that are not on this list. Listen carefully, and write them down.

Keep your list of fears handy. The next time you start to feel anxious, ask yourself what's making you anxious. If you have no idea, take out your list of fears and ask yourself about each one separately. For instance:

"Am I feeling scared of losing someone or something?"
"Am I feeling scared of being rejected?"
"Am I feeling scared of being alone?"

Try to be aware of what you were doing, thinking, or feeling just prior to becoming anxious. Consider also what stresses are in your life right now. It's helpful, if possible, to nip your anxiety in the bud before it becomes overwhelming. It's also easier to be clear about what triggered it if you can deal with it right away.

If you have trouble figuring out what the immediate trigger is, or which of your fears has been activated, ask your inner-child. She knows. Give her enough compassion and support, and she'll tell you. Remember the techniques of empathic communication that you learned in chapter 11, and use them in your inner dialogues. Turn to your inner-child and ask her in a non-judgmental way what she's worried about.

Often with nonspecific anxiety, just knowing what you are anxious about helps. For instance, maybe it's a rainy weekend when you have no plans. Instead of enjoying your free time around the house, you feel antsy and tense. Nothing satisfies or interests you. By talking with your inner-child, you discover that she feels lonely and is afraid of being alone forever. When you realize what's bothering you, your anxiety abates and you feel less anxious—not less lonely, but less anxious. Discovering what you're anxious about is like being afraid of the dark, and then turning on the light. Whatever you see is not as upsetting as the unknown, nameless fear.

Once your anxiety abates, that may be all you want. If so, that's fine. Say good-bye to your inner-child and go on. However, you may want to take this opportunity to help yourself with your underlying fears. Also, recognizing which of your basic fears has been stirred up is not always sufficient to ease your anxiety. You may first have to deal with your fear. In this example, you can continue to talk with your inner-child about her fears of being alone. You can tell her that you're afraid, too (if you weren't afraid, you wouldn't have had to hide your loneliness from yourself). You can let her know that you're doing what you can to meet someone or make new friends, or perhaps you haven't been doing that and now you'll start to do more. Give her encouragement and support. Let her know that you accept and care about her feelings, and that you'll work it out together over time. Talk about what positive steps you could take. CARESS your inner-child. When you give her Compassion, Acceptance, Respect, Encouragement, Support, and Stroking you are helping yourself to feel calmer.

Celeste was anxious because she knew that her lover Peggy was about to pull out of their relationship. Though she was aware that her anxiety stemmed from her fear of being left alone, she remained anxious. Eager to help herself, Celeste asked her inner-child about her fears. Her "child" expressed hopelessness about ever being found lovable and desirable again. Celeste reminded her of all her wonderful attributes that make her a desirable partner, and assured her that many women would want to be involved with her. She also told her inner-child that she (Celeste) would always love and care for her, and stay with her as a nurturing presence. This helped her inner-child to move from feeling that Peggy was her only source of nurturance and that without Peggy life would be nothing but bleakness, to believing that even if she were to be without a partner for a while, she'd get through it and be all right. With this shift, her anxiety abated.

The threat of abandonment and fear of being alone is a primal fear that goes back to early loss, and we all have some kind of early loss, because no one received perfect parenting. If you are frightened of an impending loss, let yourself know that you are no longer a helpless child. Loss is painful, but if you support yourself you have the strength to get through it and beyond it. Your emotional survival no longer depends on one relationship.

Paradoxically, it is often easier to make a relationship work if you feel that you could survive its dissolution. Believing that you could go it alone, if necessary, allows you to be in your relationship in a more powerful and committed way. Then you can work on your relationship because you really want it, not just because you're afraid to be without it.

Lastly, in dealing with pervasive anxiety, it is very important to remember that, if you've been significantly anxious most of your life, it's not going to go away overnight. The techniques in this chapter work, but not perfectly (nothing's perfect) and not each and every time. Don't be discouraged if you can't find a trigger—this is sometimes hard to do, but gets easier with practice. Just keep talking with your inner-child. Remember, she contains all your feelings and can and will tell you everything you need to know, if you're genuinely kind and patient with her. CARESS your inner-child and she will help you. Attack her for being anxious and you will remain anxious.

PHOBIAS

Phobias are an irrational, excessive, and persistent fear of some thing or situation. They usually produce intense anxiety, but only when the phobic person is near or anticipates being near the feared object. People can be phobic about many things. Common phobias are of dogs, snakes, elevators, bridges, and flying. Some people have social phobias, which stem from a fear of being embarrassed in public (this is different from being shy), and therefore avoid eating, drinking, or speaking in public. If forced to do so, they sweat, tremble, get nauseous. They are sure that others are aware of these reactions, and can't wait to flee this "humiliation." Social phobias are the only kind of anxiety that afflicts both men and women in equal numbers. All other phobias, like anxiety in general, afflict women much more often than men.

The way to get over a simple phobia is by exposing yourself in small graduated steps to the feared object at the same time that you reduce your anxiety by pairing in your mind the feared object with relaxing images. This is best done with professional help. First, though, make sure that your inner-child knows intellectually that the feared object, if handled properly, presents no danger (she probably already knows this). For instance, it is safe to look at snakes in a glass cage at a zoo, and travelling by plane is safer than by car.

If your inner-child knows why she fears the phobic object, talk to her about her underlying fears, and help her to dissociate them from the feared object or situation. For instance, tell her that you know she's afraid of going over bridges because she feels out of control, but really she's just as much in control of herself when driving on a bridge as when on a highway. Ask her to tell you more about her fear of loss of control, and listen empathically.

Then talk with your inner-child about why she would like to get over her phobia, what the rewards are for her. In trying to make any kind of change, motivation is very important. It is much more important than the degree of difficulty, or the amount of desired change. Ask her if there are any reasons why she may prefer to remain phobic. If so, explore these feelings with her. Before going on, make sure that your inner-child agrees that getting over your phobia is important and that she really wants to do it.

Next seek out a phobia clinic, counseling center, or private practitioner familiar with phobias who can help you face your feared object and to make friends with it. Names of clinics and therapists in your area with expertise in treating phobias are available from the Anxiety Disorders Association of America (ADAA), 6000 Executive Blvd., Suite 513, Rockville, MD 20852 (301-231-9350). For $3.00 they will also send you general information about anxiety. Many people have been helped to overcome their phobias—you can be one of them!

PANIC ATTACKS AND AGORAPHOBIA

A typical panic attack consists of a sudden onset of anxiety that seems to come out of the blue (some people even have panic attacks that start while they are sleeping), accompanied by shortness of breath, heart palpitations, sweating, trembling, dizziness or unsteadiness, and perhaps chest pains or discomfort, a choking or smothering sensation, faintness, weakness in the legs, hot or cold flashes, tingling in the hands, and a feeling that death is imminent. These symptoms are indicative of an intense fear reaction and are produced by the sympathetic nerves when triggered by adrenalin which sets off the fight or flight reaction. These physiological changes are a natural and helpful response in the face of real danger and prepare you to be better able to protect yourself by fighting or fleeing. However, when there is no recognizable danger that triggers an attack, the sufferer has nothing to fight, and instead remains painfully focused on these frightening physiological changes from which she desperately wants to escape.

Twenty to thirty percent of Americans have had one of these terrifying attacks at least once in their lives, while one to three percent of the population, that is between three and a half to seven million Americans, have recurrent panic attacks. Women compose the majority of those who suffer from panic attacks, with the typical age of onset being twenty-two.

While the precise cause of panic attacks is not known, there is some evidence that there is a genetic susceptibility to panic attacks, just as some people are genetically prone to react to stress by developing an ulcer. Panic-prone people, especially when they have been under physical or emotional stress, are particularly susceptible to reacting to fears or conflicts by having a panic attack. They are also sensitive to caffeine, which stimulates the adrenal glands, and may suffer an attack after as little as one to two cups of coffee.

While panic attacks are extremely upsetting, in and of themselves they pose little obstacle to a woman's functioning in the rest of her life. They usually only last a few minutes, and a woman is then free to continue with her planned activities. However, it is rare for someone to calmly accept such an attack as an occasional happening (like an ulcer flaring up) that will soon pass. Instead, once a woman has experienced the terror of a panic attack, she typically begins to live in dread of repeated episodes. Unfortunately, this fear of fear, and the adrenalin surge it engenders, often serves to trigger the very panic attack she dreads.

Panic attacks are typically, yet mistakenly, associated with the place in which they happen to occur. For instance, if a woman's attack occurred while she was driving, she will most probably associate driving with the attack, even though there is no real connection. The next time she is driving, she may, with or without realizing why, find herself starting to get anxious (because she fears having another attack). This anticipatory anxiety (i.e., anxiety produced by the fear of becoming anxious) scares her still more and may trigger another attack, thereby reinforcing her association of anxiety with driving and making her even more nervous at the thought of being behind the wheel. Subsequent feelings of anticipatory anxiety while driving, and the panic attacks they cause, ultimately lead her to be afraid to drive at all. Perhaps she experiences another panic attack in the supermarket. Now she becomes anxious there, too, so she starts avoiding supermarkets. For some women their agoraphobia (fear of going outside or of going to places from which escape might be difficult or embarrassing) becomes so severe that after a while, the only place they feel safe is at home. It should be stressed, that unlike simple phobics, agoraphobics are not afraid of "outside things" such as snakes or spiders—they are afraid of their own feelings and the bodily sensations their fear engenders.

Panic attacks, while they seem to come out of the blue as other forms of anxiety do, have a trigger: most often a thought, feeling, image, or expectation that is upsetting. Usually they first occur when a woman is under stress and is in some kind of conflict.

Rose, the woman whose dialogue between her "in-control" and "frightened" selves was presented in chapter 10, entered treatment precisely because of this problem. At the time I first met her, she avoided going to many public places—concerts, movies, restaurants, department stores—for fear of becoming anxious and having an attack. Needless to say, this severely limited her social life. By learning to identify the immediate triggers of her anxiety, connecting them to her underlying fears, and then being able to effectively calm the worried child within her, she has greatly reduced her anxiety, and now freely goes wherever she pleases.

Rose's anxiety and panic attacks started in her early twenties at a time when she was in great stress. Her father, at that time, was in the midst of a prolonged illness and recovery process that entailed his being in the hospital for two years. She was very worried about his survival and recovery, and was also troubled and upset by her relationship with him. Previously he had been distant and self-involved, and preferred her brother. By the time she was a teenager, Rose had learned to protect herself against feeling rejected by denying her love for her father and retreating into angry withdrawal from him. His illness broke through her defenses and she was eager to get close to him. However, in the hospital he was indifferent to her daily visits, but lit up whenever her brother arrived, thus adding to Rose's feelings of rejection and abandonment.

When Rose first became anxious, she did not connect her anxiety to her very understandable worries and fears about losing her father both through emotional abandonment and by death. Rather she blamed herself for being weak and out of control. The more she tried to hide her anxiety and blamed herself, the more frequent her panic attacks became, which in turn produced anticipatory anxiety that led to her phobic avoidance of many places. During her father's long hospitalization her anxiety, and anxiety about becoming anxious, became firmly rooted in her, and continued long after her father was recovered and home again.

When, in our work together, she was able to recognize the fear of loss that lay beneath her anxiety, and to accept and support her inner-child, her anxiety abated. She stopped hating her inner-child for being anxious, weak, and fearful, and instead learned to CARESS her; to give her the Compassion, Acceptance, Respect, Encouragement, Support, and Stroking that her inner child needed to feel less worried and fearful. (Some of this process is contained in her dialogue presented in chapter 10). I also taught her some self-relaxation techniques similar to those presented at the beginning of this chapter (deep breathing, tensing then relaxing her muscles, imagining being in her relaxation place, then positive imagery about the tense situation) for calming herself when she began to feel anxious. Rose now freely attends those places she previously avoided, and knows how to handle her anxiety when it arises.

Most women who have panic attacks, like Rose, are very concerned with being in control of themselves. They are deeply ashamed of the lack of self-control that these attacks represent to them, and view them as a sign of weakness and as a personal failing, rather than as a physiological reaction to fear and perceived danger. They dread being noticed during a panic attack, which only makes them more tense, fearful, and anxious, and therefore more driven to avoid social situations. Some women are able to ask for help during an attack from a close family member, but this again usually prompts them to stay home where the help is. It can be very liberating for a woman with recurrent panic attacks to tell her friends and colleagues her problem. They are usually supportive, and she has relieved herself of one of her fears: that she will appear weak and foolish.

WHAT TO DO ABOUT PANIC ATTACKS AND AGORAPHOBIA

If you suffer from panic attacks or agoraphobia, to free yourself from such crippling anxiety, you need to:

1. **Understand that panic attacks are not your fault. You are not experiencing them because you are weak, bad, incapable, or being punished, and it is no disgrace to have them, anymore than it is a disgrace to have an ulcer.**
2. **Learn to accept your attacks and help yourself through them.**

A. LET YOURSELF KNOW THAT THE ATTACK IS TIME-LIMITED. It will pass. Despite how you feel, reassure yourself that you are not dying, or in real danger. Most panic attacks last only a few minutes. (Though those few minutes can seem like an eternity).

B. IMMEDIATELY CONTROL YOUR BREATHING so that you don't hyperventilate, thus making your symptoms worse. Take a deep breath and hold it as long as possible, then slowly exhale through your mouth. Then take SLOW, deep breaths inhaling through your nose into your diaphragm so that your stomach moves out, and exhaling through your mouth. Count the seconds as you breathe and concentrate on making your breathing slow and rhythmical. If you start by only being able to inhale and exhale for one second each, try to make your next breath last two seconds, then three, then four, then five, then six. By the time you are up to six slow inhalations and six slow exhalations you will be breathing slowly and deeply. This kind of breathing helps you to relax, thus reducing your anxiety.

Practice this slow deep breathing when you are not having an attack, so it will be familiar when you do. Those of you who have had a Lamaze birth are familiar with how practicing breathing helps prepare you for when you really need it.

C. ACCEPT YOUR ANXIETY, RATHER THAN FIGHTING IT. The more you try to cover up or fight your anxiety, the tenser and more fearful you will become, thus setting off more adrenalin which will only make your symptoms worse. Instead of trying to fend off your symptoms, let yourself ride them out. The less you fear your fear, the less anxiety and panic you will experience. Dr. Claire Weekes in her helpful books (see Suggested Readings) recommends having a mind-set of floating through tense and feared situations, rather than fighting yourself or escaping.

3. **Identify, and help yourself cope with, your underlying fears.** Ask your inner-child what was going on in your life when you first started having panic attacks. Had you been ill? Were you in conflict over making some life

change? Had your parents recently divorced? Were you about to go away to school? Were you angry and afraid to express it? See if you can get some sense of the stress you were under when these attacks began. Then consider what kinds of stress and problems are in your life now, and what your fears are. Focus on understanding, accepting, supporting and calming yourself rather than consuming yourself with worry.

4. **Disassociate your panic attacks from the places in which they happen to occur.** As we saw above, once panic attacks occur, your anticipatory anxiety keeps them going—even though their original trigger may be long gone. To overcome your agoraphobia you need to systematically venture into your feared situations and locations without overwhelming yourself with the fear of having a panic attack. Unfortunately, space doesn't allow me to go into detail about how to do so; however, this information is readily available in the books I have recommended in Suggested Readings. I suggest you read several of them as they all offer somewhat different information. A good book to start with is *Free From Fear* by Ann Seagrave and Faison Covington, two recovered agoraphobics who are the founders of CHAANGE (The Center for Help for Agoraphobia/Anxiety through New Growth Experiences). You can also get a listing of clinics and therapists in your area that specialize in treating panic attacks and agoraphobia by writing to or calling The Anxiety Disorders Association of America (see page 191 for address and number).

Finally, a word about medication. Panic attacks can frequently be prevented with medication. While such drugs are not a cure, they can provide short-term help while a woman is learning to face and overcome her panic, and to stop avoiding the places associated with it. Medication should be prescribed by a psychiatrist who has experience in treating panic disorders and who uses it as an adjunct to a broader treatment approach. All medications have at least some side effects, so it is important that medication be used in the proper dosages, which vary for each person, and be monitored for adverse reactions.

POST-TRAUMATIC STRESS DISORDER

Panic and severe anxiety are only two of the symptoms of this syndrome that may follow a trauma such as rape, combat, assault, abuse, or a natural disaster. Other symptoms include guilt, depression, flashbacks, recurring nightmares, irritability, difficulty concentrating, being easily startled, a numbing of responsiveness, withdrawal from the world, and drug and alcohol addiction. If you have suffered such a trauma and have some of the above symptoms, it is important to get help either from a professional or from a self-help group.

Remember, whatever kind of anxiety you experience, whether it be situational, generalized, phobias, panic attacks, agoraphobia or post-traumatic stress disorder, you can lessen your anxiety by CARESSING yourself. When you approach yourself with compassion and support, when you respect and encourage yourself, when you accept yourself and give yourself credit for your efforts and achievements, you not only calm the worried and scared child within you, but you also increase your self-esteem. The higher your self-esteem, the less likely you are to expect negative outcomes or to view them as calamitous. CARESS YOURSELF AND YOU WILL FEEL LESS ANXIOUS.

CHAPTER 14

Nurturing Yourself
When Depressed

*D*epression is a widespread and debilitating condition, and is twice as prevalent in women as in men. This preponderance of depression among women is seen throughout many different countries and ethnic groups. In the United States alone there are at least seven million women who are suffering from depression.

A recently published study by the American Psychological Association sought to identify the factors that put women at such increased risk for depression. After a thorough review of all relevant research, the study concluded that "women are at a higher risk for depression due to a number of social, economic, biological and emotional factors" that include low self-esteem; personality styles that are avoidant and passive; thought patterns that are negativistic and self-critical; focusing too much on depressed feelings instead of action and mastery strategies; stress and conflict in interpersonal relationships; unrealistic expectations of physical perfection; coping styles and expectancies, including helplessness and hopelessness; discrimination; poverty; the prevalence of sexual and physical abuse (perhaps as many as 50 percent of women have been abused at some time in their lives); and having young children.[5]

It is not surprising that low self-esteem is cited as a risk factor for depression. A depressed person typically feels worthless, and someone who views her- or himself as inferior and inadequate is prone to becoming depressed. In fact, low self-esteem and depression often revolve in a vicious cycle where the more people don't like themselves, the more depressed they feel; and the more depressed they feel, the more they don't like themselves. Women, by virtue of belonging to a gender that is devalued in our society, are particularly prone to being caught in this vicious cycle.

We can learn to break out of this self-defeating cycle when we learn to treat ourselves with compassion, caring, and respect; when we learn to give ourselves encouragement, support, and credit for our efforts; that is, when we learn to CARESS ourselves.

Depression can vary from the blues (feeling down, lacking energy or desire to initiate anything), to a moderate depression (the above, plus loss of appetite, fitful sleeping or desire to sleep a lot, and feelings of hopelessness), to a severe depression (all of the above plus great difficulty functioning and suicidal thoughts and impulses). If you're depressed, you're upset with yourself and your life, and probably feel helpless and hopeless about things getting better.

It may be outward pressures that are weighing on you: too little money, a dead-end job, illness, problems with your children, a troubled relationship, caring for your aged parents or other family members, difficulties at work or being unemployed. However, no matter what obstacles you are facing, it's likely your treatment of yourself is dragging you down still further.

Earlier we looked at how self-criticism leads to low self-esteem. It also leads to depression. If your inner-critic is telling you that the reason you don't have enough money is because you made mistakes or didn't plan your life right, or that your relationship isn't working because you're such a mess, or that your children are having problems because you're a bad or inadequate mother, or that you're unemployed because you're not worthy, and that none of this is going to change because you're just hopeless, how can you feel anything but depressed?

Our problems get us depressed only when we blame ourselves for them and feel hopeless. Yes, stresses that are out of our control can and do make life very hard for women and of course may lead us to feel worried, scared, upset, and angry. However, in even the most debilitating of circumstances, there are women who manage to keep their moods up by believing in and supporting themselves, rather than blaming themselves.

Depression is not the same thing as feeling sad. There are many times in life when it is natural and appropriate to feel sad, particularly when you suffer a disappointment or a loss. At such times, it is very important that you give yourself the space and support you need to deal with your feelings, rather than urging yourself to get over it. As you deal with your feelings, in time you will be able to move on. If you deny your feelings, they will stay and fester. Remember, as we saw in chapter 2, the more you can acknowledge and accept your feelings, the more they will change. The more you deny and suppress your feelings, the more entrenched they become and the more trouble they can cause you.

In the professional literature depression is often divided into two kinds: reactive and endogenous. A reactive depression is described as one that arises because things are going badly for a person, or perceived as going badly. An endogenous depression is considered to be based on a biological predisposition to depression and is usually treated with anti-depressant medication.

I, myself, have found this latter definition to be limited in its usefulness. While research seems to indicate that some women are biologically or genetically vulnerable to depression, as definitely seems to be true of the depression associated with premenstrual syndrome (PMS), I don't agree with the implication that follows—i.e., that these women are helpless victims of their endogenous depressions and that the best they can do is get through it with antidepressants, and then continue with their lives until their next depression strikes. My clinical experience is that this isn't necessarily so.

Depression, whether or not you are predisposed to it, is intensified when you feel bad about yourself or some aspect of your life, blame yourself, and feel hopeless and unable to improve things. In other words, depression has a lot to do with how you regard and treat yourself. When you learn to treat yourself with compassion and acceptance, when you can respect, support, and praise yourself, and most of all give yourself the encouragement that you so badly need, you give yourself the power to lift yourself out of depression. To understand how this works, consider first how most people treat themselves when they're depressed. I call these:

EIGHT WAYS TO MAKE AND KEEP YOURSELF DEPRESSED

1. *Holding Yourself Responsible for all the Negative Events in Your Life:* Depressed people characteristically overestimate their own responsibility for the unhappy circumstances in their lives. Whatever goes wrong, they assume that it is their fault. Actually many economical, societal, or other uncontrollable factors may have contributed to their situation.

Pamela, a divorced mother who worked as an administrative assistant in a brokerage firm, was laid off after being there three years. Though her dismissal was part of large-scale cutbacks and reorganization, she blamed herself for not having made herself indispensable. If only, she told herself, she had taken off less when her children were sick, or been able to stay late when needed, or had somehow been more creative and innovative, she would have been chosen to remain.

Actually Pamela's layoff was due to circumstances beyond her control: her company's falling profits in these recessionary times.

Furthermore, the major things she was blaming herself for (being out when her children were sick, and having to leave work on time to care for them) were also due to factors beyond her control (lack of adequate hours at child-care facilities, and not having the money to pay for additional sitters because of the low wages paid to women in traditional female jobs, like hers).

A striking example of overassessing personal responsibility while underplaying outside factors is how many people evaluated the reasons for their losses during the Great Depression of the 1930s. In his book *Hard Times,* published in 1970, Studs Terkel interviews person after person who blamed him- or herself for such losses.[6] They chastised themselves for poor judgment in such things as buying a house, choosing a job, buying stock, and so on. In emphasizing their personal responsibility, these people were clearly minimizing the existing overwhelming economic factors that were not of their making.

2. *Criticizing Yourself:* We all do this. We feel bad, and blame ourselves. We tell our inner-child:

"Now you really messed up. You never do anything right."
"The speech you gave was awful. You're a jerk."
"You're an awful mother. How could you have blown up over such a small thing?!"
"Of course you're alone. Who would want you?!"

I'm sure by now you realize how self-destructive such self-criticism is. For a person prone to depression or already depressed, it's even worse—like kicking someone who's already flat on her back.

3. *Name-Calling:* Does this sound familiar to you? When you're depressed, do you make it worse by calling yourself "a failure," "no good," "incompetent," "stupid," "lazy," "weak," "boring," "fat," or "unlovable"? Rather than motivating your depressed child, such name-calling just makes her and you more depressed.

4. Berating Yourself for Being Depressed: This is a favorite of many of us. It's adding insult to injury. In case you're not feeling bad enough already, and don't have enough to deal with, you now have something else to dislike yourself for: being depressed. It often is combined with name-calling. Here your inner-critic is saying something like:

> "You're just feeling sorry for yourself. You're such a loser, sitting there and doing nothing. You can't even get yourself out of bed in the morning. I'm disgusted with you."

> Or, "Other people are accomplishing so much, and you can't even get a job (or a date, or a decent place to live, or a promotion). Instead, all you do is go around feeling depressed. You're so weak and such a cry-baby."

5. Threatening Yourself: This is the old "shape up or I'll punish you" approach, together with self-fulfilling negative prophecies. A self-fulfilling prophecy is a prediction that is meant as a threat or a warning, ostensibly to get you to shape up; however, the covert message is that you are expected to mess up in the predicted way. The covert message becomes self-fulfilling because most people tend to live up (or down) to what's expected of them. For instance, if a teenage daughter comes home late and her father starts calling her a whore, the message the girl hears is "I expect you to be a whore," and the girl may then start to act out sexually. Examples of self-threats together with self-fulfilling prophecies are:

> "You'd better pull yourself together or else you'll never get your work done, and you'll lose your job and end up a failure." (The message is: I expect you not to finish and to fail).
> "If you don't stop moping around, Sue [or Lou] will really be angry at you." (The real expectation is that you're going to continue to mope.)

"Keep going on this way, being depressed and not doing anything, and you'll end up even more of a nothing than you are now." (Again, the expectation is that you'll get more depressed and mess up your life.)

Needless to say, these threats just make your inner-child scared as well as depressed, which in turn further immobilizes you, and perhaps produces anxiety to boot.

6. *Comparing Yourself Unfairly and Unfavorably to Others:* In our highly competitive society, this one comes real easy. We're constantly looking at how much we do, and especially don't, measure up. And when we're depressed, all we can see is how we're not as good as others. Examples of this self-approach are telling yourself:

"Just because your daughter is sick, you're falling apart. Look how Mary Sue is coping, and she has so many more problems."
"You should be depressed. Look at how much worse you're doing than everyone else."

When people who are depressed compare themselves to others, they frequently stack the deck against themselves by using inaccurate and overgeneralized comparison, as in these two common ways:

Looking at superficial attitudes or manners, and taking them at face value

Alice is depressed. She runs into Mary Sue, who is going through a bitter divorce. Mary Sue is smiling and chats with Alice about her vacation plans. Alice smiles and chats back. At home Alice berates herself for having so much difficulty dealing with her problems, when Mary Sue is doing so well.

Is Mary Sue really doing so well? Alice has no way of knowing. Mary Sue might be feeling great, being finally separated from her extremely critical husband. Or she might be more depressed than Alice is, and just putting on the same smile Alice did.

Cindy has just started law school. She's feeling overwhelmed by the work, which is both voluminous and difficult, and thinks they must have made a mistake when they accepted her. She runs into Tara in the hall and starts to talk about how inundated she feels. Tara gives Cindy a strange, somewhat condescending look, and says she finds the courses so exciting and interesting. Cindy quickly mumbles an excuse and moves off, feeling even worse about herself. She tells herself that, if Tara can handle things so well, then there really must be something wrong with her (Cindy), and she becomes depressed.

In truth, Tara may not have opened a book yet, may have a much stronger background in the field, or may just be very competitive and good at acting superior. Cindy doesn't know, but she instantly took what Tara said at face value.

Focusing on someone, or a few people, who are doing better and then overgeneralizing that everyone is doing better

Charisse got promoted and Jessica didn't. Jessica thinks to herself, "Everyone's getting ahead and doing better than me."

Lydia doesn't have a date Saturday night and some of her friends do. She thinks, "Everyone is dating, and I'm the only one who's alone."

Both Jessica and Lydia are making themselves feel worse by telling themselves that everyone else has what they want, with the implication being that they themselves aren't getting what they want because they are deficient. Of course this isn't true. There are plenty of women who are unattached, and many women who not only aren't receiving promotions, but whose jobs are not as well-paying or satisfying as Jessica's.

When you overgeneralize, you add to your depression by exaggerating the number of people who are surpassing you, and then reasoning that you must be inadequate because you are not doing as well as "everyone else."

7. *Humiliating Yourself*: This is a particularly vicious (and common) approach. It plays on one of our worst fears: being publicly ridiculed. And it's so easy to do. All you have to do is tell yourself that the whole world sees and knows how inadequate and terrible you are. The easy thing about this attack is that it requires no evidence whatsoever—just a strong statement is good enough. For instance, some things you could tell yourself are:

> "Now you did it. You went to a dance, and no one asked you to dance. Now the *whole world* knows how unattractive and undesirable you are."
> "After the stupid thing you said at the meeting yesterday, the *whole office* must be laughing at you."
> "After you spilled coffee on your blouse, you don't dare go out to eat with those people again. Now they *all know* how clumsy you are."
> "After you screamed at your children in the park, you'd better stay away from there. Now they *all know* what a mean and awful mother you are."

Of course, none of these accusations are based on fact. Sure, some people *might* think you're undesirable, stupid, clumsy, or a mean mother, but it's not likely. Most people are too focused on themselves to be counting your errors, and most people take others' imperfections as a sign of their humanness, not of their inadequacy. The only kind of people likely to hold your minor acts against you are very critical, competitive people—the very people in whose opinion you should put absolutely no stock whatsoever, because they have their own axe to grind and are looking to build themselves up by putting you down.

8. *Rejecting Your Inner-Child:* This is the most destructive of all the above approaches. This is real and total self-hate, bound to produce deep depression. Examples of this are telling yourself:

"I can't stand you. I wish you would go away and leave me alone."
"You're a wimp and a nothing, and I want to be rid of you."
"I hate you and wish you would die."

If you weren't feeling hopeless before, guaranteed you are now. Abandoned by your inner-caretaker, how can your inner-child have any hope? How can you make any moves to improve your mood and your life when your inner-child feels absolutely bereft and alone, deserted even by herself? It's hard enough to initiate any kind of action when you're feeling depressed. It's impossible to do so when your inner voice is telling you that you're hopeless and that she is giving up on you.

To rise up out of your depression, you need to learn how to give yourself hope. You need to help yourself believe that you are a competent, capable human being who can problem-solve, who can find your way out of difficulties, who can persist in the face of troubles, who is worthy and deserves respect and support.

Raise your spirits first by ceasing to attack yourself in the eight ways that are guaranteed to make and keep you depressed. If you find this hard to do, it's because your inner-critic is entrenched and doesn't want to leave. Take out your INNER-CRITIC list that you made in Step Four and identify again where these self-criticisms came from. If you've discovered some new self-criticisms, add them to your list and then deal with them by going through the process in steps three through six. Talk back to your original critics and tell them to get packing. Let go of negative identifications. Rewrite your true self-criticisms into goals, and focus on ways to meet those goals.

Remember, change is a difficult and often slow process. Don't be discouraged to see your inner-critic rearing her ugly head. After a lifetime of bullying your inner-child, she's not going to go away so fast. Just keep standing up to her as much as you can, and with continued practice her voice will get quieter and quieter. Remind yourself that you don't have to do it all at once. Any step you take to muffle the voice of your inner-critic, and to magnify the voice of your inner-caretaker will help you.

Write down the eight ways to make and keep yourself depressed, and carry them with you. Use them to help yourself to become aware of when you're treating yourself in any of these destructive ways, and do your best to stop yourself. Then start to nurture yourself instead, because the way out of depression is by CARESSing yourself.

SIX WAYS TO CHEER YOURSELF UP

1. *Show Yourself Compassion:* When you're depressed and feeling bad, it helps a lot to feel that there is someone on your side who understands and cares about what you are going through. It helps even more if that person is you. Instead of criticizing yourself, be as compassionate as you would be towards a friend. Tell yourself that it's hard to be so upset, and you do have a lot to deal with. Tell your inner-child that you care about her and that you're here to help her.

2. *Accept Yourself:* Instead of berating yourself for being depressed, accept your depression. Tell yourself that it's OK to have that feeling. You're human, and all people get discouraged and depressed sometimes, or a lot of times. Let your inner-child know that you don't love her any less for being depressed. Tell her that you're not sitting in judgment on her. On the contrary, you care about her and want to help.

3. *Respect Yourself*: Think about the things you like about yourself. Take out your WHAT I LIKE ABOUT MYSELF list from Step One, and reread it slowly aloud. Then talk to your inner-child and tell her that you prize each of these qualities in her. Tell her that whatever she is upset with in herself is just one piece of who she is. Tell her that there is so much of value about her, and you want to help her to be in touch with her worth. If she's been comparing herself unfairly and unfavorably with others, set her straight. Help her to stop overgeneralizing, and instead to focus on all the assets she has and the things that have been, are, and can be right in her life.

4. *Encourage Yourself*: This is the most important thing you can do for yourself, because what you need now more than anything is hope. If you think you'll never find someone to love, or a good job, or a way to deal with your children, or a way to improve your relationship, you will stay depressed. The more hopeless and helpless you feel, the more depressed you will become. You need to tell your inner-child that she is worthy and that together you will find a way to reach your goals, and that you will stay with her and help her. If certain goals are not possible right now, see if you can encourage her to consider other ways to satisfy her longings. If she's depressed because she feels she hasn't achieved enough, let her know that she doesn't have to achieve for you to love her. Let her know that you love her just the way she is.

Many depressed women find it very hard to encourage themselves. They would like to, but they just don't believe in themselves. Instead, their inner-caretaker stands mute, while their inner-critic has a field day. The essence of their inner dialogues is:

INNER-CHILD: I feel hopeless and helpless.

INNER-CRITIC: You are hopeless and helpless.

If this is your inner dialogue, you need to silence your inner-critic and summon your inner-caretaker. A very helpful way to get your caretaker's voice going is by imagining yourself talking to a friend who has the same problems you do. Imagine that this is a friend that you really love and care about. Think about what you would say to encourage her, and *write it down*. It is important to write it down so you will have it for later. You may find it helpful to imagine and record a whole conversation with your depressed friend. Be creative. See how many different encouraging things you can find to say to her. Perhaps you have even known people with some of the same problems you have. Remember the encouraging things you said to them, and say them in this written imaginary conversation. See if you can come up with at least ten different encouraging things to say. If you can't, ask someone you trust for help with ideas about encouraging things to say. Then ask another friend. Here are some sample encouraging things you can tell yourself, if they are appropriate to your situation:

- You've gotten through bad times before, and you can get through this one, too.
- You may feel trapped, but there is no problem that doesn't have a solution. Let's try to figure out what we can do.
- You've been focusing on what you haven't accomplished. Let's look at some things you have done, and done well.
- Such and such is getting you down now, but in five years you won't remember it happened, or you'll think about it and be proud of how you got through it.
- You can handle this situation, just give yourself a chance.
- You don't have to stay a victim. Let's figure out something active we can do.
- This is *not* our last chance at happiness. Life has many opportunities to get what we want. Let's look for them and make them happen.

- I may not be able to control the people around us so that you can get what you want, but I can take care of you. Let's see how I can give to you right now.
- I know you're feeling helpless, but that's only because you haven't figured out what to do yet. Let's see what we can plan.
- We can stand together and survive the breakup of our relationship. Love is important, and right now being alone feels terrible, but we will get through it together. No one ever died of a broken heart. I love you and I'm going to be here for you.
- I know you don't feel like doing anything today, but when we spend the day in bed like this, we just feel worse. Let's try to do something for fun, even if you don't feel like it at first, and see how you feel after a while.

A common sign of depression is a lack of interest in doing things you previously enjoyed. Despite this lack of interest, if you can get yourself to do something, it usually lifts your spirits. Sometimes even doing non-fun things, like cleaning out a closet, can improve your mood.

When you've come up with as many encouraging statements as you can and have written them down, start a dialogue with your inner-child. When she says she feels hopeless and helpless, tell her all the encouraging things you told your imagined friend. It doesn't matter if you don't entirely believe them all yet. Keep repeating them and you'll start to believe in them, and so will your inner-child. You'll be surprised how much better you'll start to feel when you tell yourself things like, "I can make my relationship work," rather than, "I'm trapped." Or, "If I persist in looking, sooner or later I will find a job," rather than, "I'll never find a job and I'll lose my apartment and have nothing." Or, "I'm lovable and I can find someone special to love me." Tell your inner-child that you're on her side and you believe in her, and she will start to feel better.

When I first decided to write this book, I didn't know the first thing about writing or about getting published. I didn't even own a computer or know how to word process. (Now that I do, I think it's amazing that people managed to write books in the pre-computer era). As I persisted in writing, some people encouraged me, while well-meaning others told me that it was foolish to write without a book contract, agent, famous name, or any connections. There were many times as I sat alone in my attic writing (which I squeezed in between working and caring for my family) that I felt discouraged and depressed. At those times I was grateful to my inner-caretaker for telling me to go on, for telling me that she believed in me, for reminding me that I had nothing to lose—except almost all my "leisure" time—and that I wouldn't be doing anything great with this time if I weren't writing (except maybe sleeping). She told me that whether I was ever published or not, she was still proud of me for trying, and proud of my determination and doggedness. Had she not encouraged me in this way, you would not be reading this book today.

Try to give yourself that same kind of encouragement. Tell yourself, "I believe in myself, and I will find a way to reach my goals." This isn't *Peter Pan,* where believing in fairies brings Tinkerbell back to life—in reality change doesn't take place that quickly or smoothly—but believing in yourself can work slow magic. It frees up your energy to help yourself, and enhances the way you present yourself.

5. *Support Yourself:* Along with giving yourself Compassion, Acceptance, Respect, and Encouragement, it is important to give yourself Support. You've already started to support yourself by being there emotionally for yourself. There may also be more concrete ways you can support yourself when you're depressed, like hiring someone to clean so you don't have to face the mess that you have no energy to deal with. If you're depressed because you're unemployed, you could go to the library and read about

types of jobs you could apply for; or join a support group for women who are job-hunting.

Most importantly, though, you can be there for your inner-child—ready to talk things out with her, ready to get her a decent meal despite the fact that she doesn't feel like eating, ready to buy her flowers to cheer her up or take her to the movies, ready to be her friend. Remember, support means giving your inner-child the feeling that you love her and will always be there for her. That support can go a long way towards healing depression. Talk to her now and let her feel you there.

6. *Stroke Yourself:* Women generally love to be physically stroked, and we need it more when we're depressed. It's great if there's someone in your life, be it a mother, father, grandparent, aunt, husband, sibling, lover, friend, child, or grandchild, whom you can go to and ask for a hug when you're feeling down. However, it is also vital to be able to stroke yourself. Stroking yourself is all the more imperative if there is no one you can turn to who will hold you.

There are several ways you can stroke yourself. One way is to caress your body with one of nature's elements. It always lifts my mood to lie in the sun or take a hot bath. My family knows this, and whenever I get cranky or down, they always suggest I go take a bath, knowing it will make me more pleasant to live with. Another way to stroke yourself is physically. Gently caress your face and feel the love in your hands, or stroke your body and feel the caring in your touch. Lastly, but certainly not least, you can stroke yourself with words. Speak to yourself tenderly and compassionately. Tell yourself what you appreciate and value about yourself. Praise yourself and give yourself credit. Then do the following:

Sit down with a stuffed animal, doll, or pillow on your lap. Get comfortable, close your eyes, and breathe deeply, slowly in and slowly out, to relax yourself. When you feel relaxed, imagine that your inner-child is on your lap and in

your arms. See yourself holding her and speaking softly to her. Rock her gently in your arms, while you let your love envelop her. Tell her you believe in her and that you will always love her, no matter what. In your mind's eye, see yourself gently caressing her as she nestles against you. Caress the object you are holding that symbolizes her. Run your fingers through her hair, stroke her face, and hold her close to you. Give her all the stroking she needs. Take your time. Only when you feel truly ready, open your eyes and return to the room.

Now see how you feel. Do you have a little more hope, or even a slightly brighter outlook? Let yourself know that you can keep giving to and helping yourself in this way.

When you CARESS yourself, you are giving yourself the helping hand you need to lift yourself out of your depression. However, some of you may be so deeply depressed that you can't summon the desire to help yourself. You may just want to die and end your misery. IF YOU FEEL SUICIDAL, YOU MUST GET PROFESSIONAL HELP NOW.

You are an important person and your life is important. You may not think so now. You may feel like you are a nothing and a nobody and will never amount to anything or ever be happy again. That's your depression talking. Don't listen to it. It's wrong. You can get your zest back. You can learn to enjoy living. Most important of all, you can learn to value yourself and your life.

Suicide may seem like a solution to all your troubles, but it isn't. It's an escape, but it's no solution, and it leaves a mass of problems for those you leave behind. Relatives and loved ones of people who commit suicide are usually plagued for years, if not their whole lives, with enormous guilt as well as anger, loss, and a sense of abandonment and betrayal. Committing suicide also makes it more likely that your children or someone else you love will follow suit.

Think of the lost, frightened, sad, hopeless little girl inside of you, and let your heart go out to her. Become determined to do

whatever you can to rescue her. Even in your depressed state, if
you saw a real little girl in danger of dying, you would pull out
all stops to rescue her. Don't do less for yourself. You have nothing
to lose by trying. Suicide is an option you never lose, but wouldn't
you like to feel differently about yourself? Wouldn't you like to
value yourself and your life? Give yourself the chance you need.
IF YOU'RE CONSIDERING SUICIDE, GET PROFESSIONAL
HELP NOW.

You can seek out a social worker, psychologist, psychiatrist,
or other qualified mental health worker in private practice. Or
you can go to your community mental health center or other
private or public clinic or agency, a psychotherapy training institute, or if you need immediate help, the emergency room of a
hospital. If you want someone to talk to right away, you can call
a suicide prevention hot line. For a hot line in your area call 411.
You can also call the American Association of Suicidology at (303)
692-0985 or write to them at this address: 2459 Ash Street,
Denver, CO, 80222. They have a directory of suicide crisis lines
all over the country, but are open only 9:00 A.M. to 5:00 P.M.
Mountain Time. There is also a national twenty-four-hour suicide
prevention hot line run by the Humanistic Mental Health Foundation that you can reach at (800) 333-5580. Whatever you do,
DON'T WAIT!

When you are depressed, in addition to the six ways to cheer
yourself up, there are also some other things you can do to lift
your mood. Aerobic exercise can be effective in combatting
depression. Some people find it helpful to meditate or to write
in a journal. Anything that gets you mobilized will be helpful.
Taking action, no matter how small, will help raise your spirits,
while staying bogged down will lower them. Make a special effort,
therefore, to give yourself the encouragement you need to actively
approach your life. Try to do something you previously enjoyed,
such as going to a movie or museum, seeing a friend, or painting
a bookcase. David Burns in his book on depression, *Feeling Good,*
recommends predicting ahead of time the percent of satisfaction
you will derive from a particular activity, and then writing down

afterwards how much you actually enjoyed it, and whether you did it alone or with others.[7] People typically are surprised that their actual enjoyment is often much more than they predicted. As you encourage yourself to take action, keep talking to your inner-child. Remember, the more depressed you are, the more you need yourself on your side. CARESS yourself and you will feel better; attack yourself and you will stay depressed.

CHAPTER 15

Nurturing Yourself
While Raising Children

*I*f you're hoping to find out how to be a supermom, and raise perfect children, I can't help you. My own children are far from perfect. They are frequently loud; rarely remember to say "please," "thank you," and "you're welcome" without prompting; fervently believe that, at the ages of thirteen and eleven, they know much more than I do and don't hestitate to tell me so; consider cleaning their rooms to be an arduous task; and think the only nice thing about having a sister is that they are not left alone to perform exhausting work like emptying and loading the dishwasher or setting the table. In addition they have responded to a strong familial emphasis on reading and other intellectual pursuits by becoming TV addicts. In short they're normal kids, the kind you can be awfully proud of, even if you don't dare take them out in public.

While I can't help you become a perfect mother, what I hope I can help you with is learning how to survive motherhood with your self-esteem intact. As any mother knows, that's a lot easier said than done. Women are raised to view children as a reflection of the self: according to society, they are our creative products—our novels, paintings, sculptures, expressing our inner being—and we easily buy into that view. We believe that, if our children act up, misbehave, do poorly in school, or otherwise have difficulties, it is because we as mothers have failed. And my field, psychoanalysis and psychotherapy, has not helped. With the discovery, since Freud, of the connection between faulty parenting and emotional problems, the blame for many of society's ills (juvenile delinquency, high school dropouts, drug addiction, crime) has been placed on Mother. If only she were more there, more involved, more nurturing if you will, then all would be well with her children. Father receives some blame, but only in a minor way because, after all, everyone "knows" it is Mother's responsibility to raise the children—no matter how poor, discriminated against, deprived, and alone she may be. It's true that we've learned a few things since Freud (not least of all the oppressive results of a patriarchal society that confines both women and men to roles that limit our potential as people and as parents); still, when our children have difficulties, we join the world in pointing the finger at ourselves.

Before I had children, I thought I would be the world's best mom. After all, I told myself, didn't I have all the prerequisite qualities? I was warm, caring, patient, creative, able to be there for other people, a good listener, and everyone had always told me that I was great with kids. If this weren't enough, I assured myself, I was also conversant with child psychology and child-rearing techniques, and in my experience doing family therapy I had often been successful in enabling parents to help their children to blossom. Then I had my first child.

From the time Nuri and I came home from the hospital, and for the next two and a half weeks, she was colicky. This meant that she was up all night, every night, crying unceasingly for no reason known to medical science, and nothing I did could soothe her—except perhaps holding her and walking her around the house for hours on end, and even this only reduced the level of her crying, it didn't stop it. I had had a difficult birth and could barely stand without pain, let alone walk for hours. My husband Steve, who has been very involved in the day-to-day raising of our two daughters, did what he could—but he had to be up by 4:30 A.M. to go to work, so wasn't much help during the worst hours. I didn't get much sleep during the day, either, since Nuri got up every two hours to nurse. I had no relatives nearby to help out, was new to my community so had no friends around, and no paid help.

Perhaps two and a half weeks may not seem like a long time to you, and indeed I have met mothers whose children had colic for two years. I don't know how they survived it. After a week of no sleep and the anguish of not being able to soothe my distraught child, whenever she cried I would cry. After a while all I wanted to do was throw this child that I had so desperately desired out the window, and jump after her. For the first time in my life I understood how parents could abuse their children. Not that I felt in danger of doing so, but I could understand the impulse.

By the time Nuri got over the colic, I had totally revamped my assessment of how I was going to be as a mother. I decided that I would be doing well if I just managed to survive the experience with myself and my child (at that point I couldn't even imagine having a second) somewhat intact. The weeks, months, and years that have followed have done nothing to change that assessment.

I think that unless someone has spent continual, day-in and day-out time with young children, there is no way he or she can appreciate what a totally demanding task it is. In those first years of Nuri's life, I worked two twelve-hour days, the two days Steve had off, and was home the rest of the time. Those two days were like a vacation. Steve felt the same way about returning to work after forty-eight hours of being the primary parent. We both agreed that working was far less demanding than parenting. As Nuri grew and we had Robyn thirty-two months later, work remained the easy part of the week. At work only one person at a time talked to me, and I didn't have to deal with whining, constant demands, and absolutely no time to collect my thoughts or to sit still.

I don't want you to think I'm against motherhood. On the contrary, having my children is a joy to my life, and even on the worst of days I've never regretted it. However, if you're raising children, I think that it is vital that you appreciate what a difficult job you have. It is especially imperative that *you* recognize this fact, because most of the world does not.

Those men who have never been alone day after day with a small child or children cannot begin to appreciate what an overwhelming job it is. One of my favorite stories is about my husband coming home from work one day when Nuri was a newborn and finding the disposable diapers (in those days we didn't know that they were bad for the environment) piled ten high on the diaper pail. Steve looked at that pile of dirty diapers and said in a disgusted tone, "Look, I don't expect you to cook, I don't expect you to clean, but at least can't you put the diapers in the pail?!" Angry at being criticized, and secretly feeling inadequate, I explained that I wasn't able to hold Nuri still on the changing table with one hand, change her diaper with my second hand, and then hold it while I lifted the top of the diaper pail with my third hand. Steve continued to look disgusted, though he didn't say anything, and I knew he was thinking that there must have been some time during the day when I didn't have Nuri in my arms when I could have put the diapers in the pail. Six weeks later, when I came home after my first day back at work, I found the diapers piled ten high. I opened my mouth to say, "I told you so," but before I could, Steve said in his most sheepish voice, "Don't say anything. I understand now, and I'm very sorry." This is something he would never have understood without the experience of what it means not to have a free hand, or a free moment. From that time on the ten-high pile of diapers became our shorthand for acknowledging that things are often much more difficult than they appear.

I have found that some women also have forgotten how difficult raising children is, especially if their children are grown. They sometimes tend to remember only the good parts. That's fine, but as they wax nostalgic about how much fun it was to raise their children, don't take what they're saying at face value and start to feel inadequate. Remember, too, that women in your mother's or grandmother's generation likely got a lot of concrete help from a network of friends and family members. Some of you may have such a network, but many of you do not. You may live far away from your families or be estranged from them, and your friends may be too busy juggling family and work responsibilities to be able to offer you much help.

When my children were little, I found the most difficult part of mothering was the boredom, and the reality of never having uninterrupted free time at home in which I could get anything done. I had always been someone with a lot of energy and interests, used to being involved in activities that stimulated and fed me. Also, while our arrangement of Steve being home when I worked and vice versa was great for our children, it meant that we had very little time home together, leaving me feeling even more isolated. For years I had no idea of what was happening in the world and went from being an avid reader to reading about one book a year. I would wait for my child or children to go to sleep at night, planning how I would use my time, and then be too exhausted to do anything. (I couldn't plan on using Nuri's nap time because Nuri inherited her mother's energy and desire for stimulation, so she napped only briefly, and when awake was never sedentary, even as an infant.)

Now that my children are older, life is very different, and I have a lot more time to myself, but it reminds me of an old story. This very poor Jewish woman who's living in a one-room hut with her husband and six children is going crazy with the crowded conditions. She goes to her rabbi and asks for a solution. He tells her to put her cow in the house. She thinks this is crazy, but he's the rabbi, so she does what he recommends. The next week she is back at the rabbi's complaining how much worse things are. He tells her to put the chickens in the house. She starts to argue, but he insists. The next week the woman returns, saying she can't stand it another day. The rabbi tells her to bring her sheep into the hut, too. The woman says there is not one inch of room left, but again the rabbi insists. The following week the woman returns and says she doesn't want to go against the rabbi, but this is it. No one in the house can stand it. The rabbi then tells her to remove all the animals and to return in a week. The following week the woman faithfully returns, and when the rabbi asks her how things are going, she says, "Rabbi, I live in a palace. There's so much space."

So now I live in a palace of time because, when my children are home, they do not need me every moment. Never mind that much of my week is taken up working, doing errands, cleaning, carpooling, and so on. At least some of my time at home I can use to pursue my own interests (like writing this book). It feels like a tremendous boon.

I have shared so many of my experiences as a mother because I think they're fairly common. If anything, I have had it easy: being able to work part-time at a job I love, having a husband who was able and willing to participate in the day-to-day raising of our children, and having a middle-class standard of living. Many women have it much harder, especially if they're single parents, poor, teenagers, ill, or have a husband who is unsupportive and critical. Yet even from my advantaged position, I still often felt harried, overextended, inundated, and guilty.

Guilt is such an endemic feeling among mothers that I almost think it should be called the "mothers' disease." If anything goes wrong with our children, we feel guilty. If Susie falls while we are out, we feel we shouldn't have gone out, or we shouldn't be working, or we should have found a better childcare person or center. It's as though we believe that it is our job as mothers to shield our children from whatever ills there are in the world, and if anything bad does happen, it's because we didn't do our job right, because we are inadequate.

In fact, we don't even need to have something go wrong to feel guilty. I remember going to work, knowing that my children were with my husband who is an excellent father, and still feeling guilty. Something nice would happen, and I wouldn't be there to share it with them. Something upsetting would happen, and I wouldn't be there to comfort them. Or maybe they would just miss me, and I wouldn't be there.

On the rare occasions I went someplace during the day (besides work) without my children, especially if it was to do something for myself, I felt guilty. How could I be choosing to spend even more time away from my children, when I was away from home "so much" as it was? My guilt stood in sharp contrast to Steve's feelings. His attitude was that he was a great father, was doing ten times more for our kids than he had been raised to do, and had absolutely nothing to feel guilty about.

My guilt was especially noticeable to me because, prior to having children, I was not particularly prone to feeling guilty. Now it was always lurking in the shadows when it wasn't planted firmly in my chest. I pondered the difference between Steve's lack of guilt and my own constant guilt. Clearly the difference lay in what we expected of ourselves. His expectations were rooted in a traditional male/female division of roles, so whatever childcare, housework, and cooking he did made him feel great about himself as a father and husband. My emotional expectations, despite my feminist politics, were also rooted in traditional male/female roles. While I might be quick to rail against Steve if he shirked household duties, in my heart of hearts I still felt primarily responsible for the house and children—and I also knew that society would hold *me* responsible if things were not right. If people dropped by and my house was a mess, no one would talk about what a poor housekeeper Steve was. If my daughter went to nursery school and fought over toys, no one would call Steve in to discuss it. The eyes of the world were upon me as "Mom," and I knew it. No wonder I felt such intense pressure to measure up.

I also felt that one wrong move, and I could ruin my children for life. The first time I ever yelled at Nuri I felt like the worst mother in the world. She was only two, and here I was yelling at her. Surely I knew that wasn't the right way to handle a child. How could I do that to her?!

After longer and in-depth experience with toddlers, I came to believe that, if I managed to survive life with a two-year-old and did no more than yell occasionally, I was doing quite well. Now, several thousand shouts later, I'm less worried about my yelling intimidating my children for life and more concerned that it fails to even capture their attention, let alone mold their behavior.

In short, over the years I learned that my children, though sensitive, were also resilient. I also came to recognize that they had their own personalities, which were not formed by me or Steve, and weren't going to be changed by us, either. It became clearer and clearer to me that, while we were responsible for a lot, like being empathically there for our children and teaching them proper values and behavior, there were also many aspects of their behavior that stemmed from who each of them was as a person, and that the best we could do would be to accommodate ourselves to their personalities. Holding myself responsible for every negative aspect of their personalities, behaviors, and adjustment only made my consequent guilt get in the way of my accepting them as they are.

Guilt is helpful to the degree that it encourages us to act in a moral, ethical, and honest way. However, often guilt is a destructive emotion because it makes us punish ourselves for crimes we haven't committed, and it also produces anger towards the very people whom we feel we have let down or failed in some way. Guilt leads to anger because we don't like feeling guilty—it's uncomfortable and makes us feel bad about ourselves—so we often look for someone else to blame. After all, if it's someone else's fault, then we're not responsible and we don't have to feel guilty.

For instance, say you go out for the evening and return to find your young children up and crying for you. The baby-sitter says they have been crying inconsolably ever since she started trying to put them to sleep hours ago. You start to feel guilty about having left them, but you really wanted and needed the time away. You don't want to feel guilty at taking time for yourself.

So your guilt turns into anger at your children, and you yell at them for being up, and for not listening to the baby-sitter. What you're really angry about is that they resent your being out, and that makes you feel guilty. If you didn't feel guilty, you could accept that they have a right to resent that you're out and to miss you, but that doesn't mean that you did anything wrong. The less you feel guilty, the less likely you are to get unreasonably angry at your children.

Over the years I came to realize that there had to be room for my children to have unsatisfied needs and faults without my feeling bad about myself as a mother and a person. Not only that, but the more I could cut myself some slack, the more I could cut *them* some slack, too.

The more you are able to see your children as separate people, rather than as the proof of your adequacy or worth, the easier it is to correct them without angrily blaming them.

When my children argue, as they frequently do, and put each other down, I find it comforting to recall that sibling rivalry has been in existence since the beginning of recorded history, and that my brother and sisters and I gave each other a similarly hard time. Hopefully my children, like my siblings and myself, will survive their competitiveness and be there for each other as adults. While the squabbling and noise level frequently gets to me, it doesn't make me feel bad about myself. I have ceased trying to be Solomon, always coming up with the just solution to their differences, because I have come to realize that, no matter what I decide, their rivalry will not dissipate. The less I feel I have to "cure" their rivalry, the less angry I become at them and the easier it is for me to respond empathically to their concerns.

It's not that I now never feel guilty. I think such a goal is beyond the reach of any mother. Nor are any of us so perfect that we never say or do things to our children that we shouldn't have, or neglect to say or do things that we should have. However, I have learned that, at times like these, if I apologize to my children and allow them to vent their feelings, they readily get over it. I have also learned to forgive myself for not being perfect, rather than letting my inner-critic have a field day.

A big problem that many mothers have in struggling not to feel guilty is deciding how to balance our own needs with those of our children and families. The demands often are constant and unending. Where is the dividing line between giving ourselves the nourishment that we need, and depriving our children? How much of our time and resources can we devote to ourselves without taking away from those small and not-so-small creatures that need and want us? This question doesn't necessarily disappear even when our children are grown. I have known grandmothers who can't refuse to baby-sit a grandchild or a grown child's pet without feeling guilty.

This is such a difficult balancing act for so many women because we are raised to believe that our needs don't really count. We are to serve everyone else first and only then can we feed ourselves. If we dare to put some of our needs first, we often feel selfish and think that we are depriving our children. This just isn't so. In fact, while raising children, you must realize that:

Your needs are important.

I can't emphasize this enough. You're not only a mother, you're also a person, and your needs count. You will not harm your children by focusing on yourself. On the contrary, the more you can find ways to recognize and meet your own genuine needs, the more you will also be able to be there for your children.

If you feel exhausted, unrecognized (while "motherhood" is often lauded in a lip-service way, it has very low status as a profession), unsupported, isolated, bored, depleted, or overwhelmed, it is important to acknowledge these feelings. This may be hard to do. You may want to think that you can cope, and that you're doing fine as a mom. No doubt you are. That doesn't mean, however, that you can't also feel at times, or even every day, that you have had it.

Some mothers are afraid to acknowledge just how stressed out they feel. Maybe you are, too. Perhaps you know that you have no one to back you up, and are afraid that, if you acknowledge how much you're longing for help, you'll just feel more alone and bereft. Or perhaps you're proud of the kind of mom you are, and are afraid that acknowledging your negative feelings will make you feel less good about yourself. Or maybe you were eager to have chidren, and don't want to be perceived as complaining after you got your heart's desire. Or perhaps you're just barely managing to make it through each day, and fear that acknowledging the difficulty that you're having will push you over the edge. Whatever your fears may be, let me reassure you: acknowledging your feelings to yourself can only help.

When you acknowledge and accept your inner feelings, you open yourself to your inner-child. Perhaps, though, you don't feel like doing this. Maybe you feel you have enough to do in dealing with your actual children, and don't want any more burdens. Nonetheless, just as you can't deal with your real children only when you're in the mood for them, the same is true for your inner-child. She is always with you, like it or not, so you're much better off dealing with her. Otherwise the worse she feels, the more she'll undermine you to get your attention.

Speak to your inner-child. Ask her how she's feeling. Ask her what she likes about being a mom, and what's getting her down. Ask her what she'd like from you, and listen to her answer. Maybe you can't give her some of the things she desires, like paid help, or relatives nearby, or a child who's not chronically ill. Maybe you *can* give her other things she wants, like more time to herself, or permission to go out more often without feeling guilty. Whatever she asks for, be aware that the most important thing you can give her you do have in abundance, and that's your caring and concern about what she is feeling.

As a mother you have to put out so much on a daily basis. If you do not replenish yourself, your well will run dry. It's great if you get replenishment from the outside, but there also has to be replenishment from the inside. By nurturing your inner-child, you are providing for yourself the supplies you need to keep on giving. Make it a priority to set aside time just for you, and stay in touch with your inner-child. CARESS yourself by doing the following:

RESPECT YOUR NEEDS AND LIMITATIONS WITHOUT FEELING GUILTY

Whatever your needs are, and whether or not they can presently be satisfied, you are entitled to them. Accept them as your right. Every human being in the world has needs. Without them we wouldn't be human. Think of your needs as part of what makes you a vulnerable woman capable of connecting and caring.

Make peace with your limitations. Accept that you are not going to be as good a parent as you would like to be. There are no perfect moms (or dads) out there, and you are not going to be one, either. So lower your expectations. Expect to make lots of mistakes. I find that, if my goal is a B⁻ as a mother, then I often exceed this aim and I feel good about myself. When my goal was A or A⁺, most of the time I fell short and was upset with myself and less relaxed with my children. This is an important principle:

The more accepting and approving you are of yourself, the more approving you will be of your children, and the more relaxed with them you will feel.

This is only common sense. If you approve of yourself as a person and a mother, it is easier to stay centered and approving of your children even when they are less than angels. If, however, on the other hand you are trying to stave off feelings of inadequacy by proving to yourself that you are a good mother, you can't help but experience your children's misbehavior as a reflection on you. Then your attempts to shape them up becomes more for your

sake than for theirs. Children sense when their parents are trying
to validate themselves through their children's behavior and typically become either overly compliant (to rescue you) or overly
rebellious (because they resent having to feed your ego in this
way, and because they need to separate their needs from yours).
It is important to remember this paradox:

The more you need to prove to yourself that you are a good
mother, the harder it is to be one. The more you accept and
approve of yourself as you are, the easier it is to be a good-
enough mother.

ACCEPT YOURSELF RATHER THAN
BERATE YOURSELF

Perhaps you're a lot less patient with your children than you
would like to be (I know I am). Maybe you find yourself screaming
when you don't believe that that's the best way to handle things,
or have slapped your child on occasion even though you don't
believe in physical punishment. Perhaps you find yourself saying
or doing things your parents did to you that you swore you would
never repeat with your own children.

If so, whatever you do, try not to jump on yourself and start
telling yourself what an awful or inadequate mother you are. This
may be your first impulse, but it's the most unhelpful thing you
can do. Rather, give yourself permission to handle the situation
in the best way you can at that moment, and let yourself know
that later, when you're calmer, you will make a plan to help
yourself in the future.

Remember, as we saw in chapter 2, accepting yourself leads
not to stagnation but to change. The more you like and approve
of yourself and accept yourself faults and all, the more you free
up your energy to deal positively with those aspects of your
mothering that you most want to change.

BE COMPASSIONATE TOWARDS YOURSELF

When you're more relaxed and have a moment to yourself, think about what happened. Assure yourself that you can't ruin a child in one incident. In fact some children grow up in difficult circumstances and still come out OK. Then ask yourself compassionately why you acted like you did. Perhaps you felt stressed out in general, or maybe your son's "no" reminded you of your father's authoritarian attitude and set you off. Maybe you acted like your mother, because she was your model and her ways became ingrained in you. Whatever your reasons, don't hate yourself for being the way you are.

RESPECT YOURSELF AND PRAISE YOURSELF FOR WHAT YOU DO WELL AS A MOTHER

Think about all the things that you do well enough (not perfectly) as a mother, and write them down. Remember, as we saw in chapter 3, this is all that is needed, to be a good-enough mother, not a perfect mother. Call this your "GOOD-ENOUGH MOTHER" list. Be sure you put down everything you do adequately, even if it seems like a small thing or something you take for granted, like feeding your children, or waking them for school, or adequately clothing and supplying them. Think of the emotional things you do for them, too, like listening to them and paying attention, and praising them, and smiling at them, and holding them and comforting them. When you get through, you should have a long list. If you don't, it means that you're not giving yourself enough credit. Ask others who know you and who aren't hypercritical what they've seen you do. Ask other mothers what they would put on such a list of their own. Observe when your children feel happy or content, and see what it is you've done to contribute to their happiness. Keep going until you have a long list. Then add to it daily as you notice more things you do for your children.

Whenever you feel upset about your mothering, read this list slowly aloud to yourself, starting with "I" for each accomplishment. For instance, "I feed my children three meals a day." As you read your list, take credit for each thing that you do, and feel good about it. When you are done, say the following to yourself:

> I am a good-enough mother and I approve
> of myself as a mother.

Use this sentence as a mantra, something you can repeat to calm yourself and help you to feel centered and good about yourself as a mother. It helps to slowly inhale and exhale as you think, "I am a good-enough mother and I approve of myself as a mother." Even when you don't have time to go over your whole GOOD ENOUGH MOTHER list immediately, you can recite this mantra and take it in and feel good about yourself as a mother.

SET REASONABLE GOALS

Once you are feeling good about and approve of yourself as a mother, then and only then, can you start working on becoming an even better mother. In the past you may have set up goals for yourself that were like pass-fail tests. You may have told yourself that, to be a good mother, you had to not yell at your kids all day, or keep them from fighting, or make great healthy meals from scratch. Then if you yelled at all, or they fought, or you didn't have time to cook a great meal, you failed. If you followed the failure guidelines stated in chapter 1, you also didn't give yourself any credit for trying, and instead jumped on yourself for what you didn't do, concluding that you're a lousy mother and feeling awful about yourself.

Even worse, you may have set up tests whose outcome you have limited or no control over. For instance you may have told yourself that you'll know you're doing a good job as a mother if your kids get good report cards, or have a lot of friends, or are happy and outgoing, or keep their rooms clean and neat, or come home on time. The trouble with these tests is that you're judging your adequacy by your children's behavior. This is exactly what you don't want to do. This is where your self-worth and their behavior get all mixed up. It's hard enough trying to encourage your children to act ethically and responsibly and to foster their happy development without having your self-worth riding on it.

A more helpful approach is to identify one area of your behavior that you would like to change, and make a list of *specific* ways in which you would like to act differently in this area. For instance, if you think you're too impatient, you might write things like:

- When the kids are slow getting out of the car, I want to wait patiently rather than screaming at them.
- I don't want to yell at Johnny when he throws food on the floor.
- When the kids argue, I want to talk to them patiently rather than screaming at them to shut up.
- When Jennifer gets insolent, I want to correct her without slapping her.
- When Tommy goes on and on about something, I would like to be able to hear him out without getting distracted.

ENCOURAGE AND SUPPORT YOURSELF TO REACH YOUR GOALS

Once you have listed all the behaviors you would like to change, rank them in order from easiest to hardest, then start with the easiest. Let's say it's waiting patiently for your kids to get out of the car. First consider what bothers you about waiting. Is it the press of other things to do? Resentment at being tied down? Being upset at not being able to make things go your way? Before you can change your feelings, you first have to know what you are upset about. You may get impatient about different things for different reasons. Once you figure it out, have a dialogue with your inner-child. Talk to her about your reason for being impatient. See what kind of help she needs to feel more patient while waiting in the car.

If you're eager to get in the house so you can rest, perhaps you can get in the habit of using your car-waiting time as a mini-relaxation time by breathing slowly and deeply. If you're overwhelmed by the number of things that need doing, and you want to get on to the next one, maybe it would help to time how long the kids take getting out of the car when you don't rush them, as opposed to when you do. Likely the difference is only a couple of minutes. Let yourself know that two minutes is not going to make that much difference in what you accomplish. Maybe you could use those two minutes, while you're waiting for the kids to get moving, to feel proud of yourself for being patient.

Perhaps waiting tees you off because your whole life you had to wait for your very slow younger brother to get moving. If so, talk to your inner-child. Accept how frustrated and angry she feels. Ask her to talk to you whenever she feels angry at having to wait rather than screaming at your kids. Tell her you love her and want to help her. Don't expect her to suddenly stop feeling impatient. Try to talk with her whenever you have to wait. Tell her, "OK, now we have to wait for the kids. Talk to me. Tell me what you're feeling." Keep talking to her till the kids are out of the car and on their way into the house.

GIVE YOURSELF CREDIT FOR EACH STEP YOU TAKE AND THE EFFORT THAT YOU ARE MAKING

Be sure to give yourself credit for any attempts you make whether or not you're successful. As you experienced going through the steps in part II, the more you encourage and reward yourself, the easier it is to change; on the other hand, the more you criticize and berate yourself, the more you stay stuck.

Once you are comfortable with how you are handling the first item on your list, go on to the next one. In sequence, when you're ready, go through each of the behaviors on your list. Remember that change takes place slowly and only after much practice and

backsliding. Don't give yourself a hard time if you end up screaming at the kids for not rushing out of the car. Tell yourself that
you're only human, and that your kids know you love them. Tell
yourself: I am a good-enough mother and I approve of myself as
a mother.

Once you have dealt with your behaviors around one area of
parenting, such as being impatient, you can focus—if you like—
on another area in which you would like to grow as a mother.
Use the same method of listing, then ranking, behaviors you wish
to change. Start with the easiest and work with your inner-child
to make the desired change. Be sure to give yourself the Compassion, Acceptance, Respect, Encouragement, Support, and
Stroking that enables people to develop and flourish.

TREAT YOURSELF THE WAY YOU WOULD LIKE YOUR CHILDREN'S TEACHERS TO TREAT YOUR CHILDREN

We all know what it is that we think makes a teacher a good
teacher. For me, I want my girls' teachers to be warm, kind,
concerned, firm, consistent, creative, and caring. If my children
do well, or try to do well, I want them to be praised. If they
struggle to learn something that is difficult for them, I want the
teacher to be encouraging and supportive. If they act up or are
disrespectful, I would like their teacher to let them know that
they are capable of better behavior and that she expects them to
control themselves. If they are upset about something, I would
want the teacher to make time to listen to them and suggest ways
to cope with the situation. In short, I want the teacher to be
conscious not only of imparting information and skills, but also
of helping my children to feel good about and esteem themselves.

This same kind of regard is what you need for yourself. Treat
yourself with warmth, kindness, concern, and caring. Use your
creativity to problem-solve, at the same time allowing yourself to
make mistakes. Have reasonable expectations for yourself, and

help yourself to meet them by encouraging and supporting yourself. Praise yourself for doing well and give yourself credit for trying. Remember, it does you no good to reach your goals if you don't pause to recognize how far you've come. Repeat your mantra several times a day. Tell yourself:

> I am a good-enough mother and I approve
> of myself as a mother.

Stop to take in good feelings about yourself as a mother. When you're having a hard day, let yourself know that this is especially when you need yourself on your side. Give yourself the nurturing, the CARESS, you need to esteem yourself.

CHAPTER 16

Nurturing Yourself While Making Love

If I am not for myself, who will be for me?
If I am only for myself, what good am I?
And if not now, when?
HILLEL
(first-century Jewish scholar)

*T*his ancient conundrum states the dilemma that many women face today when making love: how to balance our sexual needs and desires with those of our partners. In this post–sexual revolution era, we often are unclear about how much we are "entitled to" as opposed to what is asking for or demanding too much. Many of us hesitate to ask for the kinds of approaches and stimulation we desire for fear our partners will become bored, tired, or resentful. At the same time, when our sexual needs are not met, *we* feel frustrated, unhappy, discontented, and angry.

Some of us, when continually dissatisfied, blame our partners and feel angry and resentful, but many others of us blame ourselves. We fault ourselves for not being desirable, or for being too greedy and selfish, or for expecting too much, or for not being passionate enough, or for not being able to communicate our needs, or for not knowing how to make our sex lives better.

Jennifer is twenty-four. She first had intercourse at nineteen with her steady boyfriend. She is now in her second relationship. Jennifer is easily and multiply orgasmic with clitoral stimulation. She loves to have her clitoris stroked for extended periods of time, having climax after climax. However, usually after about ten minutes of such stimulation, she signals her boyfriend to enter her because she thinks she has been taking too much and feels guilty.

Rhoda is thirty-nine, has been married for eleven years, and is multiply orgasmic with clitoral or vaginal stimulation. Her husband Sam greatly enjoys bringing her to repeated climaxes, and Rhoda enjoys this, too; however, she longs for more romance in their lovemaking. She misses all the hugging, kissing, and slow caressing they used to do in the beginning years of their relationship. She has told this to Sam, and each time she does, he will extend the non-genital part of lovemaking for a few episodes, but then goes back to his old pattern. She feels deprived, frustrated, and resentful, but hesitates to make an issue of it. She thinks she is expecting too much.

Tracy is forty-two and has been in a committed relationship for seven years with Maureen. While Tracy and Maureen are both tender and caring lovers, their pace is very different. Maureen comes easily, quickly, and repeatedly. Tracy never wants more than one orgasm, and requires fifteen or twenty minutes of continual clitoral stimulation to reach orgasm. While Maureen is happy to give Tracy the stimulation she requires, Tracy is often distracted during lovemaking by thinking that she is taking too long and Maureen must be getting tired. Tracy's guilt over "taking too much" interferes with her ability to concentrate on and enjoy her pleasurable feelings.

Liz is thirty and has been dating Roy for a year. She generally enjoys their lovemaking, but sometimes finds herself not in the mood. At such times she would rather not make love, or just pleasure Roy, but is afraid to say so. She fears Roy will be hurt and become more distant—perhaps even leading to the dissolution of their relationship. She blames herself for not being passionate enough.

Jennifer, Rhoda, Tracy, and Liz are all struggling with feeling entitled to what pleases and pleasures them, and with respecting their own needs. They are having difficulty accepting their likes and needs as valid because their inner-critics tell them that they are being demanding and selfish when their wants differ from those of their partners. They need to learn that their desires are the building blocks of great sex, and that they should cherish and celebrate them as an integral part of their sexuality.

Just as the need for emotional connection underlies the ability to form a relationship with another person, so does the desire for sexual pleasure and gratification underlie the ability to form a satisfying sexual partnership. When a woman acknowledges and accepts her needs as valid and reasonable, she then is free to learn to express her sexuality in ways that enhance both her own enjoyment and her sexual relationship with her partner.

Liz also needs to learn that unless she can say "no," she will never be able to say "yes" and totally mean it. Only when a woman can refuse to have sex without fear of outer or inner repercussions is she then free to wholeheartedly choose to make love. This kind of wholehearted involvement enhances sexual enjoyment, while a sense of obligation diminishes it.

The last question from Hillel, "If not now, when?" is particularly pertinent to women's lives today. With so many responsibilities and so little time, it is easy to avoid or postpone dealing with sexual dissatisfaction, especially if your partner is satisfied or not complaining. If this is the case for you, ask yourself, "Do I really want to deprive myself in this way?"

Some women deal with their sexual dissatisfaction by trying to resign themselves to the way things are. They tell themselves that sex isn't that important compared to other aspects of their relationships, or that sex can't stay exciting in a long-term relationship, or that they're over- or undersexed. This just sends their dissatisfaction underground, where it is likely to come out in disguised ways, such as in moodiness, anger, or depression. You, too, may not want to work on your sex life.

Perhaps the prospect of working and dwelling on it seems more trouble than it's worth, or you don't believe that it can improve. You may think the best approach is to allow sex to be infrequent, or conversely to do it, get it over with, and forget it. Or you may not have a sexual partner, so try to put sexual thoughts and desires out of your mind in order to avoid confronting frustration.

Whatever your situation, if you are reluctant to work on your sex life, I urge you to reconsider. By nurturing yourself, you can enhance your sexual desire and satisfaction. In my experience as a sex therapist, I have seen many people overcome sexual difficulties that had been plaguing them for years. You can, too. I am going to share with you some approaches and techniques to improve the quality of your sex life. Try them out. Sexual feelings and gratification can add much pleasure and joy to a woman's life; since most sexual problems can be ameliorated, I hope you will give yourself the help you need to truly relish and luxuriate in your own sexuality.

With sexuality, as with all areas of your life, nurturing yourself starts with giving yourself a loving CARESS. Begin this CARESS by having compassion for your feelings and needs and accepting them as they are, whatever they are, without blaming or criticizing yourself. We saw earlier how blaming and criticizing yourself fosters depression, anxiety, and low self-esteem, and mires you in a vicious cycle of self-blame and self-hate. This is all the more true of blaming yourself for what you see as your sexual short-comings. We are all so vulnerable when we take off our clothes and open up our bodies and feelings to another person. Any negative comment that your partner may make during lovemaking cuts to the quick.

We are similarly hypersensitive to negative messages we give ourselves during lovemaking, so it is especially important that you deal with your sexuality by encouraging and supporting yourself—that you take satisfaction in your strengths, and give yourself credit for trying to make your sex life more pleasurable. Most of all, it is important that you nonjudgmentally accept and respect your feelings and desires, whatever they are. Encourage yourself to put guilt and self-blame aside, and use your energy instead to focus on making changes. Start by figuring out what in your sex life needs improvement. In trying to decide, you should ask yourself four important questions:

Am I in the right emotional state when I try to be sexual?
Am I in the right mental state when I try to be sexual?
Am I getting enough and the right kind of touching?
Am I communicating well with my partner?

These questions are crucial, because to really enjoy yourself sexually you have to be able to let go and abandon yourself to the warm glow of your feelings, the stimulation of your thoughts, the pleasure of your body, and the delight of being with your partner.

BEING IN THE RIGHT EMOTIONAL STATE
Your emotions play a big role in feeling desire, and without desire sex usually falls flat or doesn't take place at all. If you feel angry or afraid, you're unlikely to feel turned on. If you are depressed, you may feel no desire whatsoever until your depression lifts. If you are feeling upset, worried, mistrustful, anxious, or guilty, you

may not be able to sufficiently put these feelings aside so that you can be relaxed enough to enjoy making love. While any kind of upsetting feelings can diminish sexual enjoyment, some are more lethal than others. Besides depression:

> Two feelings in particular extinguish passion—
> anger and fear.

When anger blocks desire and passion

If you are angry at your partner, it is vital to deal with these feelings before you try to make love. Clearly, if you are in the middle of a fight, neither one of you is likely to initiate sex. However, anger is not always expressed, or even felt, directly. You may be resentful about a lot of little things that have been building up. When your partner makes sexual overtures, you may not realize that you are angry and therefore disinterested in sex. Instead, you may think that your lack of interest comes from being too tired, or because your attention is focused on something else you are doing or planning to do at the moment, or that you're just not in the mood.

If you frequently find yourself "not in the mood," even when you are not exhausted, try to find out what is preventing you from feeling desire. Ask your inner-child what she is feeling towards your partner and about making love. If she is angry, find out what she is angry about and problem-solve together about how to best deal with what is making you angry. You may well want to talk to your partner about your feelings. When you do so, remember the rules of empathic communication from chapter 11: **reflect feelings, ask for clarification, encourage more expression of feelings, and state your own feelings.** Don't accuse or blame. Do state your concerns frankly and clearly. See if you can clear the air between you and your partner. If repeated efforts at resolving anger towards your partner only lead to fights or angry withdrawals, you may want to consider professional counseling to open up communication and help you out of your impasse.

Even if your relationship is basically a happy one, at times your passion and excitement may be dampened or extinguished by angry feelings.

Mary felt turned on and thought about approaching her lover Pat, but as she imagined making their way together into the bedroom, she thought about the clothes and newspapers Pat had left strewn about the floor and bed, and how she hated being the general and always having to nag Pat to clean up. Before Mary knew it, she no longer felt like making love, and instead continued to watch TV.

Fern and Bob were in the middle of passionate sex when she happened to open her eyes and catch sight of his messy hair. This started her thinking about Bob's annoying tendency to procrastinate many chores, including cutting his hair. The more she thought about his procrastination, the more annoyed and the less passionate she felt. What had started out as an ardent lovemaking session now fizzled into a so-so experience with Fern barely participating.

Mary and Fern didn't have to focus on their anger in this way. Think how differently Mary would have felt, if instead of focusing on the mess in the bedroom, she had thought about the pleasure she was about to have, and about what a thoughtful person Pat is in other ways. Of course if she's angry about the mess in the bedroom, it's important to deal with it, but why now? Why should Mary deprive herself of sexual pleasure in this way? Similarly, Fern could have chosen to think of how giving Bob is, or how much fun they have together, rather than robbing herself of a gratifying experience by staying focused on Bob's procrastination. The time to focus on her unhappiness with Bob's procrastination is when they can discuss it in a constructive way—and not at a time when focusing on her angry feelings can only erect barriers.

When fear blocks desire and excitement

Fear, like anger, can prevent, extinguish, or dampen desire and excitement. If your sexual feelings are blocked by fear, first try to distinguish whether you are in current danger—for instance, if your partner is violent, punitive, or highly critical—or whether your fear is based on prior painful and frightening experiences, such as rape, sexual abuse, abandonment, or having had very invasive, intrusive, or critical past experiences.

IF YOU ARE IN CURRENT DANGER, GET HELP IMMEDIATELY! Seek out professional counseling. You may also find it helpful to be in a group with other women who are trying to deal with destructive relationships. Ask your counselor about such a group. If you are being battered, GET OUT IMMEDIATELY. No one should be hit and abused. Most cities have shelters, trained counselors, and self-help groups that can offer you support and guidance. Consult your yellow pages or your local community mental health center for a list of such services, or call the hot line of the National Coalition Against Domestic Violence at (800) 333-7233.

If your fear is based on past sexual trauma, it would also be wise to get help and support from others. Recently childhood sexual abuse has been coming out of the closet, and we are realizing how widespread and devastating these experiences are. Such trauma typically causes sexual problems that may take years to overcome. If you have been the victim of such abuse and are experiencing sexual difficulties, as is common, some of the suggestions in this chapter about touch may not be appropriate for you at this time because you may need to go slower and to emphasize your control of the process at all times (as opposed to the abuse when control was all in the hands of the abuser). Fantasizing may also not be helpful as it may reproduce images of the abuse with concomitant negative reactions. For more information see the Suggested Readings for books written for survivors of sexual abuse; especially helpful is Wendy Maltz's *The Sexual Healing Journey: A Guide for Survivors of Sexual Abuse* which also contains an extensive resource guide. You may also find it helpful to join a group with other survivors, or to consult with a professional experienced in helping women heal from sexual abuse. Again, your yellow pages, hot line, doctor, or community mental health center can help you learn about resources in your area. You can also obtain information about self-help groups in your area by sending a self-addressed stamped envelope to: Incest Survivors Anonymous, P.O. Box 5613, Long Beach, CA, 90805-0613. You, like many other courageous survivors, can learn to cherish rather than fear your sexuality.

Fears based on past trauma or present danger are not the only fears that can interfere with sexual desire. Everyday thoughts or experiences that trigger an area of insecurity may prevent or diminish desire and excitement. Common fears that interfere with sexual feelings include fear of disapproval, fear of having your feelings hurt, fear of abandonment, and fear of intrusion and engulfment. However, any fear can have this effect.

If you are fearful before or during sex but are not sure why, ask your inner-child. She knows. As you did in chapter 13, ask her to check off which of the following fears she has:

Fear of Loss	Fear of Abandonment
Fear of Being Alone	Fear of Being Humiliated
Fear of Failure	Fear of Success
Fear of Rejection	Fear of Domination
Fear of Harm, Attack, or Retaliation	Fear of Intrusion, Engulfment
Fear of Being Controlled	Fear of Loss of Love, Approval
Fear of Loss of Respect	Fear of Illness and Death
Fear of Criticism	Fear of Betrayal
Fear of Being Out of Control	Fear of Going Crazy
Fear of Anger	Fear of Being Unworthy

Fear of Annihilation   Fear of Loss of Status
Fear of Intimacy   Fear of Being Vulnerable
Fear of Trusting Others   Fear of Being Overwhelmed

Any thought, image, sensation, or experience that triggers one of these fears (or any other fear you may have) may interfere with your being able to enjoy your own sexuality.

Meg, for example, felt amorous and wanted to approach her husband Tim. Then she started to worry that maybe Tim wouldn't be in the mood and would resent her for interrupting him while he was watching TV. Meg feared Tim's disapproval and rejection because it elicited her feelings of being undesirable and unworthy. The more Meg thought about possibly being rejected and resented, the less passionate she felt. She ended up watching TV instead, and felt depressed.

Meg didn't have to stir up her fear in this way. Instead of imagining Tim being distracted or resentful, she could have pictured him feeling glad and turned on, which was frequently the case. Meg also needed to learn to be less afraid of rejection. She needed to believe that if Tim rebuffed her, it did not make her undesirable or unworthy. When she learned how to build her self-esteem by CARESSing herself, her fear of being rejected diminished and she felt freer to initiate sex.

Sometimes fear takes over after you have started making love. You may suddenly begin to feel afraid that your partner will leave you, or engulf you, or that you will go crazy if you have an orgasm. At such times your sexual openness and vulnerability becomes emotionally threatening, and the need to "close yourself up" can become all important. When this happens, your body automatically tenses up, often without your being aware of it, and your pleasure rapidly diminishes or evaporates.

If you experience a lessening of pleasure in response to feeling fearful, you can help yourself by calming your inner-child and by allowing your body to relax. Listen compassionately to your inner-child's fears and give her the reassurance that she needs. Tell her that sharing sexual pleasure doesn't mean that your partner will leave; assure her that you won't allow yourself to be taken over by another; reassure her that, while having an orgasm may make you feel as if you lose all control, you really don't. (Just think how quickly you regain control if the phone rings). Then help yourself to relax your body and open it to pleasure.

A simple way to relax your body is to breathe slowly and deeply whenever you feel yourself tightening up. Try to become aware, and ask your partner to let you know, when you are tensing muscles anywhere in your body. Then take a slow deep breath through your nose and feel yourself inhaling the cleansing and relaxing air into your tight muscles. Next slowly exhale through your mouth, and as you do, exhale all the tightness out of your muscles and let your body relax. Repeat this slow breathing several times. At the same time tell yourself that it is OK to feel pleasure. That you are in no danger. Calm your frightened inner-child. If your fear continues, try looking into your partner's eyes or talking to him or her. Some women find this contact with a supportive and accepting partner helps to calm transient fears. Other women find it helpful to divert themself from their fears by immersing themselves in a fantasy.

DEALING WITH FEELINGS THAT BLOCK YOUR SEXUALITY WHEN YOU DON'T HAVE A PARTNER

Even when you don't have a partner, negative emotions can block your enjoyment of your own sexuality. For example, consider Sandy.

Sandy was reading a novel that excited her. She put the book aside and started to think about how much she wished she had someone to make love with. She then switched to thinking about how alone and deprived she felt. The more she thought about how alone she was, the more upset and dejected she became. She quickly went from feeling turned on to feeling depressed.

While Sandy's reaction is a common one, she didn't have to do this to herself. Instead she could have thought about making efforts to find a partner, or she could have just stayed with her desire and enjoyed that feeling for itself, without having to act on it. Or she might have drifted into a fantasy that offered excitement and mental gratification. Perhaps she would have wished to stroke herself. Whatever she did or didn't do, she could have savored feeling like a sexual woman capable of desire. By thus cherishing her sexuality, she would be enhancing her self-esteem as she enjoyed being the woman that she is.

BEING IN THE RIGHT MENTAL STATE

When making love you may sometimes find that, despite your best intentions, you are distracted by nonsexual thoughts. For instance, if you are worried about tasks that need doing or an upcoming confrontation, you might find your mind ruminating on these subjects rather than joining in with your body and feelings in the enjoyment of the present.

Even worse, your mind might be too present in the guise of your inner-critic, who is standing aside watching and judging you. If while making love, you hear your inner-critic telling you that your stomach is flabby and that you lack passion, how can you possibly relax enough to feel the depths of excitement and pleasure that you are capable of? Similarly, if while attempting to reach a climax, your inner-critic watches you with a worried eye lest you fail—your anxiety will build up and you may well fail. Watching yourself rather than being wholly part of what you are experiencing is called "spectatoring" and can greatly detract from the enjoyment of lovemaking.

Watching and criticizing your partner is similarly detrimental. This attitude is an open invitation to feel worried, dissatisfied, angry, and resentful—feelings that will negate passion and pleasure. For instance, if as your partner is stroking you, you are thinking about how bad your partner's technique is, you are distancing yourself from pleasurable feelings and making it less likely that you will enjoy your partner's caresses.

Banish your inner-critic and call forth your inner-caretaker. Encourage yourself to focus on your pleasurable feelings and see if you can make them more intense. Let your inner-caretaker support you in asking for what you want rather than expecting your partner to have a perfect technique. Most of all, have your inner-caretaker encourage you to immerse yourself in your experience, instead of standing aside and watching and judging yourself.

However, if you are in the habit of watching yourself and worrying, it may be hard to banish your inner-critic. Even though you may know that you are making yourself anxious and uptight, you may find it difficult to stop your distracting and critical thoughts. If your head keeps getting in the way of your body like this, an effective and quick way to get it on your side helping you is to lose yourself in a sexual fantasy. Then your head will be caught up in erotic images that will help your body to relax and enjoy.

Fantasies

Some of you may be reluctant to fantasize because you feel guilty about or ashamed of your sexual fantasies. What you find erotic may go against your politics or morality. Many women are excited by imagining sexual scenes that in real life would be abhorrent to them, such as being forced and raped, or being tied up and beaten, or being humiliated and dominated, or having sex with a woman if they are straight, or with a man if they are lesbians. Other women have fantasies about things that on some level they may want to experience, but violate their moral code, such as having sex with their partner's best friend, with their best friend's partner, in an exposed place, or at an orgy.

If you have fantasies that violate the way you want to be

treated by your partner or the way you want to lead your life, you may find yourself in conflict. On one hand you may be ashamed of your fantasies and consider them to be "perverted," "sick," "unnatural," or "unliberated." On the other hand, you are stimulated and turned on by them. You may imagine that if your partner, let alone your friends and relatives, knew what you fantasized about, they would look down on you.

You may be surprised to learn that your friends, relatives, and partner may have similar, or equally "unnatural" fantasies. It is very common for people to fantasize about forbidden partners, acts, and scenarios. Any woman who feels guilty about her fantasies, or who has never fantasized, may find it helpful to read Nancy Friday's two collections of women's actual sexual fantasies: My Secret Garden and Forbidden Flowers (see Suggested Readings).

Some women are hesitant to fantasize because they think that fantasizing will lead to action. They believe that because they enjoy **thinking** about something, this means that they will **do** it. Have you wondered about that? Actually, on the contrary, fantasy often serves like removing the top from a pressure cooker—it allows you to let out pent-up feelings in a totally safe outlet. It is an everyday occurrence to derive enjoyment from, for instance, fantasizing acts of vengeance and retaliation (like harming your boss) that you would never actually do. Yes, some women do engage in sadomasochistic sex or have an affair with their partner's best friend—but not because their fantasies alone led them to do so.

I am making such a point about the safety and normality of sexual fantasies, no matter how "unnatural" they are, because being able to enjoy your sexual fantasies is an important part of being able to enjoy your own sexuality. Your biggest sex organ is your brain. As we saw above, for your body to function properly and to fully experience pleasure, it needs your brain on its side. If your brain is distracted, or even worse filled with the voice of your inner-critic who is watching you and criticizing you or your partner, your pleasure will be greatly diminished.

Some women have no qualms about enjoying their fantasies when they're by themselves, but feel guilty about fantasizing while making love. They think they are being disloyal to their partner, especially if, as is often the case, they are fantasizing about sex with a different partner or partners. They think that if their partner knew, he or she would be hurt or angry. I have found that this is rarely the case. In sex therapy, where the prescription of fantasy is a common and useful tool in diminishing anxiety and spectatoring, partners are almost always accepting and encouraging of the other's fantasizing. This is especially true once the partner understands that fantasy is a way of tapping into a person's own sexuality, and is not indicative of dissatisfaction with the partner.

This doesn't mean that it's necessarily better to fantasize while making love. Some women find that it adds a lot to their enjoyment, while other women prefer to concentrate on their pleasurable feelings and sensations. It is helpful, though, to have your fantasy life available to use when needed or desired.

Expecting to Be Disappointed

Another way that your mind can diminish desire is to recall past unsatisfying sex and then to anticipate that this time will be "like all the rest." Such thoughts come from a sincere, though misguided, attempt to protect your inner-child, who is scared of trying and being disappointed. Encourage her. Tell her that it's OK to try, and with enough effort, practice, and communication with your partner (more on this later) you can find a way to make things better. Even as things are now, there is pleasure and enjoyment and you can concentrate on those feelings even as you strive to make things better. Most important of all, let your inner-child know that she doesn't have to be afraid, because you will be there to support her and help her through any disappointment that might arise, and that change is never achieved without progress and disappointment.

GETTING ENOUGH AND THE RIGHT
KIND OF TOUCHING

The third crucial way for you to nurture yourself sexually is to make sure you are getting the right kind and amount of touching. This is true whether you are touching yourself or being touched by your partner.

Some women, regardless of their age or sexual experience, do not know what kind of touching they need because they have never fully explored their own bodies. They may cringe at the thought of looking at their genitals in a mirror because they think they look disgusting, or because they were taught as children never to look or to touch themselves "down there." If you have any discomfort or unfamiliarity with your body, change that now. Begin to explore and make friends with your own body. You will not be able to fully enjoy your sexuality until you accept and embrace your own physicality.

Some women have never masturbated, or tried it briefly but gave it up because either they did not find it pleasurable or because it did not lead to a climax. Others masturbate solely with a vibrator, and may become "hooked" on this kind of intense stimulation, so cannot reach orgasm in any other way. It is very helpful for a woman to be able to bring herself to orgasm by her own hand because in so doing she is discovering a great deal about the kind of stimulation she needs and likes. (If you cannot readily have orgasms by your hand, see the Suggested Readings for help). She is then in a much better position to express her needs to her partner.

COMMUNICATING WELL WITH YOUR PARTNER

The last, but hardly least, factor that makes for exciting and satisfying sex is good communication with your partner. The more a couple is able to verbalize what emotionally, mentally, and physically turns each of them on and satisfies them, the better their lovemaking will be. This means being able to share feelings, thoughts, and desires with each other without fear of ridicule or rejection. For this kind of sharing to take place, you need to be able to trust yourself to be supportive and respectful of your own needs as well as those of your partner. Then, even if your partner should happen to respond negatively, you will continue to feel good about yourself. It is only when you are looking to your partner to validate you that a negative reaction makes you question yourself. So, give yourself the support you need. If you allow your inner-critic to make you feel ashamed or guilty, you will have great trouble communicating with your partner.

Martha and Jim had been married for fifteen years and had three children. Their marriage was a solid one, and their sex was regular and mutually orgasmic. However, Martha longed for more. Jim was gentle and considerate in their lovemaking, which she liked a lot, but sometimes she wanted him to be more forceful—to pretend to be taking her against her will. She also greatly enjoyed oral sex, but hesitated to ask because she knew he wasn't crazy about doing it. Martha had never discussed any of this with Jim. She was afraid he would view her desire to "be taken" as weird, and her request for more oral sex as too demanding.

After some exploration with Martha it became apparent that it was Martha herself who thought her wanting to be taken forcefully was strange, and who thought that she was being selfish for wanting something that Jim disliked. Once Martha was able to accept her desires as valid and legitimate without judging herself, she was able to talk to Jim about them. He acknowledged that he didn't find being forceful erotic, and that he was somewhat uncomfortable with performing oral sex; however, he was really turned on by the idea of exciting Martha more. He was willing to occasionally do the things she liked now that he knew how exciting they were to her. He also started to share more of his desires with her. Sparked by this openness and sharing, their lovemaking became more intimate. Each felt closer and more excited knowing how to tap further into the other's eroticism.

Like Martha, you can improve your sex life by opening up communication with your partner. Start by validating yourself. Let yourself know that you have every right to want what you want, to not like what you don't like, and to be turned on by what turns you on. Then acknowledge that your partner has this privilege, too. There is no right or wrong in sex (as long as it is mutually consensual between equal adults, and no one is hurt), only two people with different bodies, thoughts, and feelings coming together to share pleasure and intimacy. The more you can openly and compassionately accept and discuss your own and your partner's needs, the better your sex will be.

Talking about building desire

A good place to start this expanded communication with your partner is by talking about what puts each of you in the mood for sex. If you don't know, ask your inner-child. She knows. It may also be helpful to think about what in movies, books, and in contact with a partner makes you feel turned on.

Frequently for women, it's romance. Women, in general, like seducing and being seduced. We like flirting and courtship. We enjoy being treated as if we're special. We want to feel connected to our partners, whether just for the moment or in a lasting way. This is why so many women prefer being talked to during love-making—it makes us feel that our partner is making love to us and not just to our bodies. Even if the sexual encounter is a one-night stand with a stranger, a woman still wants to feel that her partner desires to be with **her** and not just with her body.

Beyond romance there may be very specific things that turn you on, or off. It is important to recognize these things and to communicate them to your partner. In exploring what arouses you, consider the following questions:

How and by whom do you like sex to be initiated?
What kind of approaches (yours and your partner's) turn you on? What kind turn you off?

What kind of ambiance turns you on—candles, music, incense, fabrics, outfits, etc?

Do you like great variety—different positions, locales, times of day, roles—or do you prefer alternating between a few tried and true ways of pleasuring each other?

When a relationship is new, everything is a discovery and exciting. There is the challenge of attracting the other, the ego boost of being found desirable, the mystery of learning about each other, the closeness that comes from sharing intimacies, and the thrill of exploring each other's body. All of this builds passion and desire.

In a long-lasting relationship these enhancements are often diminished or missing entirely. It may be less of a challenge to attract the other, ego-boosting compliments may be fewer and harder to come by, all your secrets probably have long since been shared, and you may know the other's body almost as well as you know your own. While you desire each other, it may be like loving friends coming together to give each other pleasure without the burning passion you once had. *In fact, if you are like most couples who have been together a long time, you may skip over the seduction/romance part of lovemaking altogether and go right into the physical act. If so, you are depriving yourselves of a powerful aphrodisiac.* The seduction phase of lovemaking plays an important role in enhancing desire and excitement.

If this is true for you, make it a priority to start your lovemaking before you start making love. I don't mean that you have to go through an elaborate seduction scene every time. Just let yourself consider what would really turn you and your partner on. While this may be more important to you than to your male partner, men can really get into it, too, especially if you present it as fun and spicy, rather than as an additional way in which he has to perform.

Talking about touching

A good way to discover what kind of non-genital touching you like is by engaging in the following sensate focus experience developed by Masters and Johnson. Even if you know very well how you like to be touched, you may still want to do this exercise for the pure sensual pleasure that it provides.

Make sure you and your partner have a private hour when you won't be interrupted and aren't tired. First shower or bathe (separately or together). Then, with both of you naked, lie on your stomach while your partner strokes you slowly and gently, using fingertips and lips, from the tip of your head to the bottom of your toes, slowly and sensuously. Don't time yourselves, but take about ten minutes. Then turn over and lie on your back, and have your partner caress you in the same way on the front, skipping your nipples and genitals. While you are being caressed, concentrate on your sensations. Experience what is most pleasurable to you and take in the good feelings while your partner concentrates on the sensations of giving. When ready, switch roles and repeat the process, again skipping the genitals, with you as the giver, so that in one session each of you experiences both giving and receiving. Then talk together about this experience.

This exercise is a wonderful way to learn not only how you like to be touched, but it is also a great way to learn what your partner finds exciting. It is valuable to repeat this exercise on different days, as you may experience different things each time. It may also be informative when you repeat this exercise to vary whether you receive first or give first. Notice if giving first makes it easier for you to receive, or vice versa. Which do you like better?

This kind of non-genital stroking, while pleasurable for men too, is usually more important to a woman. Even if she is easily excitable and orgasmic, a woman generally (but not always) prefers lovemaking to start in this slow, sensual way. If a sexual encounter starts off with a few hugs and kisses and fondling of her breasts, and then immediately proceeds to clitoral touching and/or intercourse—no matter how long, good, or satisfying the genital touching may be, a woman (unlike most men) may still feel that she didn't get all that she wanted or needed.

Sometimes women feel embarrassed, guilty, or angry at having to ask for what they want, let alone having to repeatedly ask for and demonstrate the kind of touching that pleases them. Many women believe that if their partners loved them, their lovers would somehow just know what they need and give it to them. This is patently untrue.

Loving someone in no way enables a person to read another's mind or feel what it is she needs.

Some women hesitate to express their needs for fear of upsetting or angering their partners, who may take such instructions as an attack on their technique. Others are afraid of appearing wanton, or too aggressive, or too naive. If you have any of these hesitancies, let yourself know that one of the biggest gifts you can give your partner is to be honest about your feelings and needs. *Whenever you take the risk of making yourself vulnerable, you are also making yourself accessible. You are putting yourself in an emotional place where another can reach you, and in so doing you are really giving not only to yourself, but also of yourself.* Yes, your partner might feel attacked or hurt. If this happens, deal with it without becoming attacking or defensive in return. Hold on to your sense of self, and don't start feeling guilty. Encourage your partner to talk about his or her feelings, and use the techniques of empathic communication that you learned in chapter 11. It is out of just this kind of real openness and talking things through that intimacy occurs. Of course, this doesn't happen all at once. Don't push yourself to voice more than you are ready to. Rather, support and encourage yourself to be as honest as you can be. Take little steps and give yourself credit for every one you take.

With time and persistent effort you can achieve a deeper level of intimacy.

In trying to walk the fine line between not adequately expressing your needs and being overdemanding and selfish, consider the following guidelines:

1. Be as specific as possible about what you want, not only in general, but at any given moment. It is your responsibility to communicate your desires and needs.

2. Do not *assume* anything about what your partner is thinking or feeling. If your partner is feeling tired or bored, it is your partner's responsibility to communicate that to you directly—not your responsibility to second-guess him or her.

3. If your lover says he or she is tired and wants to stop touching you, accept that without feeling angry or guilty. You are not responsible for your lover's physical or emotional state (and vice versa). The fact that your lover is fatigued means neither that you are asking for too much nor necessarily that your lover is uncaring or ungiving.

Even the best and most loving of couples are sometimes out of sync. This is natural. Just as a couple is sometimes not interested in the same kind of outing, they sometimes are not ready for the same intensity or duration of sex. At times like this a couple has to compromise, or go along with the wishes of one of the partners while the other partner will be "owed one." This is fine if it isn't the same partner who always does the compromising.

When you rarely get what you need

If you have ongoing concerns about not getting as much stimulation as you would like, talk to your partner about it. Ask for your partner's feelings about your needs. Perhaps he or she would be glad to give you more. Perhaps not. If so, talk together about ways that would make your sex life more gratifying for both of you. Some couples like to take turns—one time making love just the way she likes it, and the next just the way her partner likes it. Other couples prefer to find ways to simultaneously heighten each other's enjoyment. Whatever you do, don't downplay the importance of your needs.

When only one of you is in the mood

It is fine to give sexual pleasure to your partner when you are not in the mood to be sexually gratified yourself (and vice versa), just as it is fine to give your partner a back-rub when you don't want one. Fine, that is, with one proviso: that you want to be giving in this way. Part of loving is caring about your partner's pleasure and happiness. However, it is not loving to do something out of fear of the other's anger, disapproval, or withdrawal. Remember to say "yes" when you mean "yes," and "no" when you mean "no."

When you don't have an orgasm

Some women feel guilty or inadequate when they do not have an orgasm. Men, for whom orgasm is characteristically the be-all and end-all of sex, understandably are usually eager for their partners to be gratified in the same way. Many men do not understand that a woman may, on occasion, very much enjoy a sexual encounter even without a climax.

Some women, when they do not climax, hesitate to admit this for fear of disappointing their partner, or because they don't want their partner to feel inadequate as a lover, or because they don't want to feel increased pressure to produce an orgasm the next time. If this is familiar, let yourself know that your orgasm is for only one person in the whole world—and that's you. If you had one and enjoyed it, great! If you didn't, but still had a good sexual encounter—that's great, too! If you weren't able to come this time, you know there will be better times. If you have never had an orgasm, try one of the books recommended in the Suggested Readings, or consult a sex therapist. Whatever you do, don't belittle or blame yourself.

Sharing fantasies

Beyond communicating with your partner about how you like lovemaking to be introduced and the kind of touching you find exciting and satisfying, a very special and exciting way a couple can communicate is by sharing fantasies. Earlier we saw how fantasies can heighten your pleasure by keeping away distracting and upsetting thoughts. They're also a great way to spice up your love life.

Most couples, even those that have been together for many years, have never discussed their sexual fantasies with one another because they are too ashamed and embarrassed, and don't want to risk the other's aversion. In not divulging fantasies, they have been depriving themselves of a superb way to make their love-making more exciting.

A good way to introduce the sharing of fantasies is by reading other people's fantasies and talking with your partner about which ones each of you liked. Nancy Friday's books are a good place to start. In addition to her two collections of women's fantasies recommended previously in this chapter, *My Secret Garden* and *Forbidden Flowers,* she also has a collection of men's sexual fantasies called *Men in Love* (see Suggested Readings). You and your partner need not be turned on by the same kind of scenarios for the two of you to use fantasy to add to your passion. As long as each of you wants to turn on and gratify the other, differences can be worked out. Watching adult movies together can also be a good way to start to talk about fantasy, but keep in mind that most of these movies are geared to men and may therefore not be like your real fantasies.

Some of you may not wish to incorporate your fantasies into your love life. If so, that's fine and important to acknowledge. Real intimacy is based on being honest about what you feel and want. When you can know, ask for, and accept what you need when making love, then you are truly nurturing yourself; and the more you nurture yourself, the more you will have to give in return. Then you will be able to truly enjoy and pleasure yourself and your partner.

What if your partner is uncommunicative?

While talking about lovemaking and sharing fantasies may be viable for some women, others of you may not be able to have any kind of fruitful discussion with your partner about how to improve your lovemaking. Perhaps whenever you initiate such a discussion, your partner gets mad and stalks off. Or maybe your partner agrees to your requests, but never acts on them. You may have stated your needs and wishes countless times without your partner making any visible attempt to gratify them. If so, you have your work cut out for you. By now you may be so discouraged, you don't even want to bother asking, and are too seething with frustration and resentment to have a nonjudgmental discussion; but it is important not to give up. This is your sex life, and it will not get better unless you force the issue. Give yourself the support and encouragement you need to try again, and then give yourself credit for trying.

When you broach this very touchy and vulnerable subject with your partner, be careful to talk about your needs and desires in a way that is neither judgmental nor critical. Remember that if you attack, you are likely to be counterattacked or to elicit a withdrawal. But even if you are totally straightforward and empathic, your partner may still become defensively angry and attacking, or withdraw. People, and especially men, tend to be very sensitive about their sexual adequacy. If you get a negative reaction, don't give up. Initiate another conversation about your sexual needs soon. Be careful not to be angry and blaming. Keep it up until your partner cannot avoid talking to you.

When you do talk, discuss first what you like about your sex life together and your partner as a lover. Then go on to the things that can stand improvement. If you've never communicated your wishes before, acknowledge that, rather than blaming your partner for not having read your mind. If you've asked for what you like repeatedly and haven't gotten it, say you know there has to be a reason your partner hasn't responded, and perhaps the two of you can talk about what it is. If your partner will agree to anything just to shut you up, don't leave it at that. Make it plain that you want to open up communication rather than pressure him, or her, into meeting your needs. Also let your partner know that you want to meet his or her needs—and mean it! If all your attempts at discussion deteriorate into fights or get nowhere, you may need some professional counseling to open up your communication.

A WORD ABOUT SEXUAL DYSFUNCTIONS

Some of you may have a sexual dysfunction or have a partner with a sexual dysfunction. Examples of dysfunctions in women are inhibited sexual desire (a consistent lack of desire for sex), fear and avoidance of sex, vaginismus (the involuntary clamping down of the vaginal muscles, making penetration painful or impossible), and the inability to have an orgasm either by herself and/or with proper stimulation by her partner. Dysfunctions in men include inhibited sexual desire, erectile dysfunction (the inability to attain and/or maintain an erection), premature ejaculation, and retarded ejaculation (difficulty in ejaculating at all, or only after prolonged stimulation). If either of you have a dysfunction, I urge you to get professional help.

Sex therapy, pioneered by Masters and Johnson and elaborated upon by Helen Singer Kaplan and others, has been generally effective in treating these dysfunctions with a combination of a behavioral and psychodynamic approach. There also have been important advances in medical treatment available for erectile dysfunction. Thirty years ago people with sexual problems often had no effective place to turn, but now they can choose from many sex therapy clinics, as well as private practitioners skilled in the treatment of sexual problems. Sex therapy is typically short-term and involves both partners. AASECT (American Association of Sex Educators, Counselors, and Therapists) has a list of certified sex therapists all over the country. Local sex therapy clinics can be located by consulting the yellow pages or calling the hospitals in your area. A list of sex therapists in your area is available from AASECT at 435 North Michigan Avenue, Suite 1717, Chicago,

Illinois 60611; please send them a self-addressed, stamped envelope.

Be aware, also, that sexual responsiveness and functioning can be impaired by certain medications, drugs, and alcohol. Alcohol may make you feel more sexual, but it actually decreases your physical arousal. It also suppresses the sex drive in people who drink frequently or who occasionally drink large amounts.[8]

If you have any questions about the effect of a medication or drug that you are taking on your sexual functioning, it is important to discuss this with your doctor.

SUMMING UP

In conclusion, for sex to be great a woman needs:

- **TO DESIRE IT.**
- **TO BE FREE, FOR THE MOMENT, OF NEGATIVE EMOTIONS LIKE ANGER, FEAR, MISTRUST, AND DEPRESSION.**
- **TO FEEL CONNECTED TO HER PARTNER.**
- **TO BE ABLE TO LET HERSELF GO WITH HER FEELINGS AND SENSATIONS, RATHER THAN TO BE SITTING BACK WATCHING, JUDGING, OR CRITICIZING HERSELF OR HER PARTNER.**
- **TO REALIZE, ASK FOR, AND GET THE KIND OF CARESSING AND TOUCHING THAT SHE NEEDS.**
- **TO INCORPORATE HER FANTASY LIFE IN A WAY THAT IS ACCEPTABLE TO HER AND HEIGHTENS HER ENJOYMENT.**
- **TO CARE ABOUT HER OWN AND HER PARTNER'S NEEDS AND DESIRES, AND TO WANT TO MEET THEM.**

When you nurture yourself sexually you compassionately accept and respect your sexual needs, thoughts, feelings, and desires and see them as valid and important. You encourage yourself to make your sex life what you want it to be by getting to know your sexual self better and sharing this knowledge with your partner, at the same time encouraging your partner to share his or her needs and desires with you. Throughout this process you stay in touch with your inner-child, supporting her as she takes risks, comforting her when she needs comfort, and giving her credit for all her efforts.

Be proud of yourself for trying to improve your sex life, and encourage yourself to keep trying. Don't expect big changes rapidly. With sex, as with everything else, change comes slowly and unevenly and requires consistent effort. Believe that you can make it better and you can!

Nurturing Yourself
at Work

*C*onsidering that so much of our time is spent at our jobs, it is crucial that we esteem ourselves in the workplace, whether it be at a paying job or for unpaid work in the home. However, this is often not easy to do. We face special problems in valuing ourselves at work due to both external and internal obstacles that bear specifically on us as women.

EXTERNAL OBSTACLES TO WOMEN'S ABILITY TO ESTEEM THEMSELVES AT WORK

External forces that obstruct our ability to value ourselves at work include discrimination in the form of unequal opportunities for well-paid and prestigious employment and advancement; being penalized for taking time off to bear children, raise them, or take care of them when they're sick; sexual harassment; stereotypical ways of viewing women and women's work that hinder recognition, advancement, and respect; and not being accepted and supported by male peers. While not all women have to contend with these barriers at their jobs, many women do.

According to the latest figures available from the Census

Bureau[9] for full-time, year-round workers, the mean annual income for men is $35,076, with men's medium income being $28,979. Women, on the other hand, have a mean income of $23,392, and a medium income of $20,591. This means that half of all full-time working women in the United States earn $23,392 a year or less! These figures are even lower for women of color. While white women have a mean income of $23,722, black women have a mean income of $20,719, and Hispanic women have a mean income of $18,542. No wonder over nineteen and a quarter million women (15.2 percent of the female population) in the United States live below the poverty line of $6,800 for a single person.[10] Although black and Hispanic men are also paid less than their white counterparts (white men have a mean income of $36,178, while black and Hispanic men have mean incomes of $24,690 and $23,377, respectively), only Hispanic men make slightly less than the highest-paid group of women. This discrepancy also holds true between men and women who have had four years or more of college.[11] Here the mean income for men is $48,843 and for women is $31,044. This hierarchy, of course, is based on sex-role stereotyping and discrimination, not on women's inherent worth.

Lack of equal access to jobs that provide substantial income, prestige, and respect makes it harder for women to esteem ourselves because, as Sanford and Donovan point out in *Women and Self-Esteem*, our society embraces the myth of meritocracy,

. . . which holds that if a person is hardworking, bright and industrious she'll ultimately be rewarded with success. Conversely, it says that if a person doesn't succeed, it is because she deserves to fail. This myth is particularly damaging to women because of the extent to which discrimination against women due to race, age, ethnicity, and physical disabilities remains rampant in the American work force. Sadly, because of the myth of meritocracy some women are unable to perceive discrimination. If they are treated unfairly, they simply assume they must be at fault."[12]

The myth of meritocracy makes a woman think that if she is not getting the "three Rs"—recognition, respect, and rewards—there must be something wrong with her.

Women who work at home as unpaid homemakers and mothers have special difficulty esteeming themselves as workers because they are given so little status and recognition by society. Despite occasional paeans to mother as the "self-sacrificing enabler," the reality is that society views women who are homemakers as unemployed. It is difficult for a woman to value her work when she is told that she "isn't doing anything" and is "lucky that she doesn't have to really work." Even though the reality may be that she is busy from morning till night with little or no time for herself, she may still view herself as "not doing much" and have trouble seeing herself as a valuable worker. Consider Eileen.

At thirty-three, with a masters in occupational therapy, Eileen has worked at home as a mother and homemaker since her children, ages six and two, were born. Eileen likes and values being home with her children, but at the same time she feels a loss of prestige and respect. At parties when strangers ask her what she does, she feels defensive about being a homemaker. When an extra task arises at home, Eileen hesitates to impose it on her husband, thinking that because she works at home she isn't working as hard as he is. In hesitating, Eileen is accepting society's view that being a housewife and mother is not really working. In the face of our culture's denial of her and other women's labor and contribution, Eileen, like many homemakers, has difficulty authenticating her work to herself and to others.

Sexual harassment, the extent of which is just being realized in the wake of Anita Hill's charges against Clarence Thomas, is another hindrance to women esteeming themselves at work. A 1987 survey by the Merit Systems Protection Board determined that 42 percent of women working for the federal government had experienced some kind of sexual harassment.[13] A 1988 study by *Working Woman* magazine of Fortune 500 companies revealed that almost 90 percent of these companies had received complaints of sexual harassment, more than a third have been sued, and almost a quarter have been sued repeatedly.[14] These numbers likely underestimate the scope of the problem because, as in Anita Hill's case, sexual harassment, like rape, is often not reported.

Some women are denied jobs or promotions for refusing to "put out," while others are harassed by unwelcome and degrading sexual "jokes," comments, and touching. Such harassment, which treats women as objects, can lessen a woman's ability to esteem herself. Consider Sylvia:

Sylvia, a highly intelligent and hard-working college chemistry teacher, was also blond and extremely attractive. Despite her excellent qualifications and teaching performance, the members of her department—who were all male—fixated on her appearance. They responded to whatever she said with "jokes" that were full of sexual innuendo. When she objected to their remarks, she was called a "bad sport." No matter how professional, assertive, and competent her presentation of herself, her co-workers kept trying to put her into the role of "blond bombshell" and ignored her professional input. This sexual stereotyping and harassment not only was a constant irritant, but it wore away at her self-esteem. Despite her anger at her colleagues for not taking her seriously, she began to wonder if she was doing something wrong, or didn't know how to handle herself, or had chosen the wrong profession.

A woman who has external forces undermining her sense of self-worth at work finds it difficult to respect herself for the work that she is doing when those around her do not. However, she can weather the situation with her self-esteem intact by realizing that her difficulties are the result of factors other than her own inadequacy, and by constantly reinforcing herself.

Gwen, a graphic artist, worked in a small design studio where she got little credit for her excellent work. Nonetheless, she knew just how good her work was and derived satisfaction from its creative and challenging nature. Her self-esteem as an artist remained high, even in the face of scant external recognition and modest pay. After a while her positive regard for herself and her abilities led her to leave this job and take another where she was appropriately recognized and rewarded.

INTERNAL PROCESSES THAT UNDERMINE WOMEN'S SELF-ESTEEM AT WORK

It is unusual for a woman to be so free of inner insecurities that she can, like Gwen, deal with outside forces battering her self-esteem without beginning to doubt herself. Most of us have a "Swiss cheese" ability to esteem ourselves; that is, our self-esteem is solid and continuous in some areas of our self-concept, and full of holes in other areas. Some women are convinced of their competence to deal with the nuts and bolts of their work, but doubt their ability to deal effectively with people. Others feel confident of their people skills, but think they aren't technical enough, or creative enough. We can feel insecure about almost any or all aspects of our jobs, and the more insecure we feel, the more likely we are to blame ourselves for whatever is wrong. By doing so we are playing into the outside forces that are working to undermine and diminish our self-esteem. This is a very common occurrence.

Brenda, a fifty-four-year-old divorced woman with two grown daughters, is one example of how a woman's insecurities feed into discrimination in undermining her self-esteem at work. After running her own small store for many years, Brenda was forced out of business by the skyrocketing cost of rent. Capable, vivacious, and outspoken, but underneath filled with insecurities, she got a job as a buyer in a small company where she was underpaid and often ignored by her two chauvinistic bosses, despite her impressive job performance. Although she quickly learned that her bosses had a history of being condescending to women and difficult to work for, Brenda kept blaming herself for the poor relationships she had with them and for her lack of advancement. She felt that she had to be deficient, or lacking, or offensive to receive such poor treatment.

Marie entered the work force in her mid-forties because her family needed the money. She worked as a waitress in a coffee shop that was largely patronized by businessmen. When calm, Marie was a friendly and efficient waitress. When flustered, she would sometimes mix up orders and forget things. Most of her customers were friendly and pleasant, but some of them spoke harshly and critically to her. These weren't mean men, but they seemed to feel they had a right to order a woman around. Marie resented it, but she was also used to being in a subservient position. She thought that maybe these customers were right—that she wasn't good enough at her job, or deserving of respect. The more she blamed herself, the more nervous and flustered she became, and the more mistakes she made. The more mistakes she made, the nastier these customers became. She started to feel so bad about herself that she wanted to quit her job, but couldn't afford to, and felt stuck and miserable.

Even without being hindered by external discriminatory forces, some of us are buffeted by internal assaults on our self-esteem at work. We criticize and disparage ourselves out of an internalized sense of inadequacy that makes it difficult for us to recognize and give ourselves credit for our strengths and achievement, impedes us from taking in and integrating the praise we get from bosses and co-workers, and causes us to view ourselves as imposters. Men, too, can and do suffer from feelings of inadequacy; however, women are more prone to feeling inferior because of having internalized society's view of us as being less capable than men.

Debra is a thirty-year-old investment banker who is struggling to believe in herself. In the year she has been at her present position, she has won high praise from all the bank officers. Still, she constantly doubts herself and blames herself whenever anything goes wrong. On the surface she is able to recognize her strengths and achievements, but on the inside she lives in fear of being found wanting. Despite her achievements, she feels like an imposter and dreads being "found out."

Debra, like all women contending with inner assaults on their self-esteem, is struggling with feelings of inadequacy that she has carried with her for a long time. For most of her life her inner-critic has been telling her that something is wrong with her. This message started in childhood when Debra tried to make sense of her parents' emotional unavailability by reasoning that it must be because she wasn't enough for them. As she grew into womanhood, societal messages about women being passive, dependent, emotional, and needy, and men being strong, assertive, dominant, effective, and independent blended into her self-image. Notwithstanding her feminist outlook, inside she doubts her own ability and sufficiency. She is able to take only limited comfort in her achievements because her inner-critic continues to tell her that she is an imposter and will be found out. She is driven to overachieve in a vain attempt to impress and silence her inner-critic; however, her inner-critic continues to harp on her failings while giving only passing notice to her successes.

The kind of inner insecurity that Debra as well as Brenda, Sylvia, and Marie are struggling with is common in women. It stems, as we have seen, from familial and other experiences that leave a woman feeling that she is not good enough, combined with societal messages that she's a "supporting player," while men are the stars, and that her value and worth lies in being able to please others.

When you need to please others too much

The tremendous focus that women's socialization places on pleasing others is problematic throughout women's lives. This problem has recently received a lot of well-deserved attention under the label of "co-dependency," which can be described as getting one's good feelings about oneself not from within but from doing for others. It is no accident that most co-dependents are women: society teaches us to get our satisfaction by taking care of and pleasing others, while putting ourselves last. This overemphasis on pleasing others is a particular handicap on the job, where it can undermine a woman's ability to assert herself and act competitively, and renders her incapable of feeling pleased with herself without constant infusions of praise.

Not all women, of course, feel inadequate or are overfocused on receiving praise, but many of us are. Generally the less acceptance, recognition, respect, and rewards a woman has received in her life, the more likely she is to feel inadequate and dependent on outside reinforcement to shore up her sense of being a valuable person. However, even the most nurturing of childhoods can't safeproof us from having feelings of inadequacy. From early childhood we receive praise for being quiet, obedient, friendly, helpful, giving, modest, and, most of all, pretty. The media generally depict women as glamorous appendages to men. None of this is geared towards making a woman feel good about herself just the way she is or towards helping her to develop the kinds of mastery skills she needs to compete in the work force, where assertiveness and independence are usually necessary traits for success.

What role does being attractive play on the job?

The emphasis in our culture on women's value being tied to our ability to attract often poses problems for us on the job. We frequently are unsure how to handle our appearance and sexuality. Are these tools that we should subtly (or not so subtly) use to get ahead, as the media portrays? Or are they disadvantages that should be minimized and ignored? Are they something that men are going to use against us to either manipulate us or put us down? Many of us find ourselves walking a tightrope between trying to appear mildly responsive to sexual jokes and vibes (lest we be perceived as cold, strident, or "bitchy") and trying to remain businesslike (lest we not be taken seriously).

Why is my life not like Clair Huxtable's?

Another problem faced by women who work outside the home in trying to affirm our own worth is measuring ourselves against the unrealistic media picture of what our lives should be like. The TV image of a working woman is of an attractive, slim, beautifully dressed woman who is able to raise near-perfect children, have a high-powered job, keep her house immaculate, have plenty of time for family sharing and activities, and look gorgeous all at the same time. Women who work outside the home know just how far from their reality this image is. The majority of working women work out of economic necessity and many are single, divorced, widowed, aged, or childless and have far from high-powered jobs. Those who are raising children often find themselves trying to be all things to all people, and coming up short everywhere. Many of us feel deficient for not being able to live up to this idealized version of a working woman. (A rare and welcome alternative to the professional superwoman/supermom is Roseanne. Blue-collar, outspoken, forthright, vulnerable, unglamorous, imperfect, but doing her best as a person and as a mother, she is like a breath of fresh air.)

Women who are homemakers may also feel insufficient if they compare themselves to the superwoman image. After all, here's this working mom on TV who regularly has moving encounters with her children that teach a lesson and promote growth. We, on the other hand, may find our attempts to guide our children to be much less satisfying, not to mention less entertaining, and our problems don't get solved within a half hour, if at all. It's easy, in comparison, to feel inadequate.

NURTURING YOURSELF AT WORK

In the face of the many factors that can undermine women's self-esteem at work—such as discrimination, sexual harassment, gender-role stereotyping, and unrealistic images and expectations—it is particularly important that we affirm ourselves on the job. Rather than sabotaging our self-esteem by believing that we are at fault for whatever is wrong, we need to champion and CARESS ourselves.

If you feel inadequate at work, or are driven to keep achieving more and more to prove your worth and to avoid being found lacking, *talk back to your inner-critic.* She is the one who is making you feel that you don't measure up. We feel inadequate only when we tell ourselves that we **should** be doing better than we are, and that there is something wrong with us for not achieving more. Don't let her get away with it.

When you allow your inner-critic to berate you, you are doubling your problems. Then you have to both find a way to manage your work situation and to deal with your feelings of inadequacy and discouragement. The more you feel inferior and despondent, the harder it is to think clearly and creatively. To counteract your sense of inadequacy, you need to nurture yourself by replacing your inner-critic with your inner-caretaker and by putting your locus of power and self-affirmation within yourself.

Nurturing yourself at work, like nurturing yourself anywhere, entails CARESSing yourself. It means recognizing and valuing your strengths, and it means acknowledging your problem areas without berating yourself. When you are having difficulties at work, when you don't know how to successfully complete a task, or find the solution to a problem, or deal with a troublesome interpersonal conflict, or stand doing boring repetitive work, and you are feeling frustrated and worried, what you need more than anything else is support and encouragement.

For instance, say you're a new manager and have to fire someone. You may blame yourself, thinking that if you were a good supervisor, you could have helped this worker to perform satisfactorily, so take his continued incompetence as proof of your inadequacy as a manager. If at this point your boss came by and shared having had similar feelings at dismissing employees, and confirmed that this worker has been a problem to previous managers, likely you would feel much better.

Or maybe you're a secretary in a large firm, and you're having trouble performing under constant pressure, as you see your co-workers doing. You may feel inadequate and on the verge of quitting. Think how much better you would feel if your co-workers told you that they all find the pressure difficult, and it causes them to make mistakes, too.

But not everyone has a boss or co-workers who are supportive. A critical boss might choose to say that being able to fire people is the hallmark of a good manager and there's no reason to have difficulty with it, or competitive co-workers might say that keeping forms and procedures straight is easy and you're just slow.

Faced with such criticism, the way to hold on to your sense of worth, value, competence, and adequacy is to banish your inner-critic and call out your inner-caretaker. Ask her to be at your side supporting you and giving you the compassion, respect, and encouragement you so need and desire. Tell yourself that you are competent, capable, and valuable, and that even the most talented people feel perplexed, worried, overwhelmed, or scared some of the time. Even the best and brightest make major mistakes, don't know how to handle something, need advice from others, and can struggle a long time with something before finding a solution. Tell yourself that the opposite of "inadequate" is "adequate," and not "perfect."

When you nurture yourself, you replace the search for respect, appreciation, and approval from the outside with being able to respect, appreciate, and approve of yourself. It's not that outside approbation and rewards aren't important—they are very important—but they don't take the place of self-validation. To maintain high self-esteem, it is important to stop putting your sense of self-worth into others' hands, and instead to keep it centered within yourself.

When Debra, Brenda, Marie, Sylvia, and Eileen learned to nurture themselves, their esteem as workers went up and they then could react to criticism and disparagement as just one piece of the feedback they got and deal with it appropriately. When Debra, the investment banker, learned to silence her inner-critic, she no longer lived in fear of her boss's disapproval. As Brenda, the buyer, became more centered in herself she was able to move on to a job where she was appreciated. When Marie, the waitress, learned to validate herself, she no longer became flustered and nervous when confronted with bossy, critical customers. In fact, she developed a sense of pride in being able to hang on to her self-worth in the face of their attacks. As Sylvia, the woman who was being sexually harassed, stopped blaming herself, she was able to seek other ways to deal with the harassment. When Eileen, the homemaker, learned to see her work at home as being valuable and essential, she no longer felt apologetic or self-abasing. Now these women could take in and glow with the good feeling of being praised, without making their whole sense of adequacy based on continued infusions of such praise.

You, too, can learn how to replace the search for outside validation on the job with being able to validate yourself. You have already learned a great deal about how to do this by following the steps offered earlier. Now let's see how to apply the same process to validating yourself at work.

Recognize and affirm your strengths

The first step in being able to validate yourself at work is to be able to truly take credit for your strengths and accomplishments. This is the process you went through in Step One when you made a list of all the things you like about yourself, owned them as being true of you, and began to read them twice daily. Now do this specifically for your job. **Write down all the things you do well at work, no matter how insignificant they may seem to you.**

Generally there are four areas of functioning at work:

1. The task itself: selling, creating, making or fixing something, providing a service, and so on.
2. Backup to the task: writing reports, making presentations, collecting fees, etc.
3. Relationships with clients/customers.
4. Relationships with others at your job: colleagues, boss, administrators, supervisors.

Consider each of these areas and write down your strengths in each of them. For instance, if you are a teacher, the task is providing information to and fostering the intellectual and social growth of your students. Backup is correcting work, filling out forms, ordering supplies, etc. Relationships with clients include parents and community visitors, as well as students. Job relationships include other teachers, the principal and other administrators, and aides. Look at your strengths in each of these areas and write them down. Make this list of your strengths as long and detailed as possible and use "I" to start each item. Instead of "I teach well," be more specific: "I enliven discussions," "I am clear and precise in my presentations," "I am well prepared," "I voluntarily stay after school and help students," and so on. When your list is as long as you can possibly make it, ask colleagues or others familiar with your work to add to your list.

Keep this list with you at work and read it slowly three times a day: when you arrive, just after lunch, and right before leaving. Before reading your strengths, take three slow deep breaths, then read each of your work assets. Take your time and let yourself absorb and own every one of your abilities. During the course of your day, make it a point to notice more of your strengths and add them to your list.

The next step after owning your strengths is to respect yourself for having them. So often women undermine themselves by taking their strengths for granted and focusing on their shortcomings. Don't do this to yourself. Let yourself know that each of your strengths was not something that magically appeared, but something that you worked on developing. Take pride in them and in yourself!

Dealing with your insecurities at work

After you have started to integrate your work strengths, you are then ready to form a plan for dealing with situations on the job that trigger your feelings of inadequacy. Typically feelings of inferiority are evoked by work events that you believe prove you are deficient or incapable in ways that you already believed to be true. For instance, if you think that you aren't assertive enough when you are not called upon in a meeting, you may interpret this as proof that people see you as easy to pass over because you're such a mouse. This is most likely an erroneous interpretation. However, even if it is accurate, that doesn't make you inadequate—it only means that you have defined an area in which you can work towards change.

A few common areas of insecurity, and common triggers of these insecurities include:

Triggers	Insecurities
Making a mistake, or being asked to redo a task.	Thinking you aren't bright or don't know enough.
Having trouble figuring something out, or not having an idea of yours accepted.	Thinking you are not skillful or creative.
Not being greeted warmly or smiled at.	Thinking you are not likable or personable.
Not getting as big a response or reward as a colleague.	Thinking you are too passive and not assertive enough.

Being glared at.	Thinking you are too aggressive and outspoken.
Being ignored.	Thinking you are not attractive.
Having trouble with a coworker/boss/employee.	Thinking you are too or not sufficiently feminine.
Not being included in something.	Thinking you are not able to fit in or don't know how to handle people.
Being yelled at.	Thinking you are too emotional.

An interesting thing about these two categories is that almost any event in the "Triggers" column can evoke any of the insecurities in the second column. For instance, if you make a mistake, you might think it is because you don't know enough, aren't creative, are too feminine, not aggressive enough, and so on. Similarly, if you are not rewarded as much as a colleague, you could take this as proof that you don't know enough, aren't skillful or creative, are too passive, not sufficiently personable, or too emotional. This is one of the difficult and misleading things about insecurities:

> If you are insecure about something, almost any negative happening can be *interpreted* by you as proof that you are deficient in this way.

To make matters worse, it is also true, as we saw earlier, that if you are insecure positive feedback and successes can be interpreted by you not as proof of your adequacy and worth, but as a sign that you have fooled people. This is failure guideline #2: "If people praise me, it's because they've been taken in by my 'surface' virtues (hard work, talent, pleasant manner, looks, etc.). When they get to know me better they will change their opinion." The way out of this trap is to stop making these kinds of fallacious connections. **Look at the above inventory of inse-curities, and put a check mark next to those you have. Then add any other vulnerable spots you may have.** (I listed only a few of the most common: there are many, many more.) Be aware that these are your sore points—the areas that you most need help with and in which you least need to be chastised. Next look at the list of triggers. Consider which of these or other triggers you have experienced. Did you react to them in a way that in-creased your sense of inadequacy? If so, decide to work on reacting differently. Commit yourself to using your energy to help yourself. Think about how you could interpret and respond to these triggers in a self-affirming way.

As an example, let's say that you are denied a promotion. Rather than take this as proof of your inadequacy, let yourself realize that even being considered is to your credit, and that there may be factors beyond your control that influenced your not being chosen. If something is lacking in your performance, take this as an indication of an area in which you can grow, rather than as a sign of your deficiency. Help yourself to develop the additional skills you need, rather than castigate yourself for not being better.

Perhaps something seemingly trivial has stirred up your sense of inadequacy, as is frequently the case, such as your boss not returning your "good morning" greeting. Can you nurture your-self, rather than take this as proof of your not being worthy? Be aware that there may be many reasons that have nothing to do with you that could have made your boss ignore you. Perhaps she or he was lost in thought and didn't hear you, or feels guilty about overloading you with work so wants to avoid you, or is eager to make a phone call so just rushed by. Why should any of this make you feel bad about yourself? Even if your boss didn't respond because he or she doesn't like you, does this really make you less worthy? Maybe you remind your boss of a disliked mother, wife, daughter, or sister. Or perhaps your boss doesn't like women who are assertive . . . or reticent. None of this means that there is something wrong with you. Look at yourself through the eyes of your inner-caretaker and affirm yourself!

∙ ∙ ∙

Sometimes when my work isn't progressing as well as I wish, I start to feel inadequate: such as when I've been working with a couple who leave my office after a session more angry and defensive than they were coming in, or when a client remains caught up in the same kind of conflict that we have worked on myriad times, or when I become aware of a psychodynamic factor that I had previously missed. At times like these my inner-critic is quick to jump in. She tells me that, if I were good enough, the couple would be opening up to each other more, or my client would have worked through this conflict already, or I wouldn't have missed that dynamic. The more I listen to my inner-critic, the more upset and discouraged I become. This discouragement and upset, when left unchecked, further diminishes my effectiveness, since it is difficult to be tuned in to other people and stay with their process if I need them to get better in order to validate my worth.

I have learned that when I start to feel inadequate, the sooner I summon up my inner-caretaker the better. I need her to tell me that I do good work and have seen much progress in my clients, and to remind me that it is not part of my job description to be omnipotent and omniscient. When I can connect with and believe in my own competence, I am then free to consider how to improve my work without abusing myself for my deficiencies.

Accepting your mistakes

An important part of learning to nurture yourself at work is developing a positive attitude towards the mistakes you make. To do so it is crucial that you first believe that it is not only natural but *inevitable* that you will make mistakes. You are not perfect and will not perform your job perfectly. Accept that. It's an unavoidable part of the human condition. When you do make a mistake, rather than denigrating yourself, accept it as normal and natural. As we have seen, the less you criticize and attack yourself, the more you will free up your energy to creatively problem-solve.

It is also a waste of your time and energy to make up excuses or look for someone else to unfairly blame. Self-justification or scapegoating others when we make an error stems from not being able to tolerate the feelings of badness, inadequacy, and guilt that being "wrong" or "at fault" produce in us, so we look to blame others. This is a dead-end process that leaves us trapped in an either/or approach to ourselves—either we're good or bad, worthy or unworthy—rather that accepting ourselves as valuable, though fallible, human beings.

You can best help yourself when you make an error by non-judgmentally accepting responsibility, and then moving quickly to rectify it. Now is the time for your inner-caretaker to tell you that it's all right to make mistakes and that she still loves and respects you and is there for you; that she knows that you are upset and that she feels for what you are going through; that this mistake, however major, is just one piece of your work, and basically you are a good and competent worker.

Feelings that interfere with your work performance

It is common for people to have feelings that interfere with their work performance. While work can be boring, exhausting, tedious, repetitive, frustrating, perplexing, overwhelming, pressured, under-stimulating, too isolating, or too frenetic, it is more tolerable when the worker feels good about herself as a worker and is appreciated and supported by the people on her job. When she is not appreciated, supported, or rewarded by the people in her work environment, a worker usually feels some combination of anger, hurt, confusion, resentment, sadness, feelings of guilt, and inferiority.

If the lack of validation at work mirrors previous experiences, she is even more likely to be upset or angry at the same time that she blames herself and feels inadequate. For instance, a woman who was criticized as a child for being too slow may react to a similar complaint by a colleague from a well of resentment, even as she over-apologizes for what she considers to be her deficiency. Or a woman who was not popular as a teenager may respond to not being chosen for a particular assignment by feeling undesirable and unworthy.

If you have old unresolved feelings that undermine your job performance, it is essential to be in touch with them and to consider how you want to handle them, rather than acting them out in nonproductive or counterproductive ways such as: starting a fight, refusing to speak up, neglecting your responsibilities or carrying them out while sulking and pouting, or by calling in sick.

Uncover your feelings by talking with your inner-child and listening to her with your heart. Once you understand what she is feeling and why, talk with her about what action would be most beneficial and satisfying. Sometimes it is best to speak up, and other times you are better off holding your own counsel.

Allison was asked by her colleague Frank to prepare part of a report. At the last minute Frank discovered that Allison had not covered a certain area. Allison apologized and explained that she was unfamiliar with the format he had requested and had not realized that more information was required. Frank blew up at her, insisted that Allison had omitted the information on purpose to get him in trouble, and refused to accept her explanation. Allison, who had previously had a good working relationship with Frank, was shocked and speechless. The more Frank blamed her, the more she questioned herself, making it impossible for her to think clearly or to deal with Frank. She was so upset she got no work done for the rest of the day.

That evening in her therapy session Allison felt all confused. She was particularly vulnerable to being accused of competitive back-stabbing because, while growing up, she had often been similarly falsely accused by her domineering brother whenever she tried to stand up for herself. Her inner-child needed Allison to believe in her and support her, but her inner-critic wondered whether her brother and Frank weren't right—maybe she was being unknowingly vindictive. In our session she had an inner dialogue that led her to understand her inner-child's feelings of being bullied and wronged, and was able to move from colluding in the false accusations to compassionately standing by her inner-child, and her anxiety diminished. The next day Allison was able to calmly speak to Frank without being either defensive or attacking. Frank ended up apologizing for having overreacted, and the incident was over for both of them.

Kendra's co-worker Leona had a slightly superior air, frequently gave Kendra unsolicited advice, and took over whenever they had a joint project to prepare. After a while Kendra found herself just passively letting Leona take the lead, rather than fighting with her, and then would feel upset with and down on herself.

I encouraged Kendra, rather than blaming her inner-child, to ask her what made it so hard to assert herself. Her inner-child said how scared she had been by the constant arguing that had gone on between her parents, and that she wanted to avoid an argument at any price. Kendra listened empathically to her inner-child's fears, and then expressed her own strong need for them to stand up together, and promised to support and protect her inner-child in the process. After several nurturing dialogues, her inner-child felt safe enough to allow Kendra to become more assertive with Leona, with the result that Kendra insisted on sharing the leadership of joint projects. As Kendra continued to CARESS herself, and to therefore feel more inner security, Kendra also became less intimidated by Leona's superior attitude.

Both Allison and Kendra were able to recognize and deal with their feelings, rather than acting them out. These incidents may sound simple or trivial, but they are exactly the kinds of everyday happenings that impede functioning at work, undermine self-esteem, and often lead to long-standing hostilities. By giving their inner-children the Compassion, Acceptance, Respect, Encouragement, Support, and Stroking that they needed, these women helped themselves to raise their self-esteem while dealing well with a troubling work situation.

Dealing with your boss

Many of us have special difficulty maintaining our self-esteem when we get negative responses from our bosses. Ideally bosses are supposed to be there to guide and help, giving constructive criticism, teaching workers what they need to learn, fairly evaluating and rewarding. However, this is often not the case. As we all know, bosses are only human and are filled with human failings. They can be arbitrary, temperamental, cold, explosive, inconsistent, self-centered, prejudiced, chauvinistic, egotistic, or highly critical and perfectionistic. In dealing with a difficult boss, we commonly feel anger, hurt, confusion, resentment, longing, and a sense of inadequacy.

Women with a boss who is unfair, overdemanding, and hard to please, or who gives out approval and rewards in an inconsistent manner, typically alternate between anger at their boss and feeling bad about themselves. Our anger would seem to indicate that we blame our boss, and we do; but commonly deep down we blame ourselves more. We believe that somehow we should be able to turn this difficult boss into an approving authority figure. An example is Diane, the woman whose process we followed in chapters 4, 5, 6, and 8.

Diane's work situation, when she entered treatment, where her boss pounced upon her mistakes, ignored her many achievements, and denied her an appropriate title and salary while overloading her with responsibilities, mirrored her childhood experience of being both burdened and devalued by her alcoholic father. Her response at work was to feel furious at her boss, Tom, but also to feel inadequate. She reasoned that there had to be something wrong with her that made her not able to get the approval and rewards she wanted from Tom. Although in her dealings with Tom, she acted assertively (in fact, it was most likely her refusal to fawn over him that annoyed him), underneath she felt like a nothing.

Many women, like Diane, despite intellectual recognition of their boss's problems, in their guts blame themselves and feel unworthy. The more they blame themselves, the worse they feel, and the more stuck they become in a bad situation, desperately wanting recognition and respect from a person who will never give it to them. Their friends may tell them to not take their boss's criticisms to heart or to try and get out of there, but they often remain mired for extended periods of time, vainly trying to get approval where it will not be forthcoming. They are caught up in a power struggle, and as we saw earlier,

There is no winning in a power struggle.

Power struggles arise when we put the source of our power in another person (or group of people) rather than in ourselves. A person locked in a power struggle is essentially saying, "I can't feel good, adequate, and competent unless you tell me that I am." Do you want to bestow on any other person, let alone on your hypercritical, ungiving boss, this power over you? Just as un-helpful, do you want to decide your worth by a majority vote of your co-workers? If so, you are giving up control over your own self-esteem. I urge you not to do so. Take back your sense of worth and center it in yourself!

I don't mean that you should shrug off and disregard all feedback. On the contrary, feedback can be very helpful in the process of self-recognition and growth. However, it is essential to deal with feedback, and especially critical feedback, from a position of being grounded within yourself. If the feedback seems valid to you, it gives you a direction to work on change. If not, you need to have the power to reject it, without having to convince the person who criticized you that he or she is wrong.

If you need to convince another person that you are right before you can feel OK about yourself, you have temporarily lost control of yourself. You wouldn't want your daughter to believe that she was stupid, clumsy, or incompetent because her teacher called her these things. Nor would you want her belief that she is smart, poised, and capable to hinge on whether she can convince her critical teacher that she possesses these qualities. Then why do this to yourself?

To get out of a power struggle where you are enraged with your boss at the same time that you are hell-bent on gaining your boss's respect and recognition, you need to replace your focus on getting validation from your boss with being able to validate yourself. I call this learning to butter yourself up.

Buttering yourself up

When you focus on buttering yourself up, you are instantly changing your focus from outer-directed to inner-directed. **Start this process by repeating to yourself twenty times aloud:**

I AM MY OWN BOSS. I AM IN CHARGE OF MYSELF,
AND I WANT MY OWN APPROVAL.

As you say these words, put your feelings into them. Mean it! Don't worry if it seems forced or artificial at first. With time and repetition this affirmation will sink in.

Next give yourself the approval that you so want. Summon your inner-caretaker and tell yourself all the things that you value and esteem about yourself as a worker and as a person. Use your WHAT I LIKE ABOUT MYSELF list from Step One and your STRENGTHS AT WORK inventory. You can talk to yourself in your head, or if you prefer you can do it out loud or in writing. Regardless of your method, **CARESS yourself by being Compassionate, Accepting, Respectful, Encouraging,**

Supportive, and Stroking. Go into specific detail and be sure to give yourself credit for all your efforts, even something as simple as coming to work when you don't feel like it. As you talk to yourself in this way, imagine that you are a vessel of some kind and that your inner-caretaker is filling this vessel that is you with good feelings about yourself. See yourself taking in these good feelings, holding on to them, and getting filled up. Let yourself know that you can hold on to these feelings. Also let yourself know that if they do seep away, you have an endless supply of love and respect to pour back into yourself.

If there are things about your performance at work that interfere with your ability to feel good about yourself as a worker, follow the process you went through in Step Four. Consider which of your concerns are valid, and which stem from having perfectionistic, unrealistic expectations of yourself or from inaccurate self-appraisals. Then turn your valid concerns into directions for change. Set your goals and then nurture yourself as you work towards them. Give yourself lots of credit. CARESS yourself.

But, you may be wondering, what if I'm really no good at my job, or unable to deal effectively with people at work? If I CARESS myself, aren't I just blinding myself to my faults? Absolutely not. When you CARESS yourself, you open yourself up to your inner-child and thereby become better able to help yourself. Perhaps you are not performing well at your job because you are distracted by personal problems, have a high level of performance anxiety, lack motivation, feel insecure, or are even unsuited to the work. Whatever the reason, increased self-esteem can only help.

The more you believe in yourself, the more likely you are to do a good job, or to switch to a more suitable position if that is practicable. As we have seen throughout this book, and as you have experienced going through the steps herein, enhanced self-esteem frees up positive energy for growth and development. It doesn't make practical problems disappear, but it does make it more likely that you will have the inner resources to find a solution to your problems. As you go through your daily work, remember the following:

WORKPLACE GUIDELINES FOR SELF-NURTURING:
1. RECOGNIZE AND RESPECT YOUR WORK STRENGTHS.
2. STOP ERRONEOUSLY INTERPRETING NEUTRAL AND NEGATIVE RESPONSES AS PROOF OF YOUR INADEQUACY.
3. DEAL WITH MISTAKES BY PROBLEM-SOLVING RATHER THAN BLAMING YOURSELF.
4. AVOID POWER STRUGGLES AND PUT YOUR LOCUS OF POWER WITHIN YOURSELF BY BUTTERING YOURSELF UP.
5. CARESS YOURSELF.

A FINAL WORD

Before you lay this book aside, stop and CARESS yourself. Give yourself the Compassion, Acceptance, Respect, Encouragement, Support, and Stroking that you, like all of us, need. Take credit for all that you have done, and all that you are. Remind yourself that unrealized goals are just that, goals—something that you can feel good about striving towards. Promise your inner-child that you will be with her always, maintaining empathic communication, and being on her side as her protective caretaker who cherishes, approves of, and loves her unconditionally. Then take in this CARESS and the sense of self-esteem that comes with it. Commit yourself to keep CARESSing yourself for the rest of your life.

Suggested Readings

Anxiety, Phobias, and Panic: (I suggest you read several of these, so you can choose the approach that suits you best.)

GOLDSTEIN, ALAN, *Overcoming Agoraphobia: Conquering Fear of the Outside World*. (New York: Viking Penguin, 1987). (A very helpful guide that combines behavior and exposure therapy with a psychological and familial approach in curing agoraphobia.)

NEUMAN, FREDRIC, *Fighting Fear: An Eight-Week Guide to Treating Your Own Phobias* (New York: Macmillan, 1985). (Though limited in scope, I have included it because it is a good exposition of exposure therapy.)

SEAGRAVE, ANN and COVINGTON, FAISON, *Free From Fears: New Help for Anxiety, Panic, and Agoraphobia* (New York: Poseidon Press, 1987). (A wonderful book written by two recovered agoraphobics who founded the Center for Help for Agoraphobia/Anxiety through New Growth Experiences (CHAANGE). They also have a tape/workbook program for home use.) Write or call: CHAANGE, 128 Country Club Drive, Chula Vista, CA, (619) 425-3992.

WEEKES, CLAIRE, *More Hope and Help For Your Nerves* (First published in Great Britain, 1984. New York: Bantam, 1987). (One of the first writers to guide sufferers with anxiety and agoraphobia, Dr. Weekes's books are short, helpful, and encouraging.) Also, see her other books: *Peace from Nervous Suffering* (New York: Hawthorn, 1972).
Simple, Effective Treatment of Agoraphobia (New York: Hawthorn, 1976).

WILSON, R. REID, *Don't Panic: Taking Control of Anxiety Attacks* (New York: Harper & Row, 1986). (A helpful book.)

Healing from Incest and Sexual Abuse:

BASS, ELLEN and DAVIS, LAURA, *The Courage to Heal: A Guide for Women Survivors of Child Sexual Abuse* (New York: Harper & Row, 1988). (This has already become a classic.)

DAVIS, LAURA, *Allies in Healing* (New York: Harper Perennial, 1991). (A helpful book written especially for partners of survivors.)

MALTZ, WENDY and HOLMAN, BEVERLY. *Incest and Sexuality: A Guide To Understanding and Healing* (Lexington, MA: Lexington Books, 1987). (A very informative book about the effects of incest on a woman, her relationships, and her sexuality.)

MALTZ, WENDY *The Sexual Healing Journey* (New York: Harper Collins, 1991). (An excellent book with lots of practical advice and suggestions about the process of healing sexually from sexual abuse. A must-read for survivors experiencing difficulties with sex.)

MILLER, ALICE, *Thou Shalt Not Be Aware: Society's Betrayal of the Child* (New York: New American Library, 1986). (A compelling book that refutes Oedipal theory and demonstrates that child abuse is real.) Also excellent is *For Your Own Good: Hidden Cruelty in Child Rearing*.

Becoming Orgasmic:

BARBACH, LONNIE, *For Yourself: The Fulfillment of Female Sexuality* (Garden City, New York: Anchor Press/Doubleday, 1976).

HIEMAN, JULIA and LoPICCOLO, JOSEPH, *Becoming Orgasmic: A Sexual Growth Program for Women* (Englewood Cliffs, N.J.: Prentice-Hall, 1988).

Sexual Communication and Fulfillment:

BARBACH, LONNIE and LEVINE, LINDA, *Shared Intimacies: Women's Sexual Experiences* (Garden City, N.Y.: Anchor Press/Doubleday, 1980). (Women talk about their sexual experiences.)

BARBACH, LONNIE, *For Each Other: Sharing Sexual Intimacy* (New York: New American Library, 1984).

COMFORT, ALEX, *The Joy of Sex: A Gourmet Guide to Love Making* (New York: Fireside, 1972). Also, *More Joy of Sex*.

LOULAN, JoANN, *Lesbian Sex* (San Francisco: Spinsters Book Co., 1984).
———, *Lesbian Passion* (San Francisco: Spinsters Book Co., 1987).

Fantasies:

BARBACH, LONNIE (ed), *Pleasures: Women Write Erotica* (Garden City, New York: Doubleday, 1984). (A collection of erotic experiences written by women writers.)

BARBACH, LONNIE (ed). *Erotic Interludes* (New York: Harper & Row, 1986). (A collection of erotic short stories written by women writers.)
FRIDAY, NANCY, *My Secret Garden: Women's Sexual Fantasies* (New York: Trident Press, 1973). (A collection of everyday women's sexual fantasies.)
———— *Forbidden Flowers: More Women's Sexual Fantasies* (New York: Pocket Books, 1975).
———— *Men in Love, Men's Sexual Fantasies: The Triumph of Love over Rage* (New York: Dell, 1980).
NIN, ANAIS, *Delta of Venus: Erotica* (New York: Pocket Books. First Pocket Book Printing, 1990).
———— *Little Birds: Erotica* (New York: Harcourt Brace Jovanovich, 1979).

General Interest:
LERNER, HARRIET GOLDHOR, *The Dance of Anger: A Woman's Guide to Courageous Acts of Change in Key Relationships* (New York: Harper & Row, 1989). (A terrific book that teaches the reader how to recognize her anger and use it constructively.)
———— *The Dance of Intimacy: A Woman's Guide to Courageous Acts of Change in Key Relationships* (New York: Harper & Row, 1989). (Another terrific book. Emphasizes the need to honor yourself as well as your relationship.)
ALICE MILLER, *The Drama of the Gifted Child: How Narcissistic Parents Form and Deform the Emotional Lives of Their Talented Children* (Originally published as *Prisoners of Childhood*. New York: Basic Books, 1981). (A wonderful book, full of wisdom and compassion.)
VIORST, JUDITH, *Necessary Losses: The Loves, Illusions, Dependencies and Impossible Expectations that All of Us Have to Give Up in Order to Grow* (New York: Fawcett Gold Medal, 1986). (A wonderful book that is relevant to any woman's life.)

Self-Esteem:
MILLER, JEAN BAKER, *Toward a New Psychology of Women* (Boston: Beacon Press, 1986). (An important and compelling exposition of how the socio-political system affects women.)
SANFORD, LINDA and DONOVAN, MARY ELLEN, *Women and Self-Esteem: Understanding and Improving the Way We Think and Feel about Ourselves* (New York: Penguin, 1985). (An excellent analysis of the socio-cultural, familial, theological, governmental, and economic factors that foster low self-esteem in women, with suggestions for personal growth.)

THOELE, SUE PATTON, *The Courage To Be Yourself: A Woman's Guide to Growing Beyond Emotional Dependence* (Berkeley, Conari Press, 1991).

Contacting Your Inner-Child:
CAPACCHIONE, LUCIA, *Recovery of Your Inner Child* (New York, Fireside, 1991).
TAYLOR, CATHRYN L., *The Inner Child Workbook: What to do with your past when it just won't go away* (Los Angeles: Jeremy P. Tarcher, 1991).
WHITFIELD, CHARLES L., *Healing the Child Within* (Deerfield Beach: Health Communications, 1987).

Depression:
BURNS, DAVID, *Feeling Good: The New Mood Therapy* (New York: William Morrow, 1980). (This is a cognitive approach with lots of exercises.)
BRAIKER, HARRIET B., *Getting Up When You're Feeling Down: A Woman's Guide to Overcoming and Preventing Depression* (New York: Pocket Books, 1988. Published by arrangement with G. P. Putnam's Sons). (A detailed program that directly addresses women's struggles with depression.)
DE ROSIS, HELEN and PELLEGRINO, VICTORIA Y., *The Book of Hope: How Women Can Overcome Depression* (New York: Macmillan, 1976). (A book that has given many depressed women new hope.)

Notes

1. Alexander Thomas and Stella Chess, *Temperament and Development* (New York, Brunner Mazel, 1977).

2. D. W. Winnicott, *The Maturational Processes and the Facilitating Environment* (London: The Hogarth Press and the Institute of Psycho-Analysis; New York: International Universities Press, 1965) pp. 145–46.

3. Ellen McGrath et al., *Women and Depression* (Washington, D.C.: American Psychological Association, 1990) p. xii.

4. S. Provence and R. C. Lipton, *Infants and Institutions: A Comparison of Their Development with Family-Reared Infants During the First Year of Life* (New York: International Universities Press, 1962) pp. 78–86 and 163–74.
   Rene Spitz, "Hospitalism," *The Psychoanalytic Study of the Child,* Vol. 1, (New York: International Universities Press, 1965) pp. 53–72.

5. McGrath et al., *Women and Depression* p. xii.

6. Studs Terkel, *Hard Times: An Oral History of the Great Depression* (New York: Pantheon Books, 1970).

7. David Burns, *Feeling Good: The New Mood Therapy* (New York: William Morrow, 1980) pp. 280–84.

8. Julia R. Heiman and Joseph LoPiccolo, *Becoming Orgasmic* (New York: Prentice Hall Press, 1988) pp. 162 and 226.

9. U.S. Bureau of the Census, Current Population Reports, Series P-60, No. 174, *Money Income of Households, Families, and Persons in the United States: 1990* (Washington, D.C.: U.S. Government Printing Office, August 1991), pp. 109 and 111.

10. U.S. Bureau of the Census, Current Population Reports, Series P-60, No. 175, *Poverty in the United States: 1990* (Washington, D.C.: U.S. Government Printing Office, 1991) p. 24.

11. U.S. Bureau of the Census, Current Population Reports, Series P-60, No. 174, *Money Income of Households, Families, and Persons in the United States: 1990* (Washington, D.C.: U.S. Government Printing Office, August 1991) pp. 157 and 159.

12. Linda Tschirhart Sanford and Mary Ellen Donovan, *Women and Self-Esteem: Understanding and Improving the Way We Think and Feel about Ourselves* (New York: Anchor/Doubleday, 1984) p. 211.

13. U.S. Merit Systems Protection Board, *Sexual Harassment in the Federal Governments: An Update, 1988* (Washington, D.C.: U.S. Government Printing Office, 1988) p. 11.

14. Ronni Sandroff, "Sexual Harassment in the Fortune 500," *Working Woman* (December 1988) p. 69.

Index

premenstrual syndrome (PMS), 201
procrastination, 19, 34, 243
professional counseling, 215–16,
   219, 244, 262
promotions, 39, 206, 207, 268, 280

rape, 34, 198, 244, 268
reactions of other people, interpreting, 97–98
reactive depression, 201–202
recognizing good points, 75–79
recognizing the real you, 85–105
recovery programs, 127
reflecting feelings back, 146–52
rejection, 20, 21, 36–37, 42, 53, 54,
   55, 67, 68, 89, 91, 93, 94, 177,
   181, 182, 208, 246
relationships, 41–42, 45–46, 76, 92,
   100, 138; and anxiety, 176–98;
   career, 91–92, 95, 114, 118,
   265–89; and depression, 199–
   217; and independence/depend-
   ence conflicts, 43–47; parent-
   child, 50–70, 83–84, 107–24,
   182–86; sexual, 237–64
relaxation techniques, 128, 178, 180,
   246–47
respect, 29, 31, 38–40, 91–92, 102,
   129, 145, 146, 182, 210; career,
   38–39, 265, 267, 268, 275; and
   raising children, 229–34
responsibility, 16; overassessing,
   202–203
restlessness, 170, 181
risk-taking, 43

sadness, 201
salaries, 39, 41, 203, 266
sarcasm, 87, 94
self-criticism(s), 19–21, 23, 24–28,
   50, 80–84; and depression, 200–
   217; evaluation of, 85–105; and
   failure cycle, 24–28; and influence
   of parents, 50–70, 107–18; letting
   go of, 111–20; list of, 81–82; and
   physical appearance, 98–104; and
   raising children, 218–36; recog-

nizing patterns of 80–84; and recognizing the real you, 85–105;
   and separation from negative role
   models, 121–24; and sex, 237–
   264; taught to us by others, 50–
   70, 106–24; and work, 265–89
self-esteem, 72–74; believing in
   yourself, 79; in difficult situations,
   173–289; empathic communication for, 141–72; letting go and
   liking yourself, 111–20; listening
   to your heart, 141–58; nurturing
   attitudes for, 28–31, 32–49, 125–
   172, 173–289; and parental
   models, 50–70, 107–18, 120–23,
   182–86; recognizing good points,
   75–79; recognizing the real you,
   85–105
self-fulfilling prophecies, 204–205
selfishness, 34–37, 87–88, 94, 107,
   112, 113, 115, 253
separation anxiety, 119–20, 183–86
separation from negative role
   models, 121–24
sex, 38, 44, 117, 127, 204, 237–64;
   communication with your partner,
   252–62; dissatisfaction with, 239–
   240; dysfunctions, 262–63; and
   emotional state, 241–51; fantasies,
   249–51, 260, 261; lesbianism, 38,
   99, 238–39, 249; masturbation,
   248, 252; nurturing yourself while
   having, 237–64; oral, 253; and
   orgasm, 238, 246, 247, 252, 259,
   262; and partnerlessness, 274–48;
   seduction phase, 254–57
sexual abuse, 199–200, 244–45
sexual harassment, 267–68, 274,
   278
shopping, 127
shyness, 86–87, 94
siblings, 50, 52, 108, 114, 116, 118,
   185, 226, 283–84; *see also* family
single parents, 223
single women, 38, 39, 41–42, 45,
   88–89, 273
situational anxiety, 175–80

About the Author

Carolynn Hillman is a Board-Certified Diplomate in clinical social work. She received her B.A. from Barnard College, her M.S.W. from Hunter College, and her psychoanalytic training at the National Institute of the Psychotherapies. She is also an AASECT (American Association of Sex Educators, Counselors, and Therapists) certified sex therapist. For the past twenty-four years she has been helping women and men fulfill their potential and raise their self-esteem. She lives in Teaneck, New Jersey, with her husband and two daughters and maintains a private practice in New York City of individual, couple, and group therapy.